IMAGES
of America

AROUND PICTURE ROCKS

On the cover: Prof. D. B. Little is crossing the bridge over Muncy Creek in Picture Rocks. Professor Little was the principal of both the Hughesville and Picture Rocks High schools. After he retired as an educator in 1920, he became the secretary/treasurer and manager of the Lycoming Ladder Company in Picture Rocks. Little was also a burgess and member of the Picture Rocks Borough Council. (Courtesy of Wes Sprout and Bob Roller.)

IMAGES
of America

AROUND PICTURE ROCKS

Sherry A. Gardner

ARCADIA
PUBLISHING

ISBN 978-0-7385-4473-1

Published by Arcadia Publishing
Charleston, South Carolina

Printed in the United States of America

Library of Congress Catalog Card Number: 2005936971

For all general information contact Arcadia Publishing at:
Telephone 843-853-2070
Fax 843-853-0044
E-mail sales@arcadiapublishing.com
For customer service and orders:
Toll-Free 1-888-313-2665

Visit us on the Internet at www.arcadiapublishing.com

Contents

ACKNOWLEDGMENTS

This book is a culmination of efforts by so many people. I cannot take credit for doing this alone. There are two people without whom I could not have completed this book: my grandfather, Charles Gansell, and my mother Cris Gansell, both whom helped me in so many ways when I could not be in town. Thank you for all of your help!

The following people spent time with me telling their stories and sharing their photographs of Picture Rocks. Without these people, this book would never have been written. So, a very special thank you goes to: Mike Bayley, Wes and Pat Sprout, Mary Artley, Evelyn Bryan, Byrton and Marjorie Winder, Bob Roller, Eugene Daye, Jesse Haywood, Eunice Stover, Nicole Haines, Robert Webster, Janet Kohler, Dot and Bill Sandmeyer, Stewart Hill, Principal William Knapsack of George A. Ferrell Elementary, Phyllis Stevens of the East Lycoming Historical Society, and Scott Sager of the Lycoming County Historical Society.

The Muncy Historical Society purchased 55 journals written by Amos Sprout. In the beginning of each chapter you will read a little of what he wrote over the years. Thanks to the MHS, there is truly a unique piece of history in this book.

Another very special thank you goes to my publisher Erin Vogsien and Arcadia Publishing. What they do is a great service to history and making sure that every town and region can share its history. Everyone should support such a fine company.

Thank you to the rest of my family and friends who truly supported me throughout the writing of this book.

INTRODUCTION

The beginnings of Picture Rocks are legendary in both tragedy and love.

The famous rocks boasted carvings created by an American Indian named Fisher Fox, who was the cousin of the tribe's chief, Chief Wolf. Fisher Fox became friends with a French maiden named Georgie Dupre, the wife of the leader of French settlers who were on the land (around 1760). One morning, Fisher Fox was going to the mountains to look for rock paint. Georgie Dupre begged to go when she found out they would be home by dark. Unfortunately, a rainstorm came and the two were forced to seek shelter in a cave. They were there so long and Dupre feared her husband's wrath so much, that instead of returning to her settlement she went with Fox to his camp. They were not greeted warmly. Chief Wolf was so angry with Fox, mostly because he knew Fox would not be able to return to the rocks to finish the paintings, that he banished both from the camp. Fox and Dupre were taken to the Susquehanna River, near Shamokin Dam, and put in a canoe with 10 days worth of provisions. Fox eventually escaped the canoe, leaving Dupre alone and betrayed.

Georgie Dupre was later rescued by German hunters. She moved to their settlement in Clinton County and made a life there, even remarrying.

In a turn of events, Georgie was captured by American Indians and found her former husband among the captives. An opportunity arose for them to escape, but Georgie did not wish to do so. Her former husband was shot while trying to scale a wall, and she was inflicted with a fatal wound by a tomahawk. In her dying moments, she said that she never wanted to escape. There she died, surrounded with sympathetic American Indians after detesting the entire race since the betrayal of Fisher Fox.

Another town legend is that of Chief Rest Your Bones and the beautiful American Indian maid Laughing Eyes. Laughing Eyes had many who sought to be her admiring lover, but it was Chief Rest Your Bones who won her heart. Before the two could wed, Laughing Eyes became ill and died. Chief Rest Your Bones was so grief stricken that he died of a broken heart over the loss of his beloved Laughing Eyes. The two were buried together at a bend in the creek just above the rocks. The grave is still there to this day.

One

Mills and Business

February 1, 1861
Smoothed 300 lts sash and fussed with the painters. They came about 11 and went home at 12. Went to Mr. Cowles and singing school in evening. Richard Woodly died today.

—Amos Sprout

While walking home from Berrysburg, Dauphin County, to his home in Montrose, Amos B. Sprout and his nephew Asa R. Sprout came upon the land that would become Picture Rocks. He reportedly talked to John Tice about the land and the mill that was there and learned it was for sale. The two purchased the land from Tice for a mere $2,500 in 1848. It is hard to imagine why the two even bought the land. It was considered next to worthless. Three prior owners had given up on the land. The woodland was a mess with the trees being leveled by a cyclone 40 years before.

While surveying the land, they discovered paintings and carvings on the rocks and trees left by the Monsie Tribe. Those pictures gave the town its name. There was a single home and sawmill on the land. That mill was the sparkle in the eye for its settlers. Burrows and Sprout started buying new machines for the mill so they could manufacture window sash and doors, which were in high demand for home building up and down the West Branch Valley.

From that first saw mill, other industries started. Sabin Burrows, son of Amos Burrows (who was Amos Sprout's uncle), started manufacturing furniture in 1856.

Asa R. Sprout started a factory to make berry boxes and shingles. The berry boxes were used to sell his strawberries.

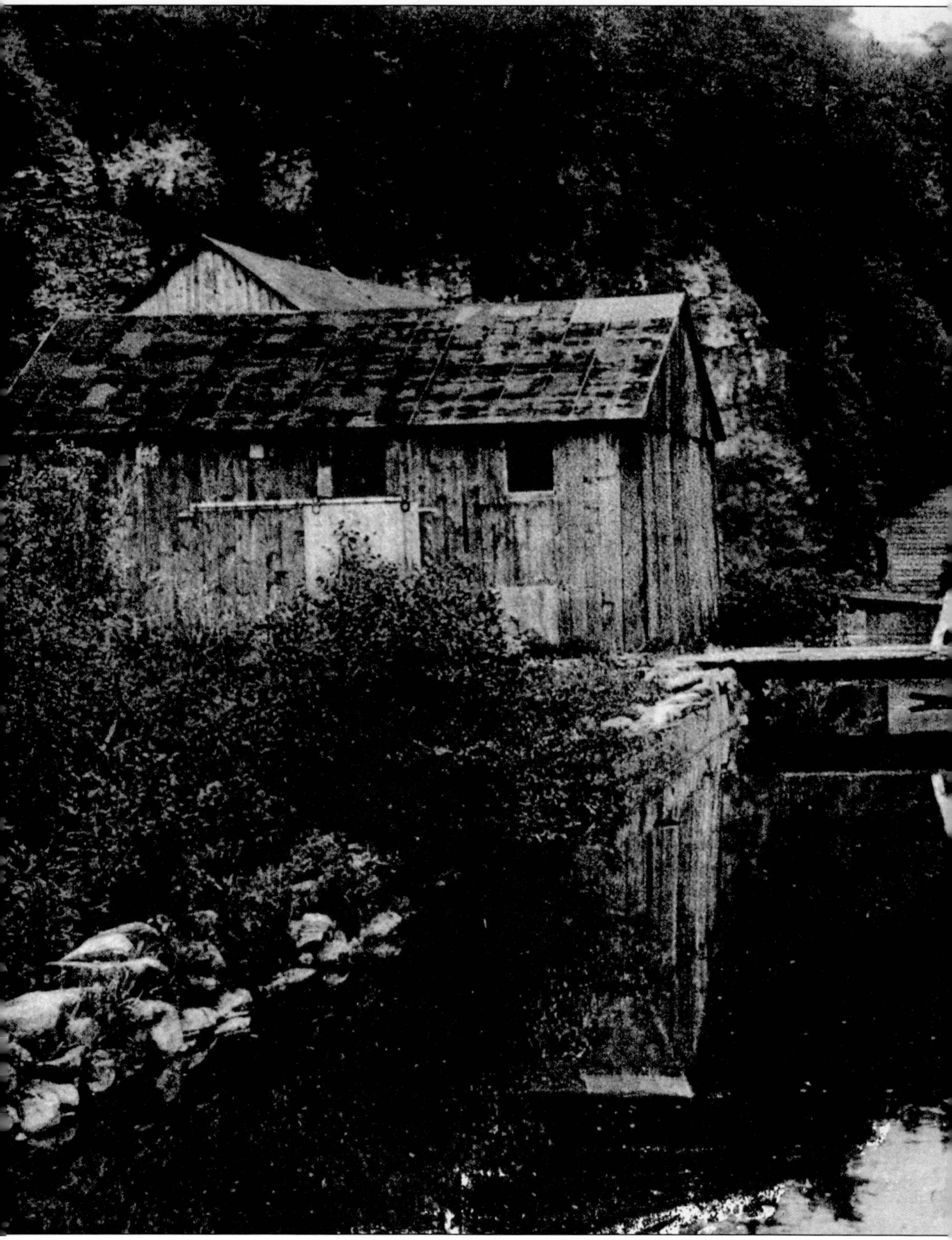

Seen here is the dam at the rocks. (Courtesy of Cris Gansell.)

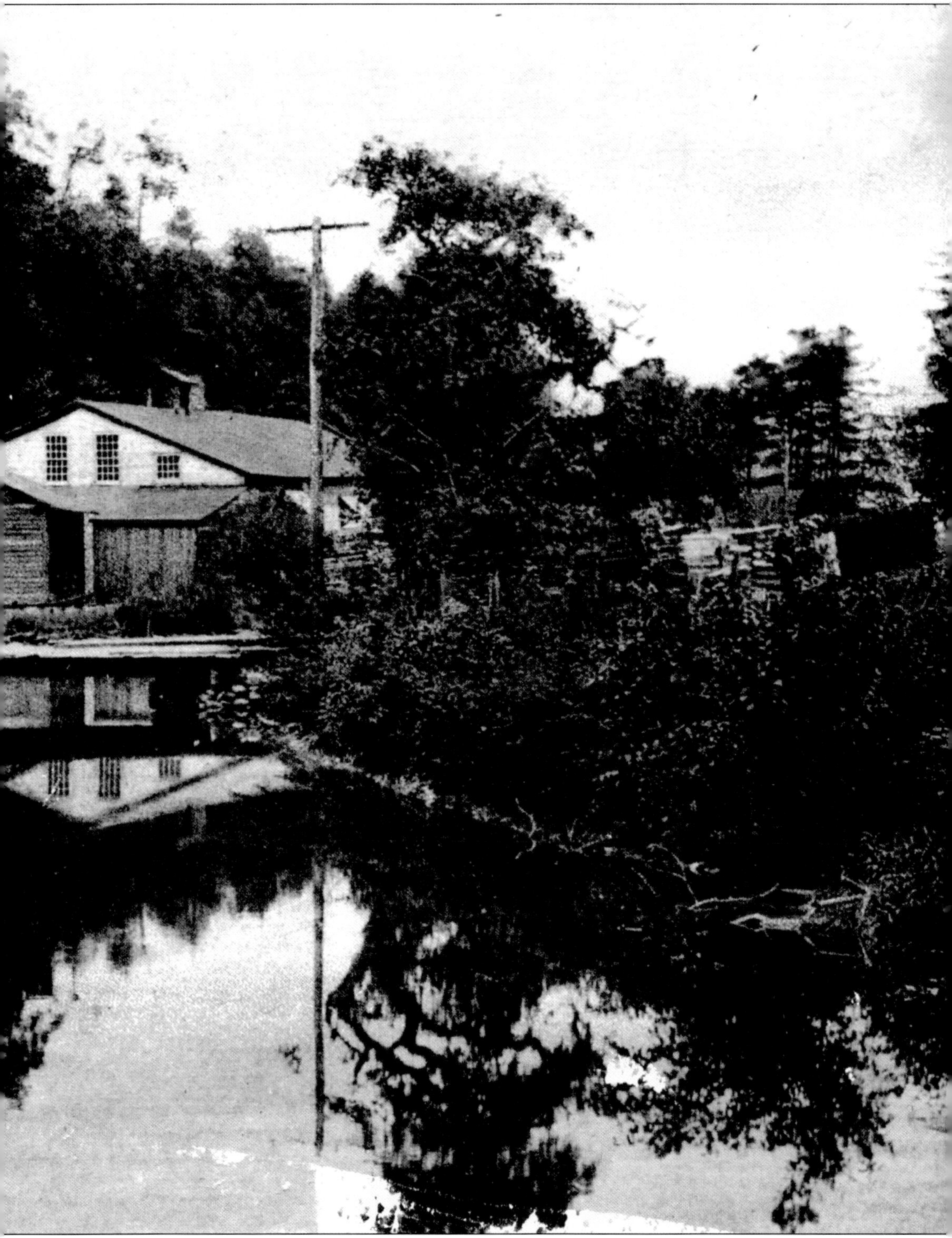

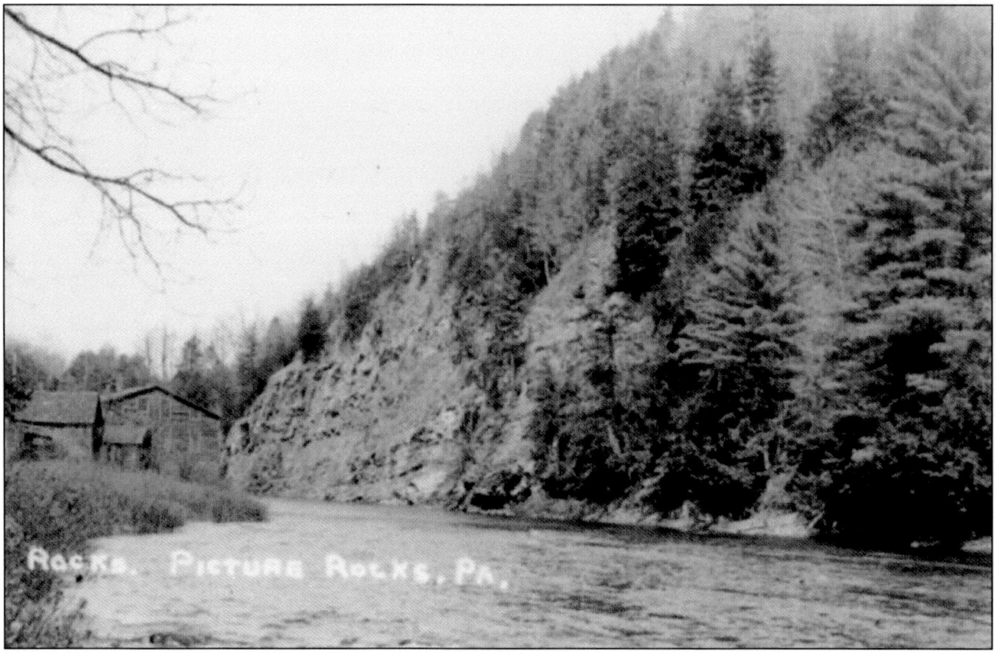

This is the mill that started it all. This mill sat along the Muncy Creek and was one of two structures on the land. The Burrows and Sprout families bought machinery to make window sash, blinds, and doors. This mill created employment, which brought many of the family's friends to settle here. (Courtesy of Stewart Hill.)

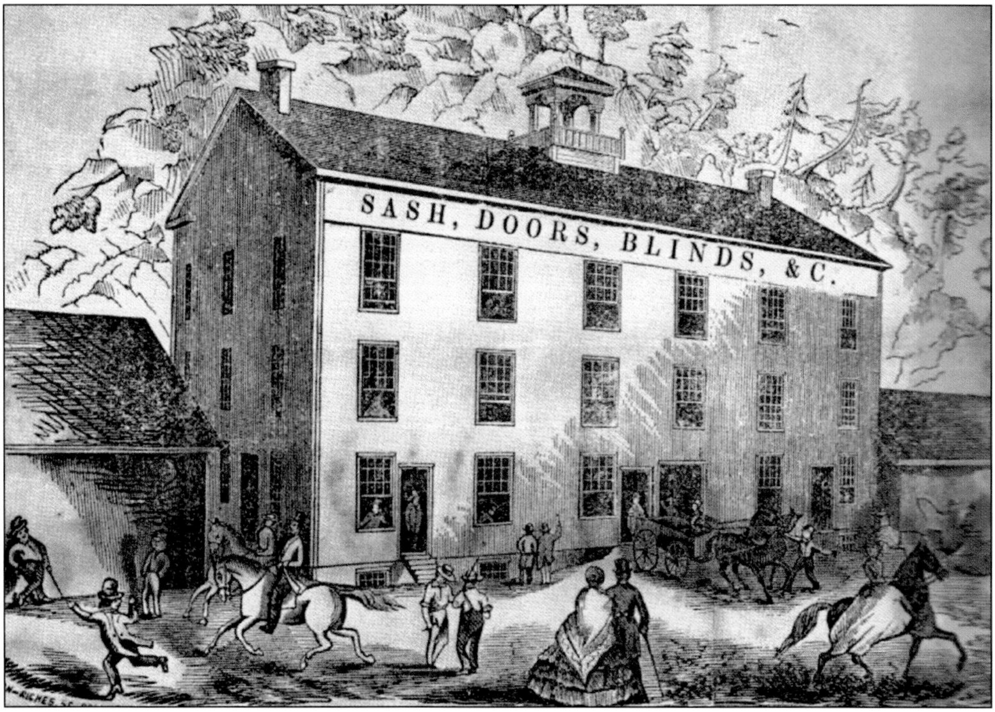

The first mill in the area was used to make window sash and doors. At the time, it was in great demand because new homes were being built throughout the area.

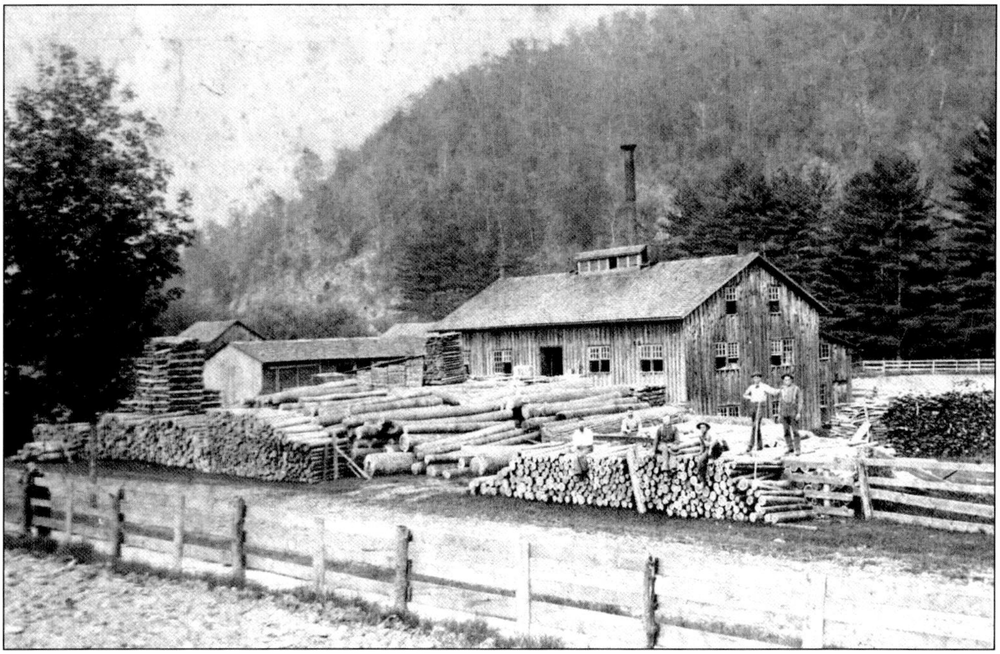

The Handle and Excelsior Company greeted people as they crossed the Muncy Creek into the main part of town. Also known as the H and E, they made handles, wooden rakes, and excelsior's for packing furniture and china. They were successful for many years. (Courtesy of Mary Artley.)

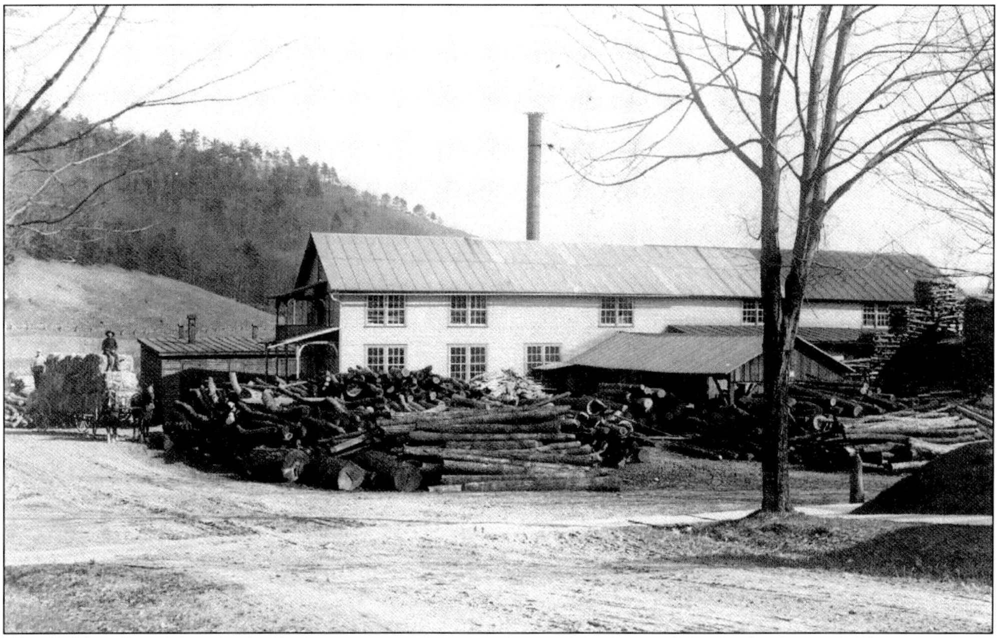

The Handle and Excelsior operated in Asa Sprout's steam-powered factory from 1870 to 1939. Then in 1939, they bought the Burrows Brothers building when the furniture company went out of business. (Courtesy of Mary Artley.)

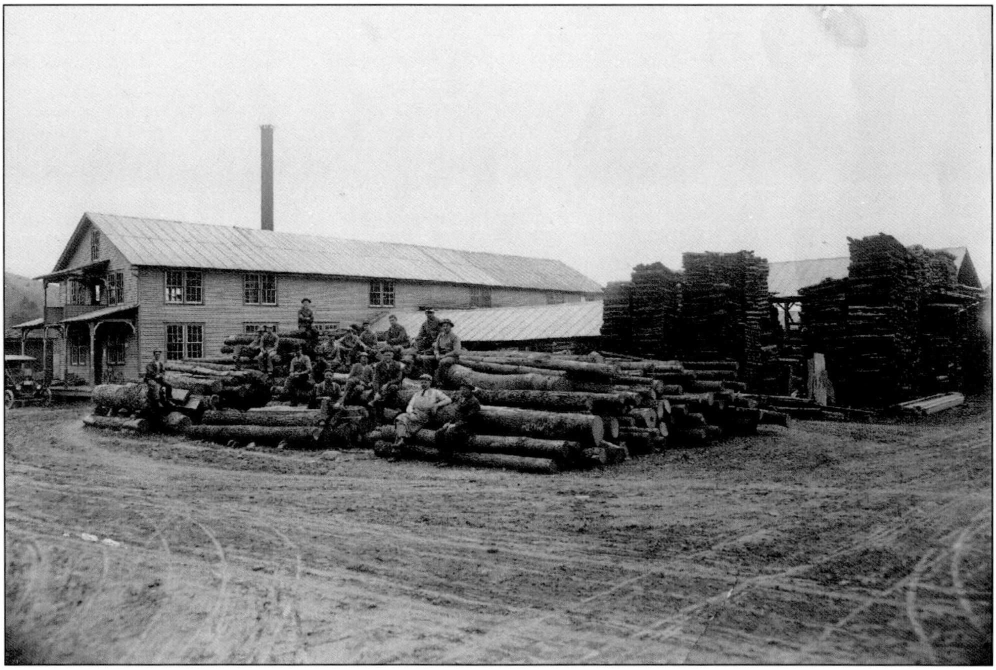

This is the original Handle and Excelsior Company, with its hard-working crew, before it moved to Main Street. This factory was operated by the Eddy brothers from 1867 until it burned down in 1870. (Courtesy of Mary Artley.)

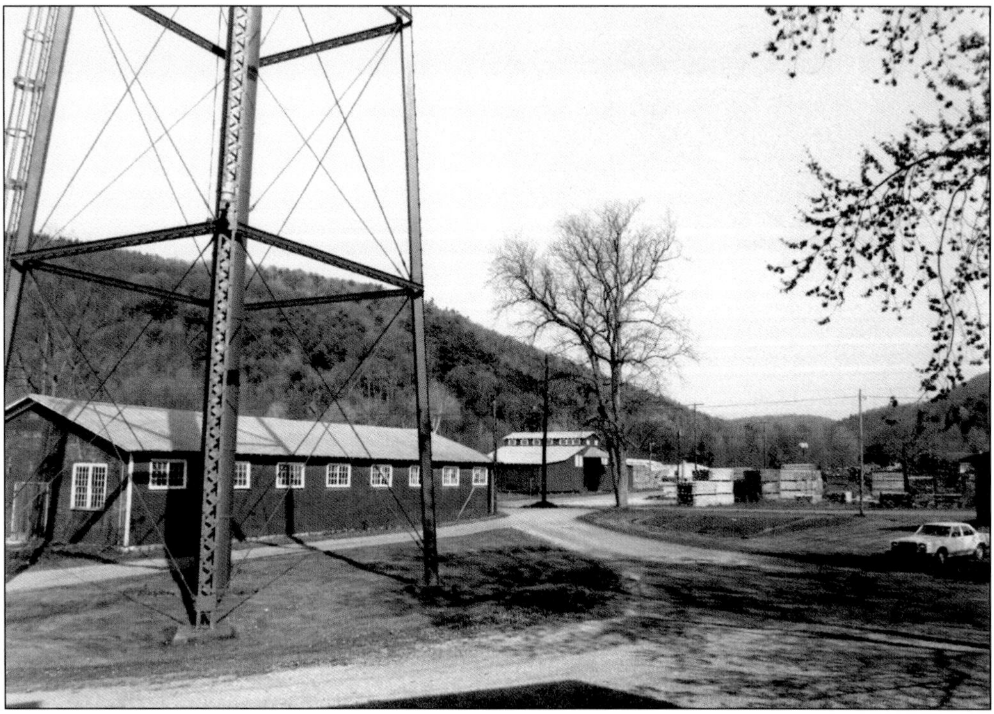

Shown here is the back lot of the H and E located on Bennett Lane around 1960. (Courtesy of Mary Artley.)

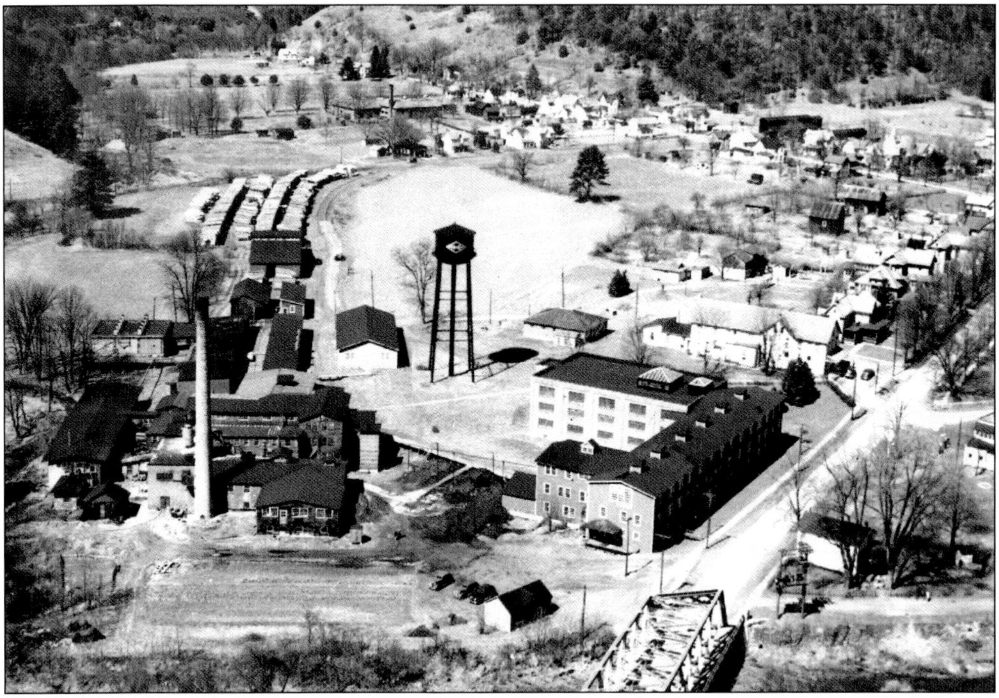

The H and E became such in the late 1920s after the Handle and Excelsior discontinued the making of said excelsiors. (Courtesy of Mary Artley.)

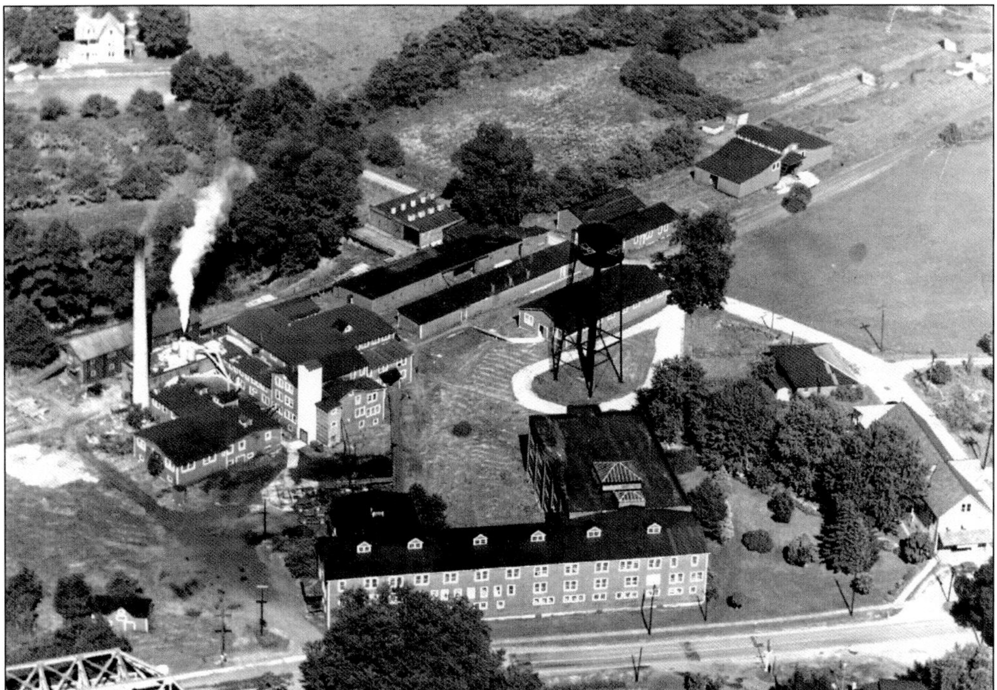

The H and E operated in Picture Rocks until the 1980s. (Courtesy of Mary Artley.)

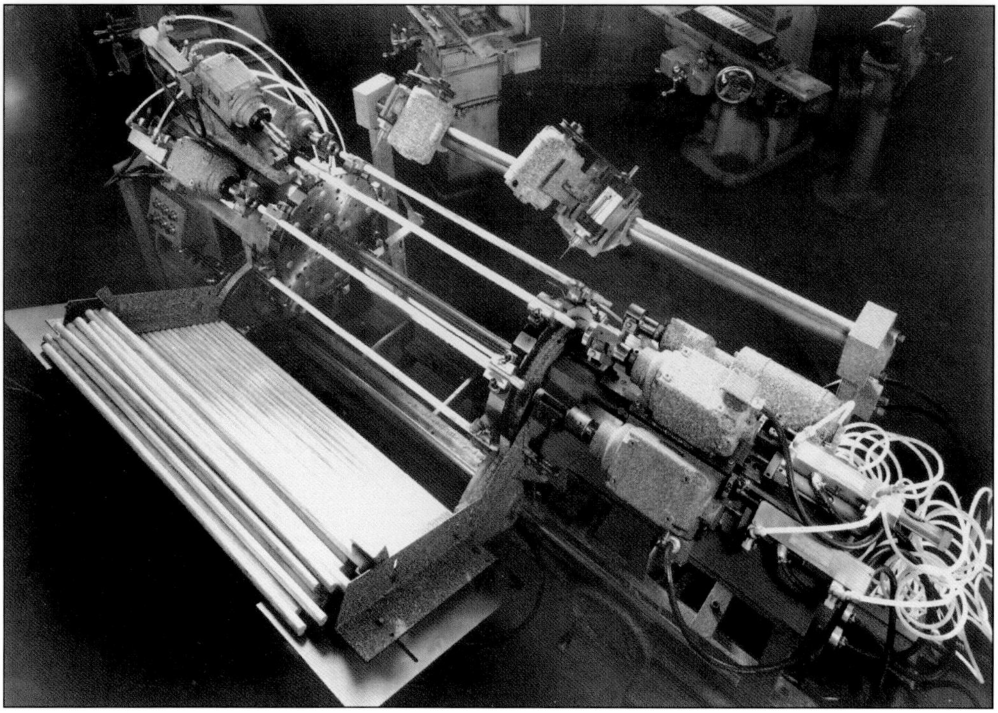

This photograph is of the H and E machines that were used to make wooden rake handles. (Courtesy of Mary Artley.)

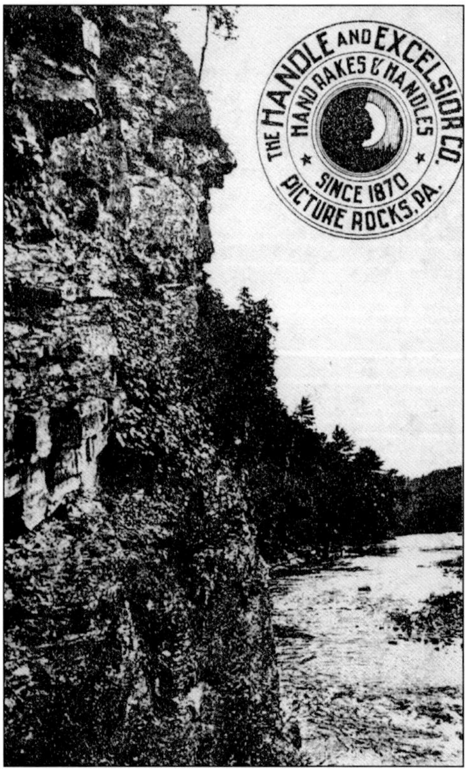

In the spirit of Picture Rocks, the Handle and Excelsior Company printed this image on postcards that the company used. The image was drawn up by Picture Rocks artist J. Wesley Little. (Courtesy of Mary Artley.)

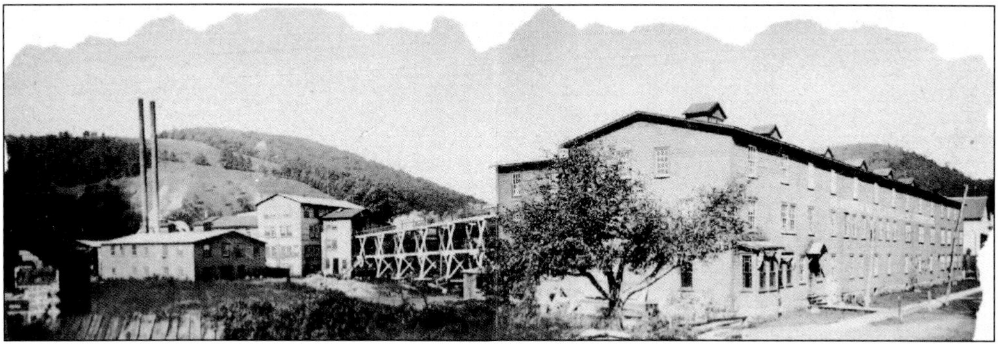

During World War II, the factory made uniform pieces for the American soldiers. (Courtesy of Mary Artley.)

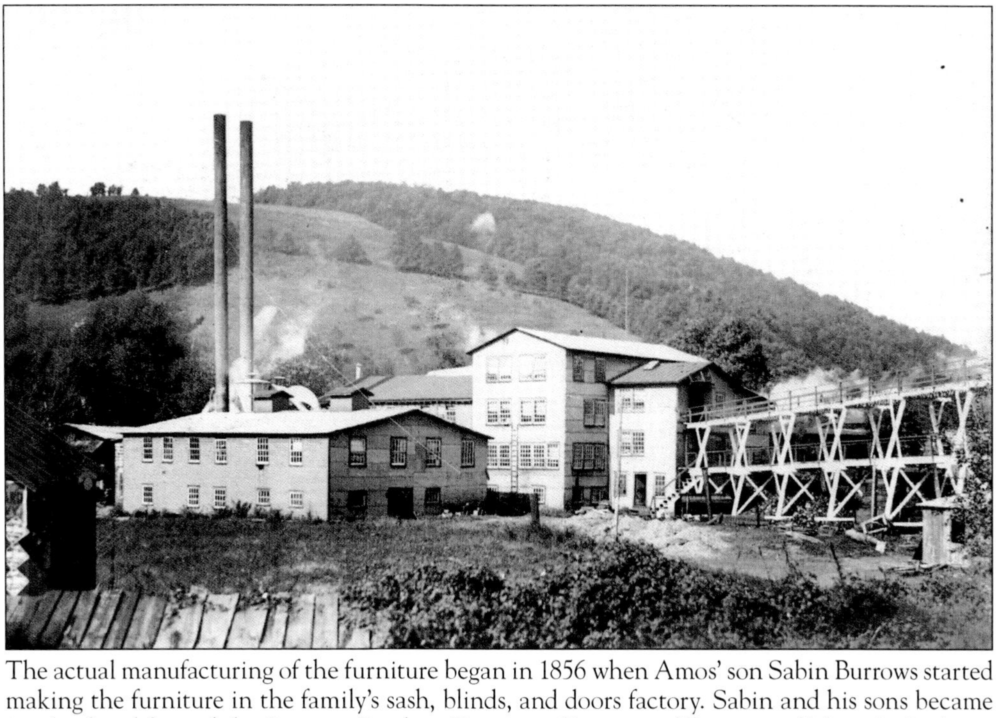

The actual manufacturing of the furniture began in 1856 when Amos' son Sabin Burrows started making the furniture in the family's sash, blinds, and doors factory. Sabin and his sons became involved and formed the Burrows Brothers Furniture Company. (Courtesy of Mary Artley.)

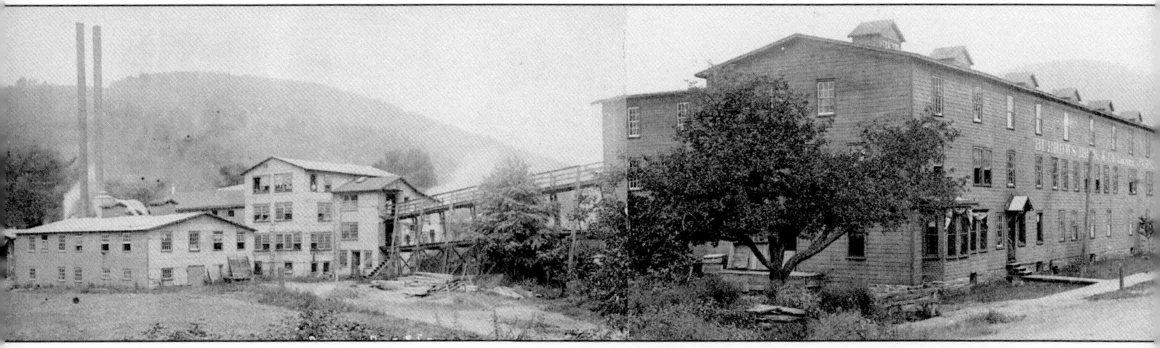

The Burrows Brothers made fine furniture from the late 1880s, through the depression, until 1939. (Courtesy of Mary Artley.)

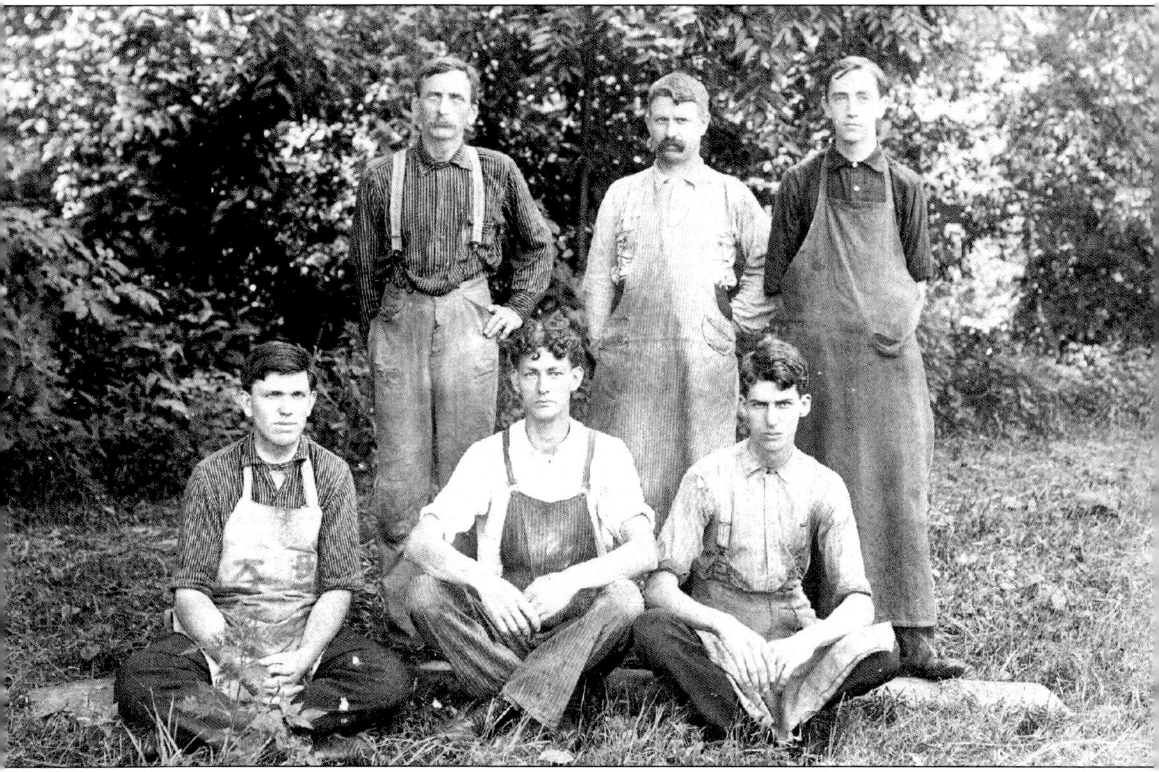

The workers of the packing room for the Burrows Brothers Furniture Company are pictured here in 1904. (Courtesy of Mary Artley.)

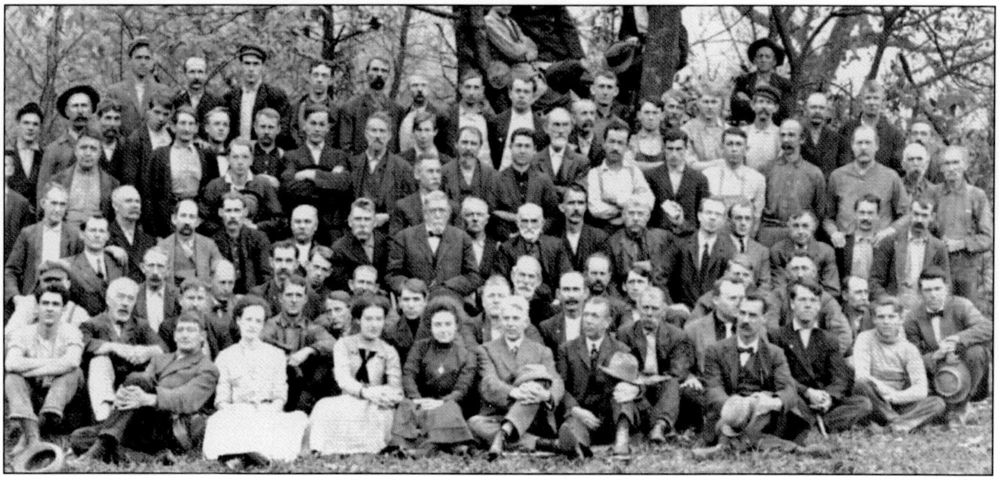

The Burrows Brothers was an offshoot of the first mill, as all the other mills in town were. The Sprout Waldron plant in Muncy is also associated with the Picture Rocks mills. The founder of Sprout Waldron was Lewis B. Sprout who was the co-owner of the Sash and Factory in town.

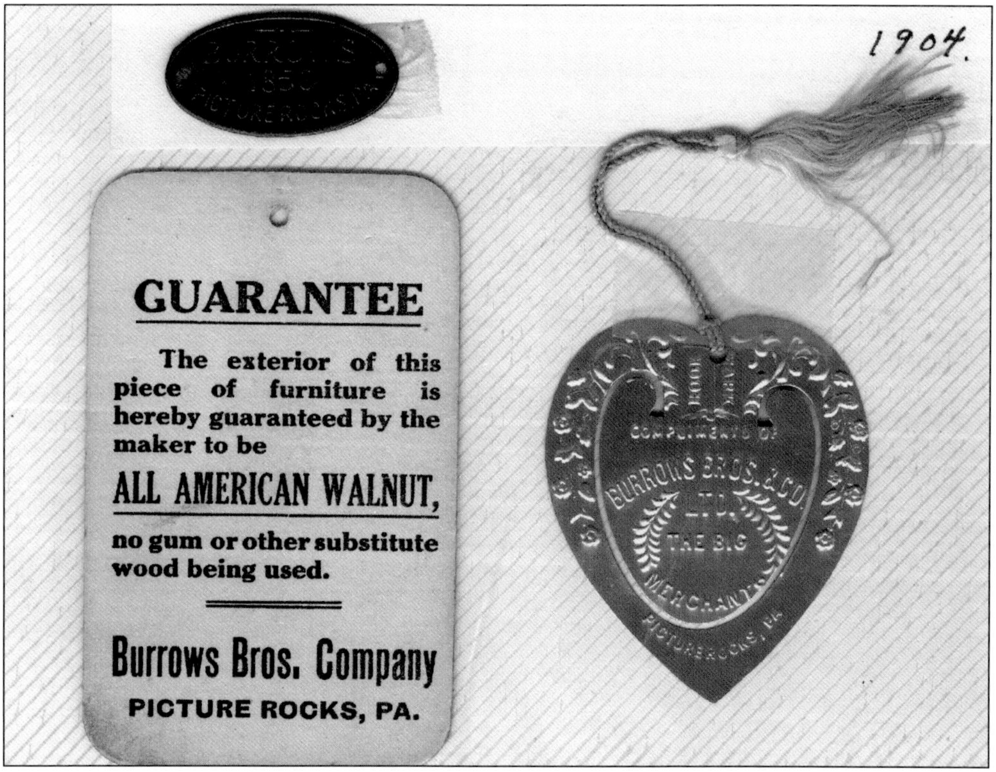

These tags accompanied the furniture made at the Burrows Brothers furniture factory in Picture Rocks. (Courtesy of Mary Artley.)

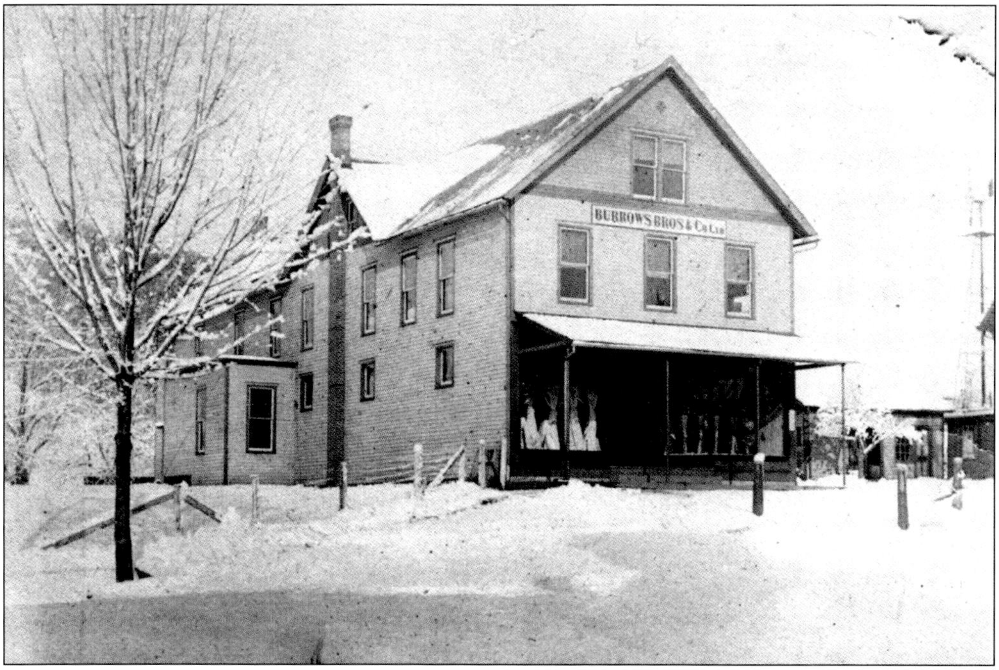

If someone wanted to buy a piece of the stunning furniture, this is were they would go. This was the retail store for Burrows Brothers, located by the factory on the corner of Main Street and Bennett Lane. (Courtesy of Mary Artley.)

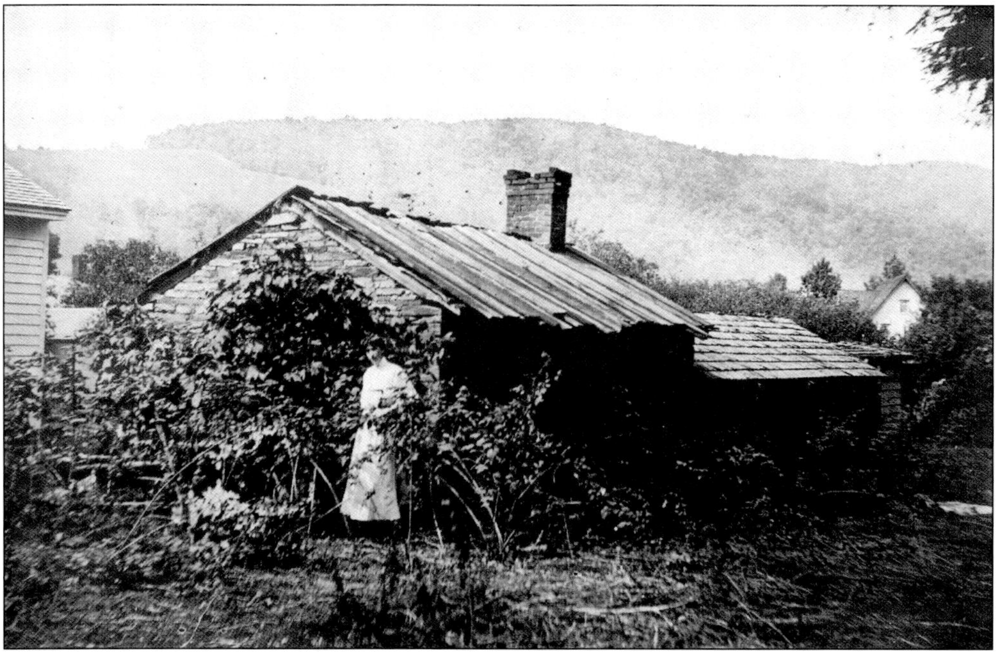

This is believed to be the workshop of founding father and inventor Asa R. Sprout. One of his most popular inventions was the berry basket. Sprout also invented many different machines. He also drew up plans for a steam streetcar, but the plan halted with the invention of the electric car. (Courtesy of Nicole Haines.)

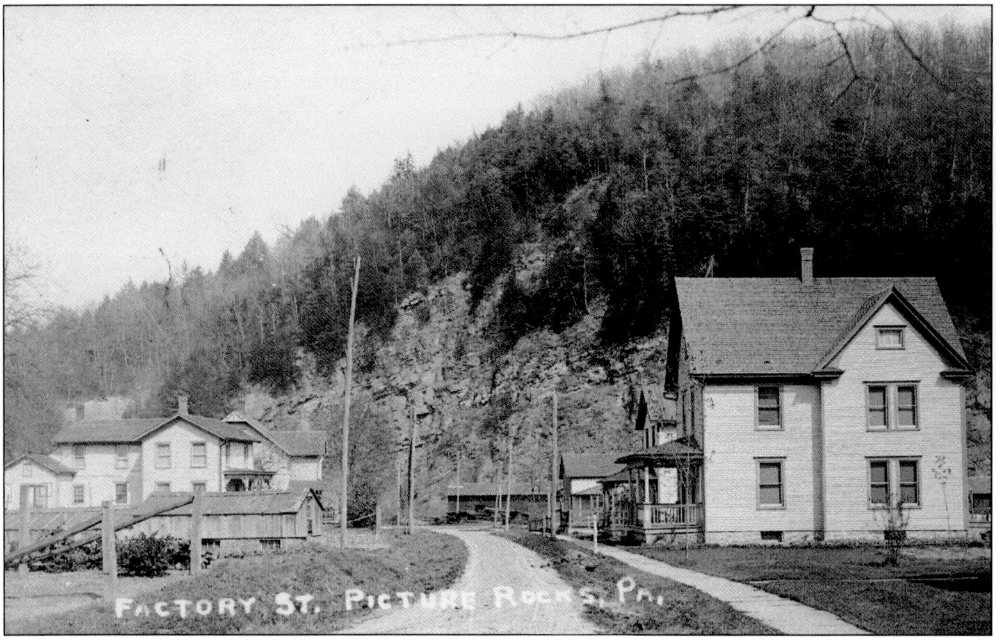

This is the mill that caught the eye of Amos Sprout at the foot of Factory Street. This, along with one home, were the only structures on the land. (Courtesy of Wes and Pat Sprout.)

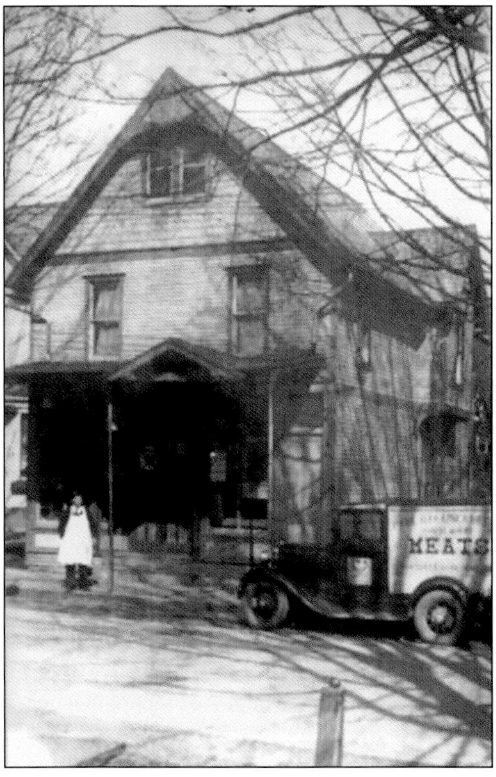

The town even boasted its own butcher store, which was operated by Paul Houseknecht. (Courtesy of Stewart Hill.)

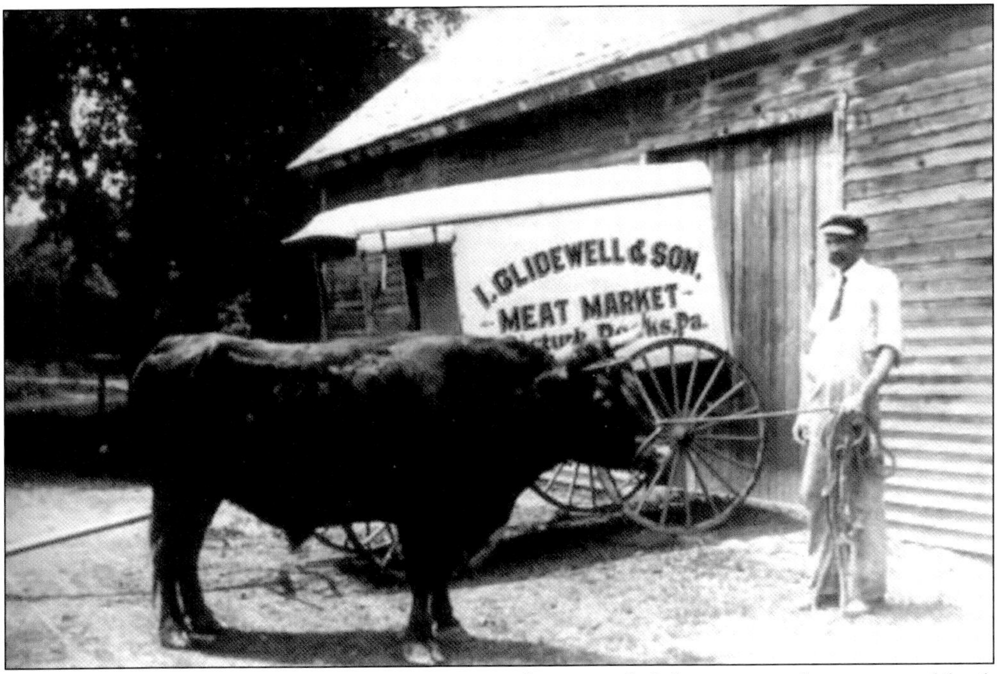

The Glidewells also had a meat market in town that provided the town with a source of food. (Courtesy of Stewart Hill.)

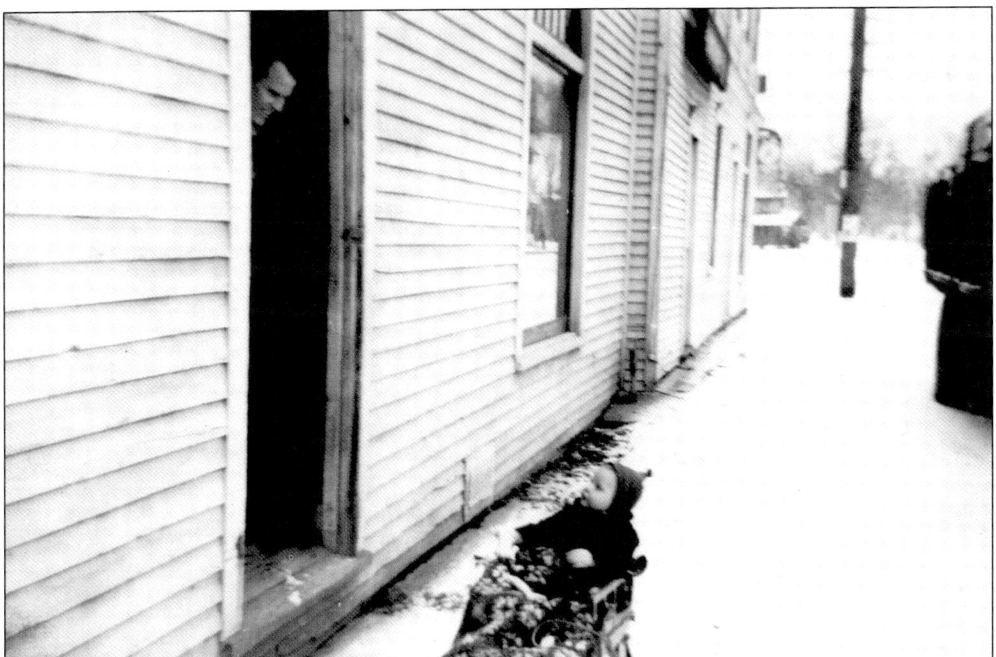

An employee at the Bayley General Store looks on as a youngster enjoys some time playing in the snow. (Courtesy of Mike Bayley.)

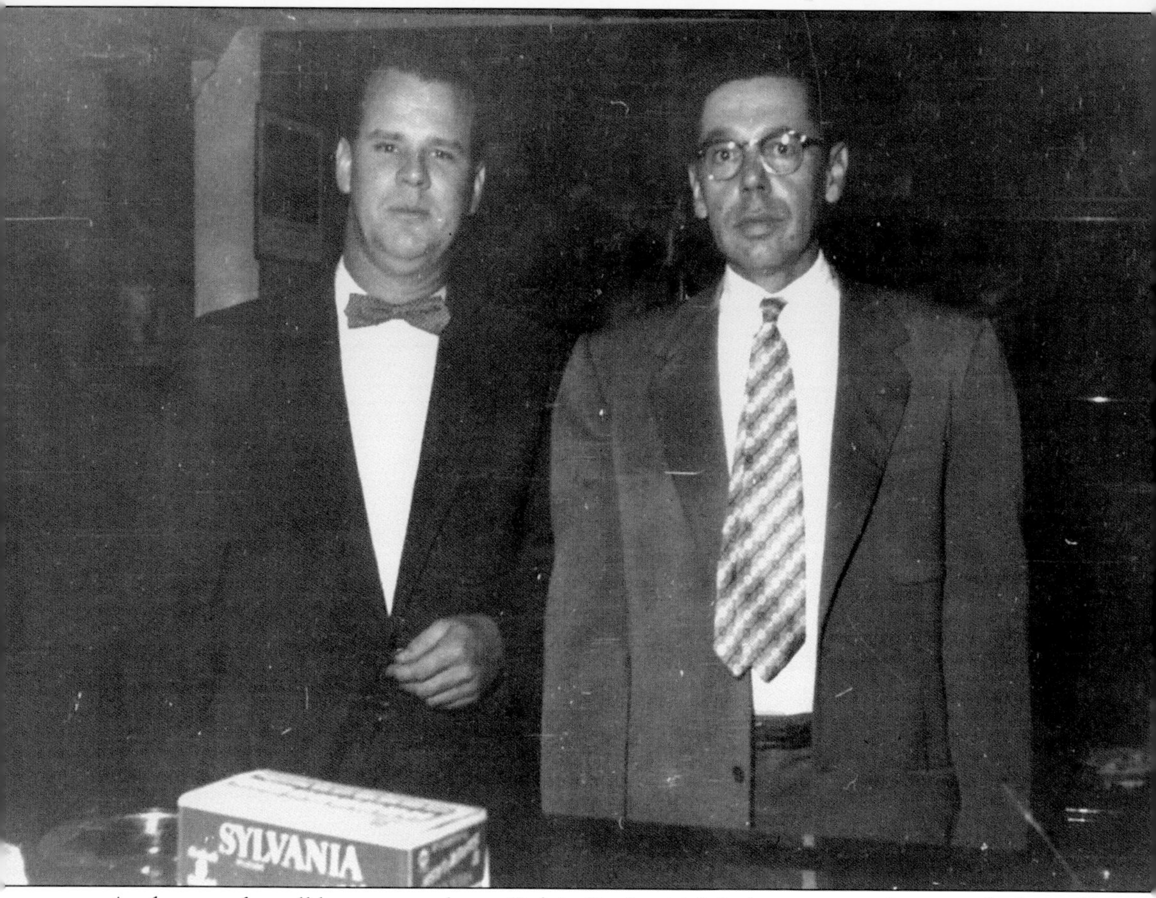

As the son of a well-known merchant, Calvin Bayley (right) also went into business for himself. He owned the coal yard, which was once located at the intersection on Laurel and Railroad Streets. (Courtesy of Mike Bayley.)

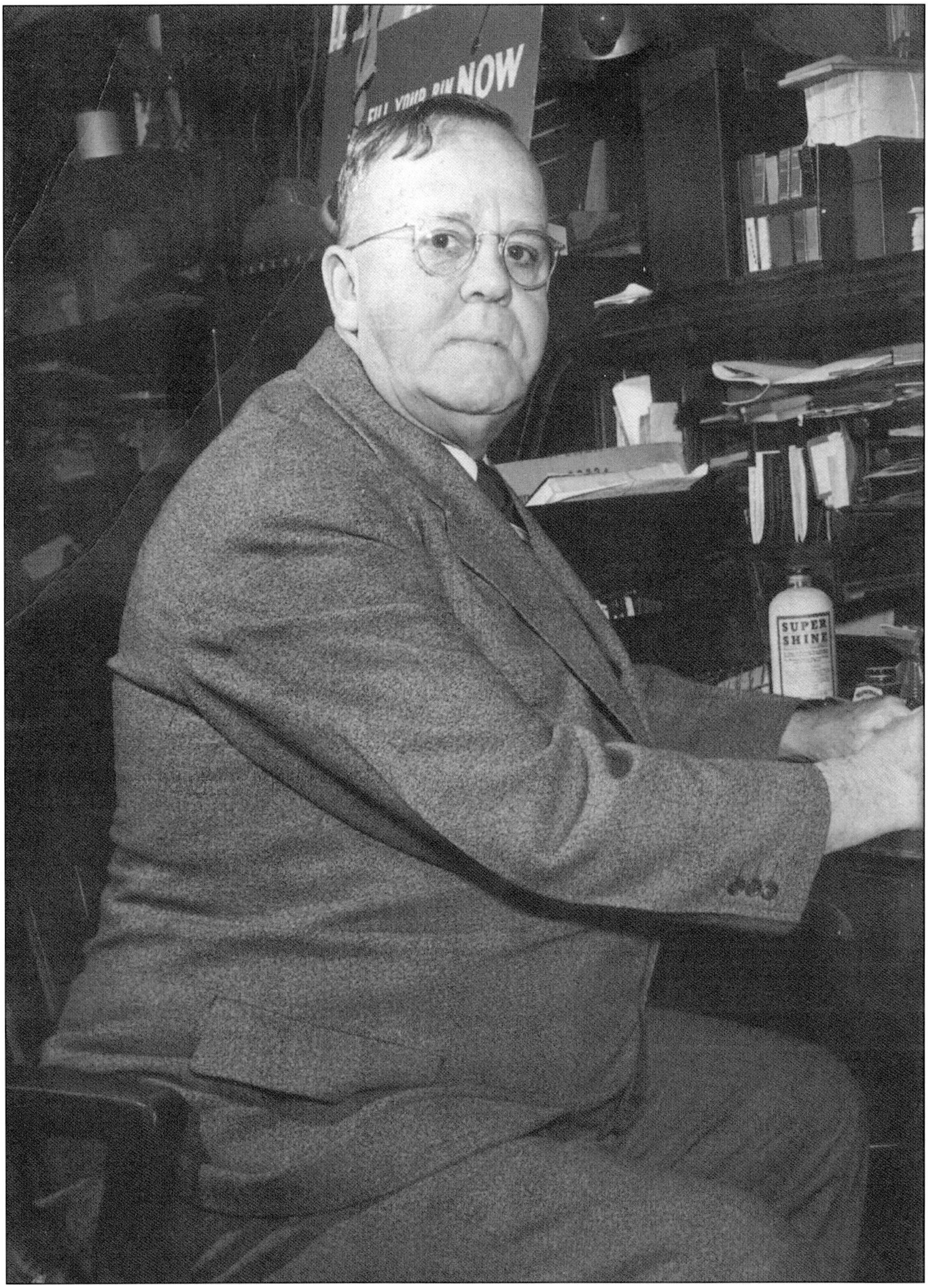

Ed Bayley Sr. moved to Picture Rocks in 1912 and established a general store that he operated until he was 65. Bayley was also the postmaster from 1914 to 1934, and he operated a hotel that was connected to his store. (Courtesy of Mike Bayley.)

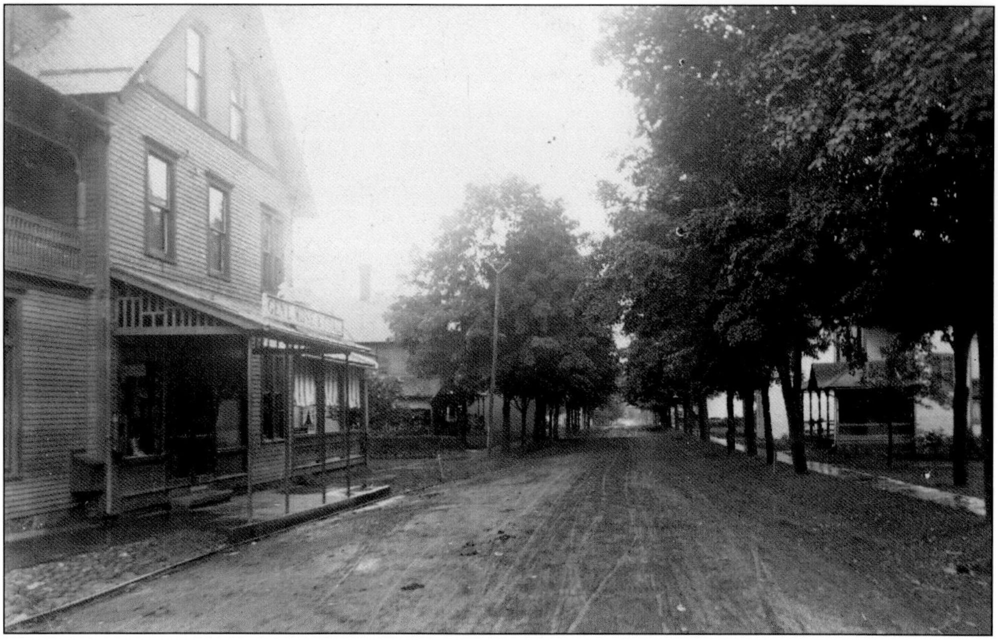

This unique building on the corner of Main and Elm Streets has been many different businesses over the years. It was most commonly known as the general store of Edward Bayley Sr. The building still stands today, although it has been remodeled over the years. The hotel no longer accompanies the building. (Courtesy of Wes and Pat Sprout.)

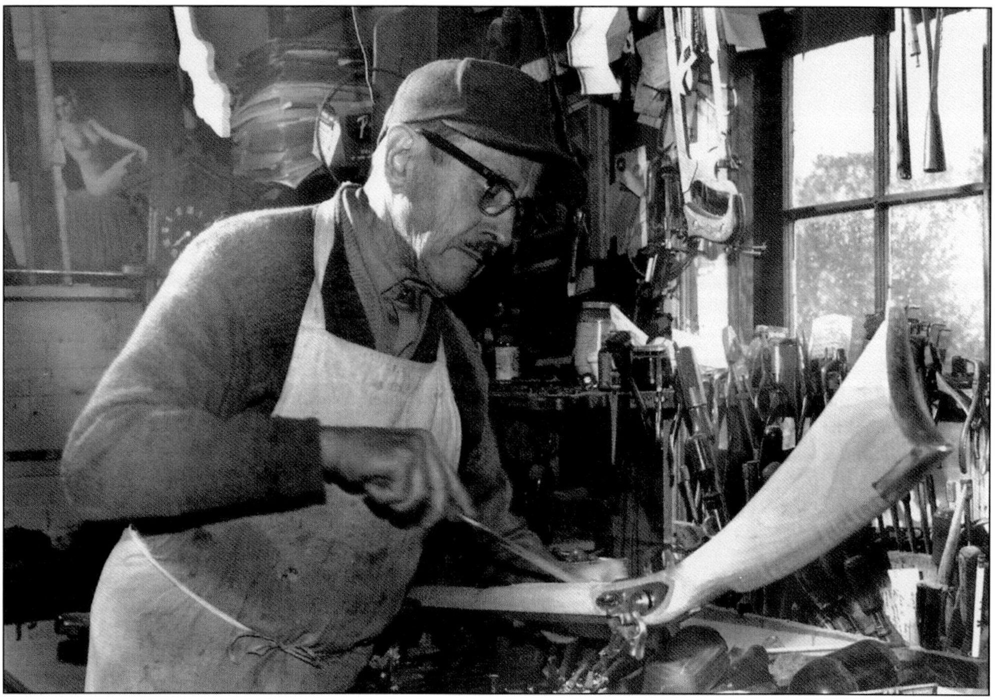

Louis Gansell operated a gunsmithing and carving shop. His son-in-law, Paul Taran, constructed a plant on Laurel Street to craft gun stocks, which was known as the Frontier Carving Shoppe. (Courtesy of Charley Gansell.)

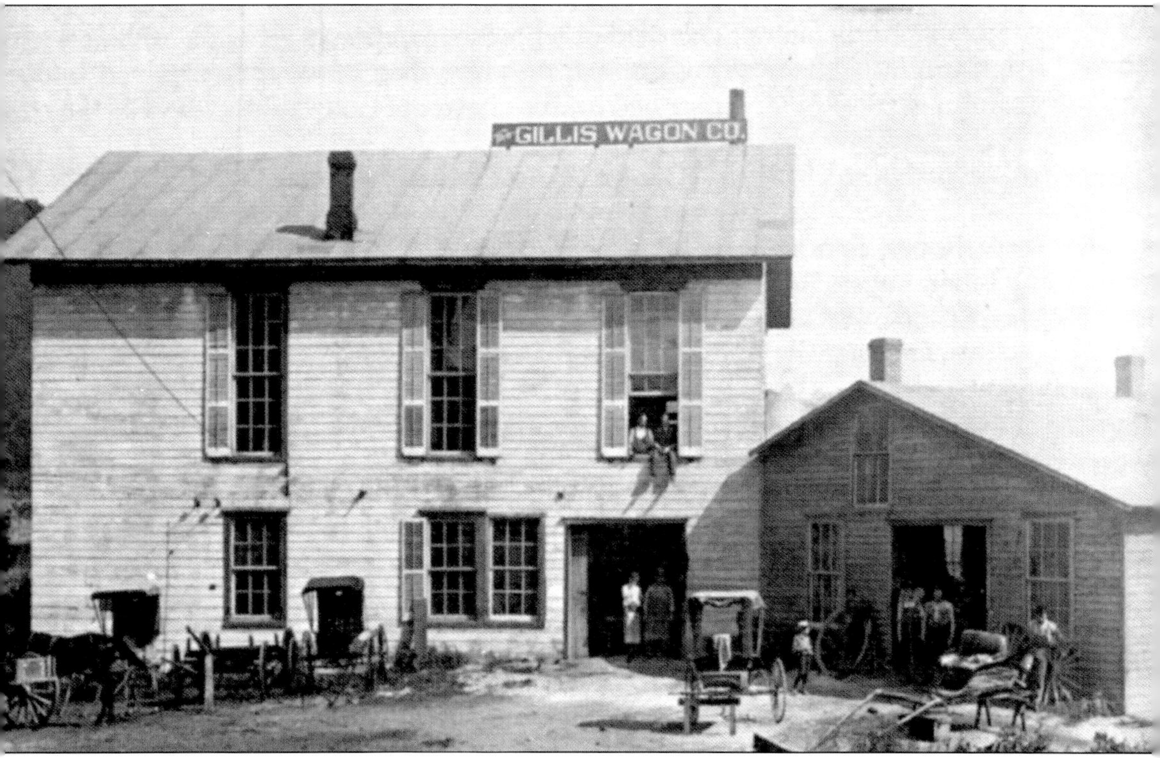

This building was once the Methodist Church on Water Street by the creek. It was moved to Main and Center Streets where it became the Gillis Wagon Company. The company made a variety of horse-drawn carriages and buggies. (Courtesy of *History and Pictures of Picture Rocks* by Ethel Cruse.)

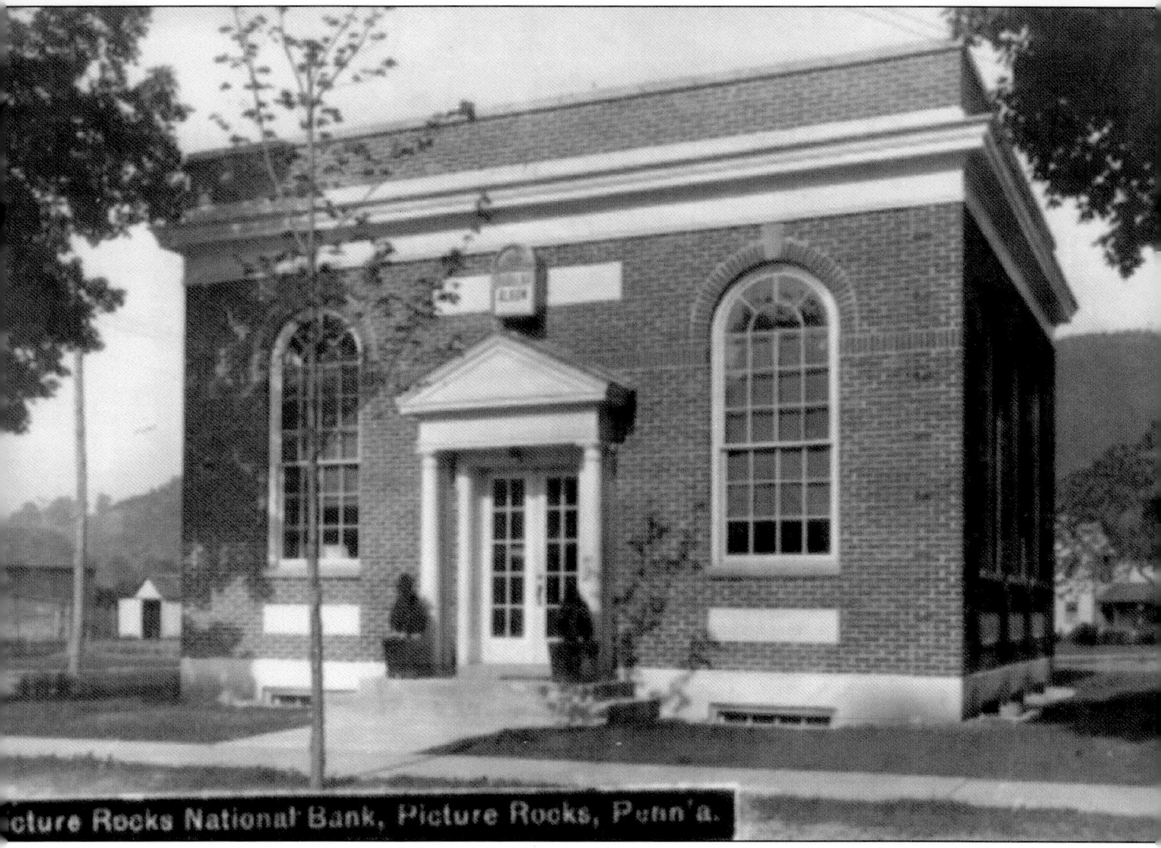

The Picture Rocks National Bank first opened its doors to the public on February 23, 1921. Morton I. Sprout was the bank's president. On February 23, 1932, exactly 11 years later, the bank was sold due to the Depression. The building also spent time as the Handle and Excelsior offices and again as a bank. Today it is the borough hall. (Courtesy of Stewart Hill.)

Two

EDUCATION

Saturday August 20, 1870
Worked 3 hours on the rails. Went to school house meeting for school board. A. C Little takes job of building new school house or $1149.00 (directors decide not) to build on.

—Amos Sprout

The first school used by Picture Rocks was the Woodly School in Wolf Township. Mary Bates taught a small class of five students. Eventually a school was built on the corner of Center and Oak Streets where Amos Sprout was the teacher. Finally in 1877, a school was built between Main and Center Streets. That school remained until the Picture Rocks High School was built off Laurel Street in 1926.

Picture Rocks was the first place in Pennsylvania to open a vocational school. Students came from all over, some even staying with families in town during the school week, just to attend.

Athletics were king for these students. Picture Rocks High School held championships in many different sports under coaches like Frank Walp and Clyde "Pat" Collins.

In 1946, Picture Rocks High School became part of the East Lycoming School District. The students were transferred to Hughesville High School. Today the school is known as George A Ferrell Elementary School, whose namesake worked in the school as a teacher and principal. Ferrell was also the assistant superintendent for the East Lycoming schools.

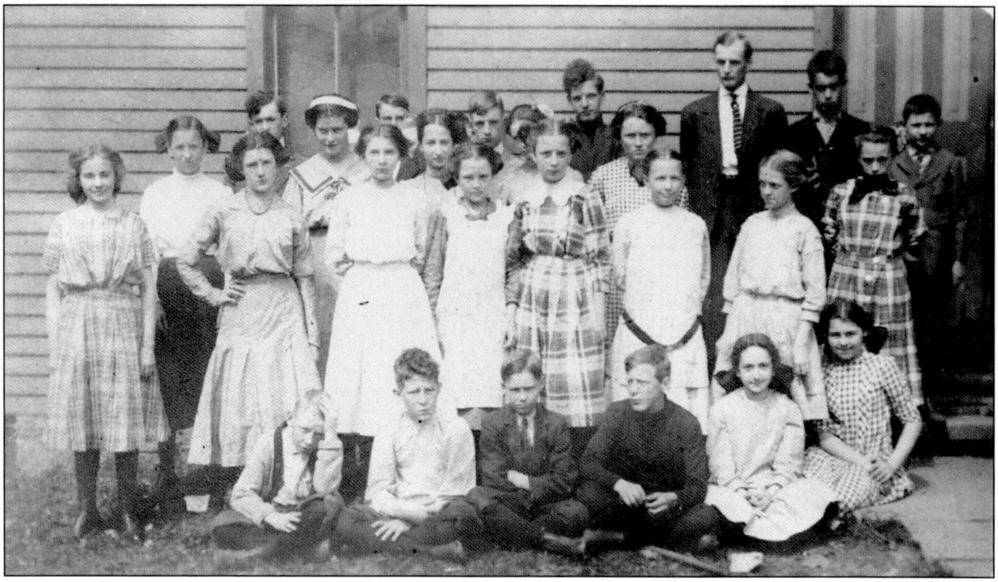

This school was built in 1877 by A. C. Little for a mere $1,100. Additional rooms were later added. The school taught primary, intermediate, grammar, and high school. Pictured here is a group of school children from 1911. (Courtesy of Wes and Pat Sprout.)

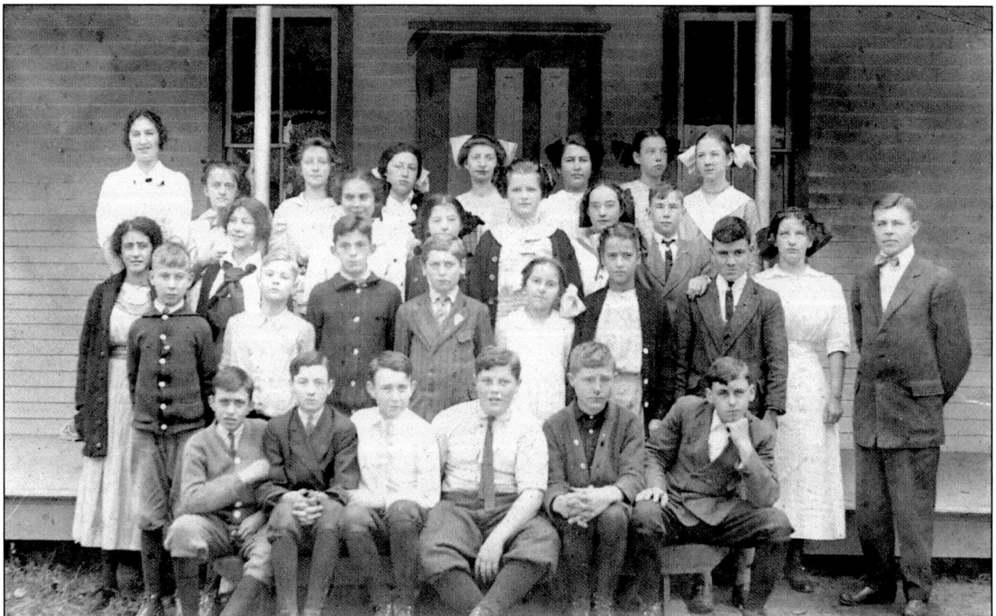

The first class from this school graduated in 1896. The class had only two people, Mitchell Persun and Benton Eddy. In 1921, the school became one of the first vocational schools in the state. (Courtesy of Bob Roller.)

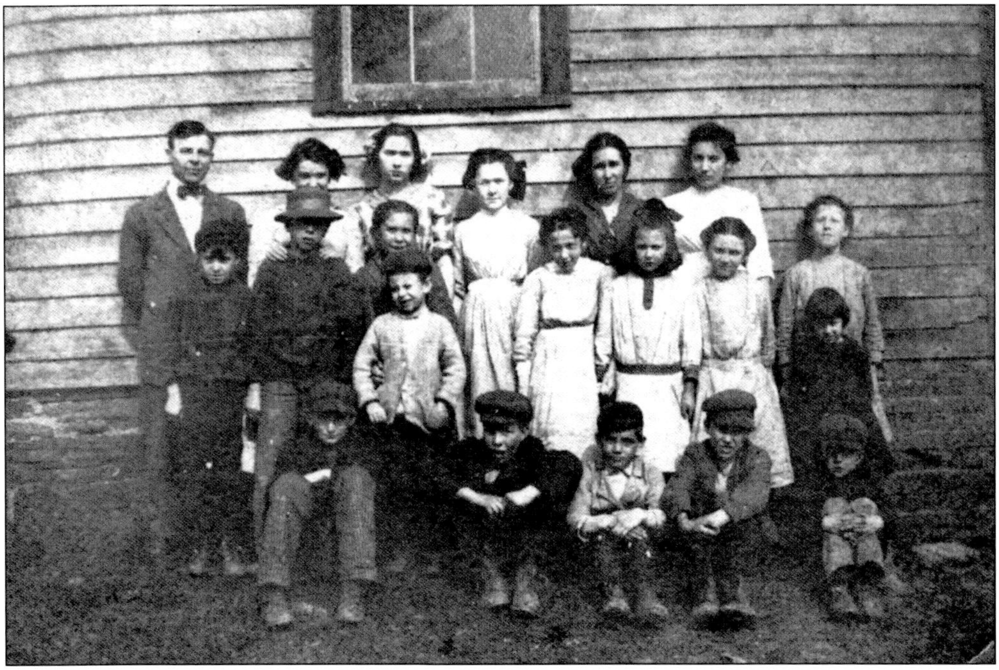

The school housed grades 1 through 12. In the minutes of a September 23, 1876, meeting, it was decided that the teachers would make $30 a month. (Courtesy of Bob Roller.)

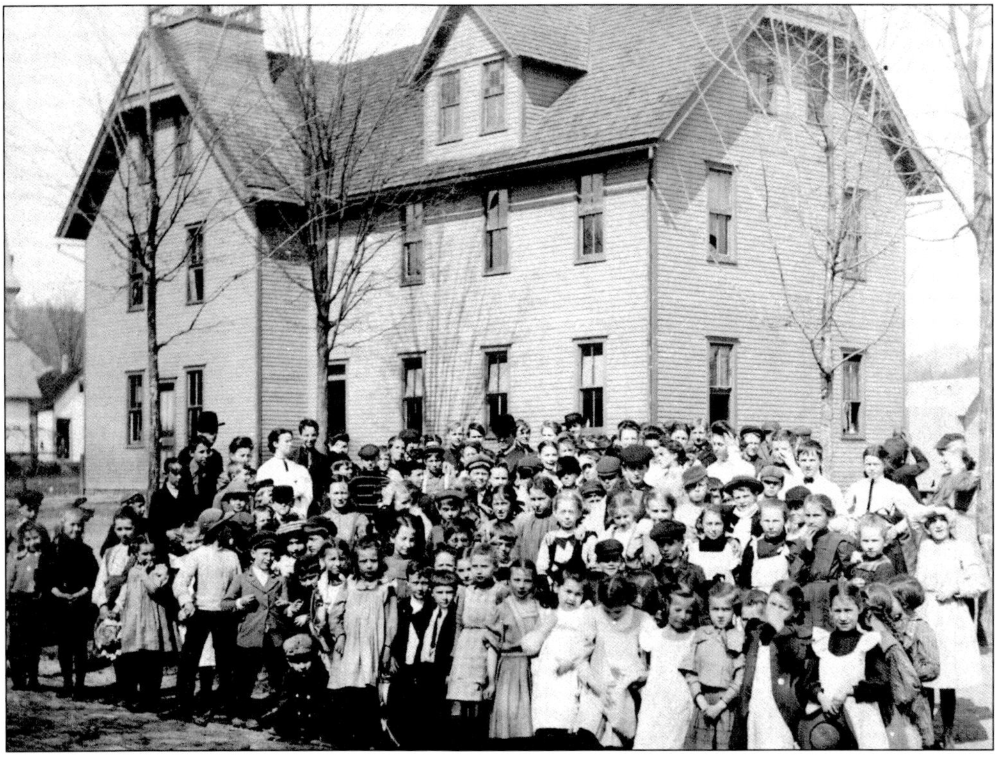

The old school no longer exists today. Homes to new generations of Picture Rockians take its place. (Courtesy of Wes and Pat Sprout.)

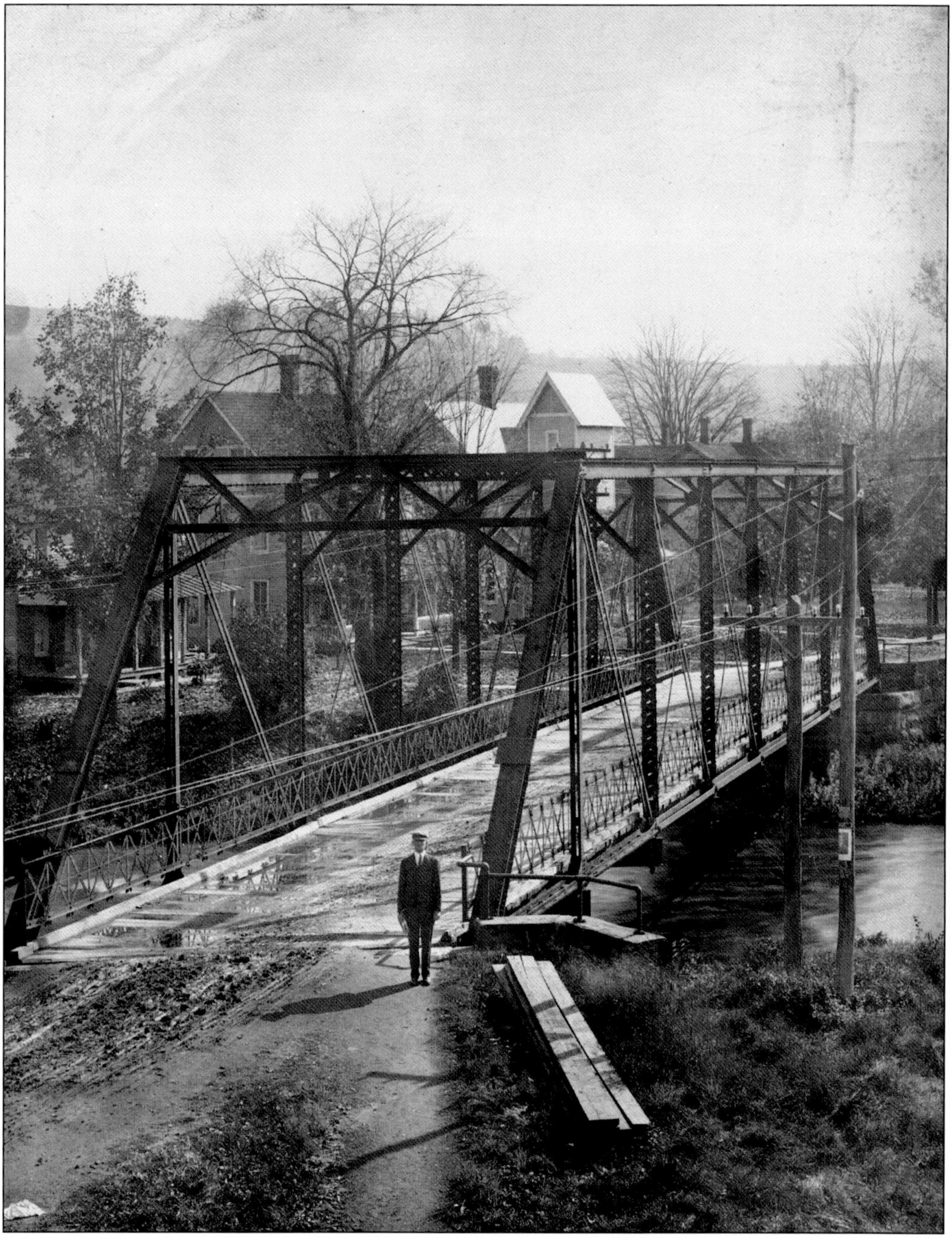

Prof. Daniel Brady (D. B.) Little was an educator. He served as the principal at Picture Rocks High School and at the Hughesville schools. His main interest was history, on which he was known to give many talks and speeches. Little later owned the Lycoming Ladder Company. (Courtesy of Wes Sprout and Bob Roller.)

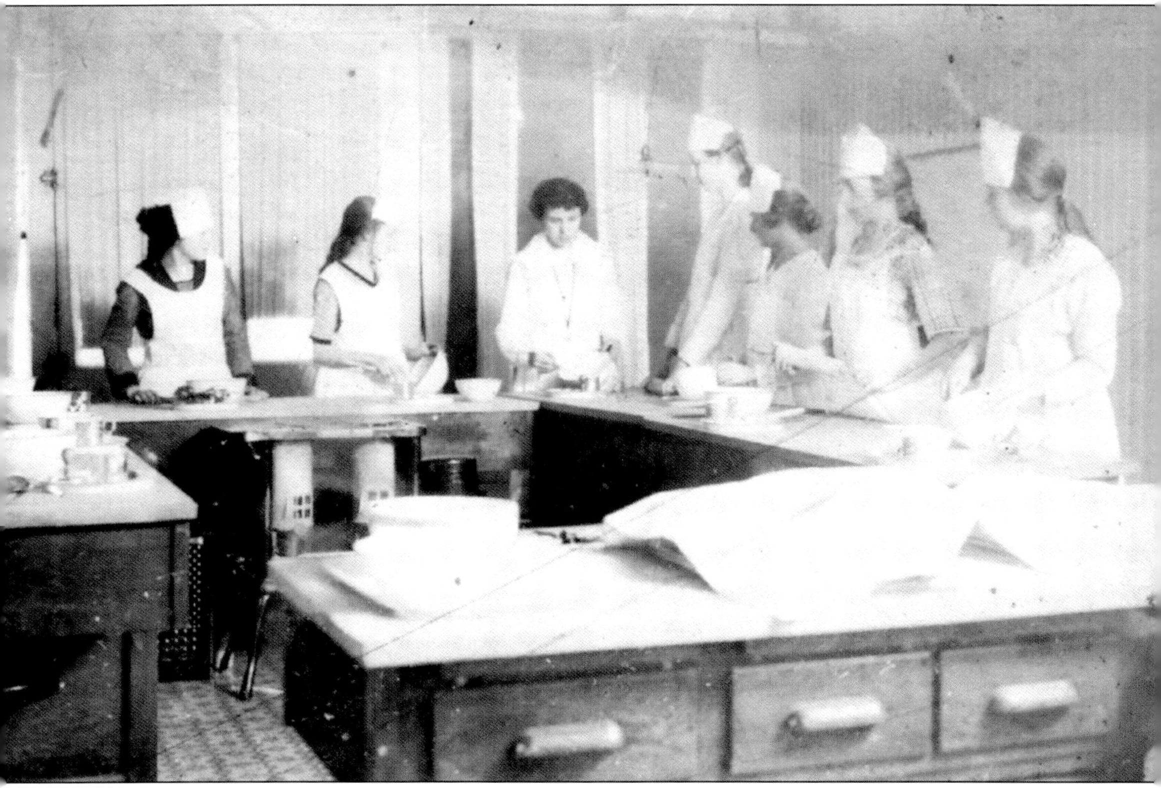

Among the branches taught in the home-making department were cookery, sewing, hygiene, general science, and practical dietetics as well as other subjects relating to the management of a home. (Courtesy of Cris Gansell.)

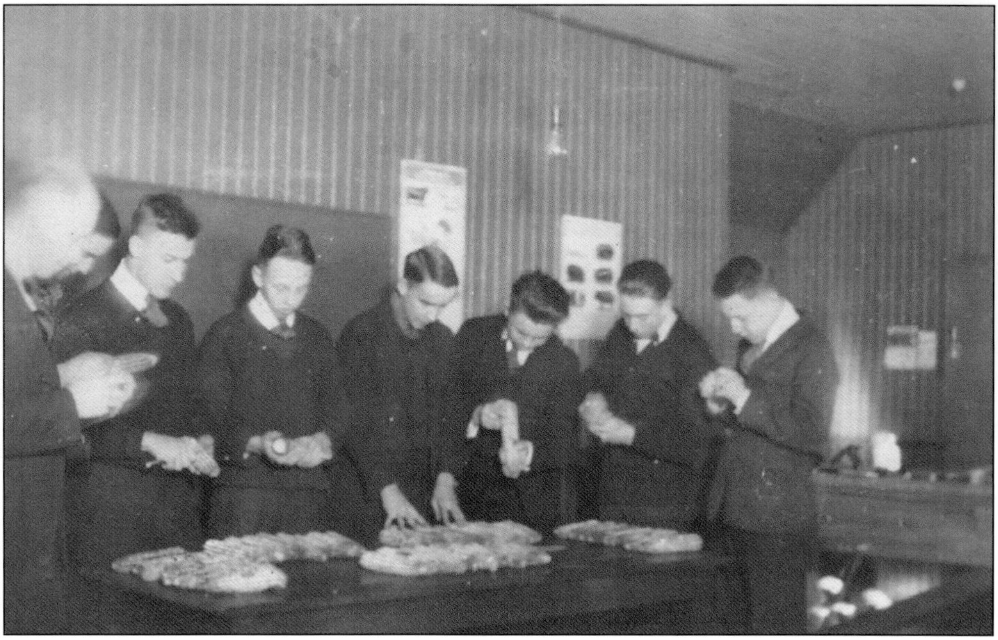

The Picture Rocks High School was a vocational agricultural school and one of the first of its kind in Pennsylvania. (Courtesy of Mike Bayley.)

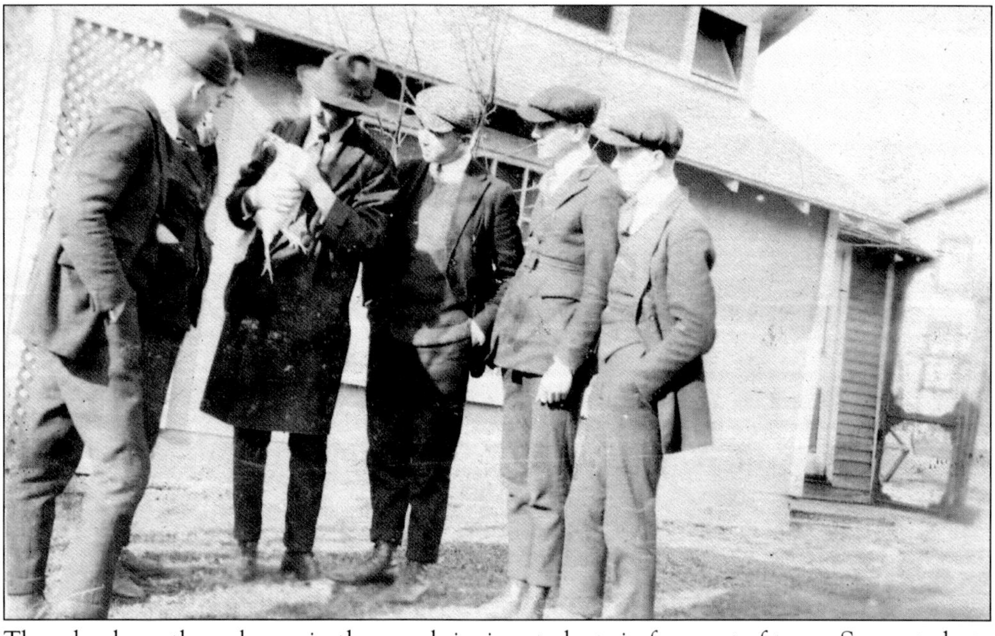

The school was the only one in the area bringing students in from out of town. Some students stayed with families in town during the week just so they could attend the school. (Courtesy of Mike Bayley.)

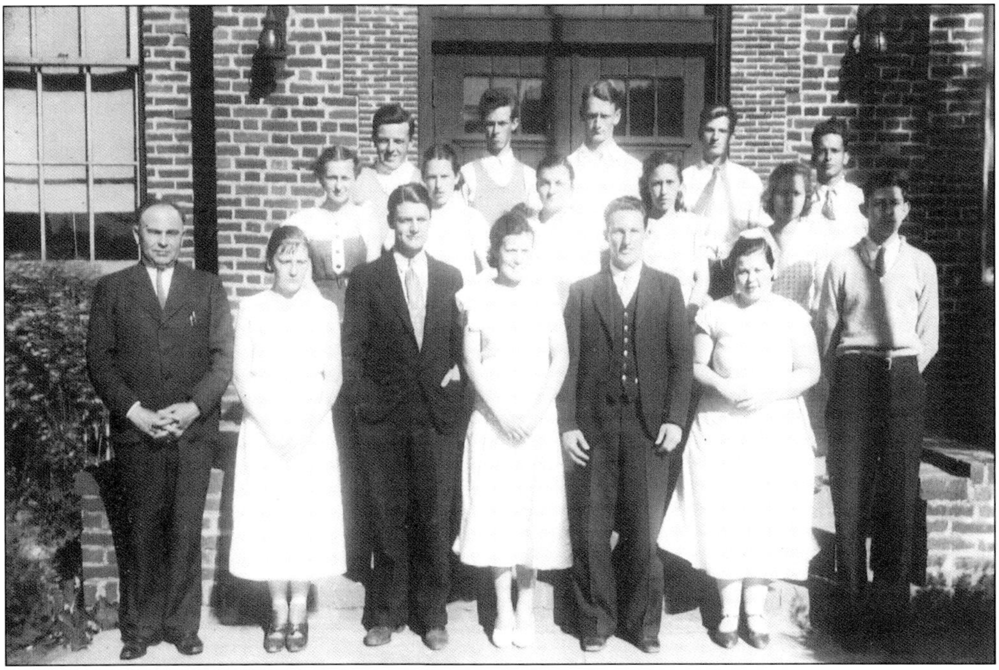

The 1934 graduating class of Picture Rocks High School is pictured here. (Courtesy of Eugene "Cap" Daye.)

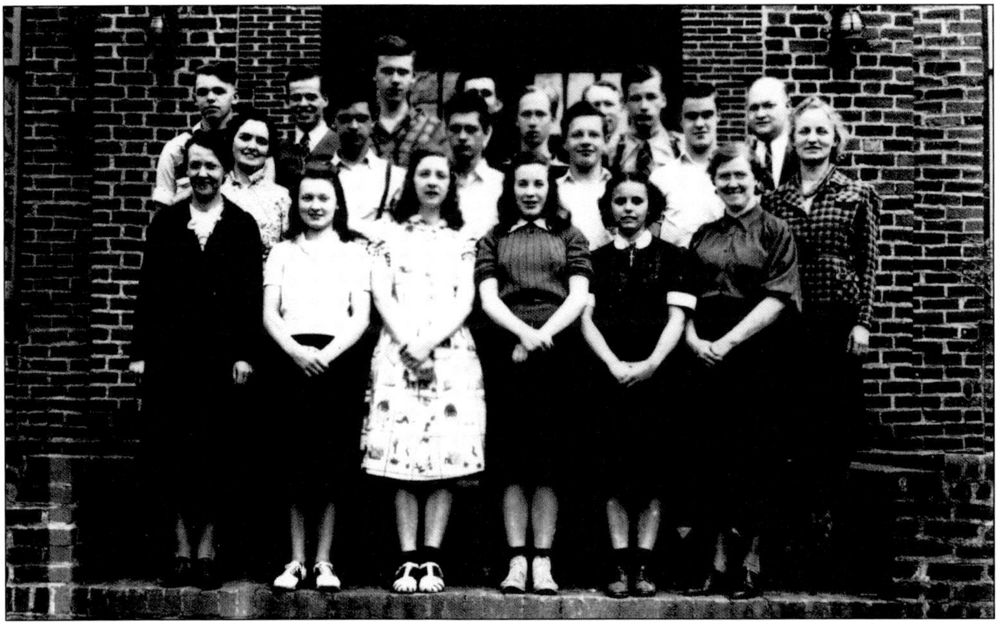

One student remembers when Principal Dinger (third row, far right) came running out of his home in the middle of the night after listening to a little radio program called "War of the Worlds." He was one of many that went into a panic that night, thinking it was real. (Courtesy of Bert and Marjorie Winder.)

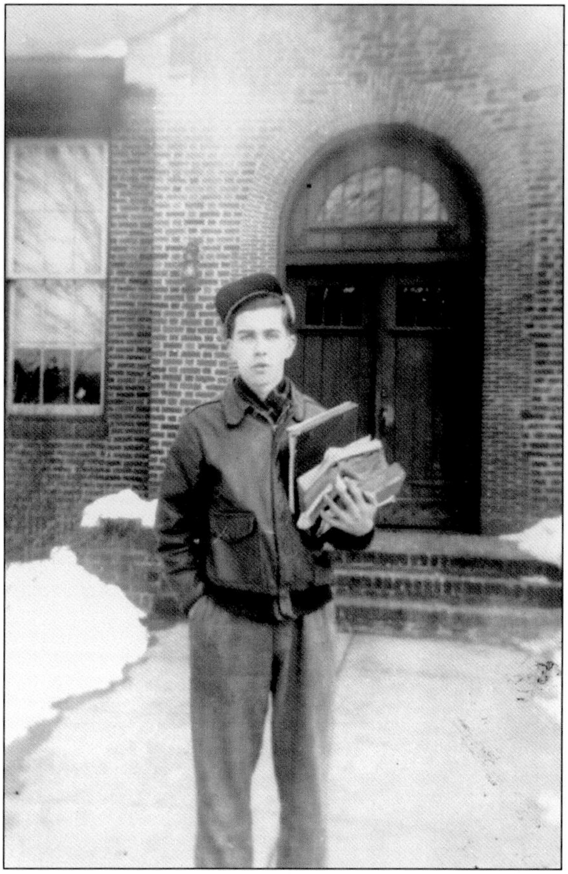

There is a large field across from the school that needed to be leveled. The school decided that it should be done by a pick and shovel. They did not want to bring equipment in because they wanted the people of Picture Rocks to have good paying work. In this picture, schoolboy Charley Gansell poses in front of the high school. (Courtesy of Cris Gansell.)

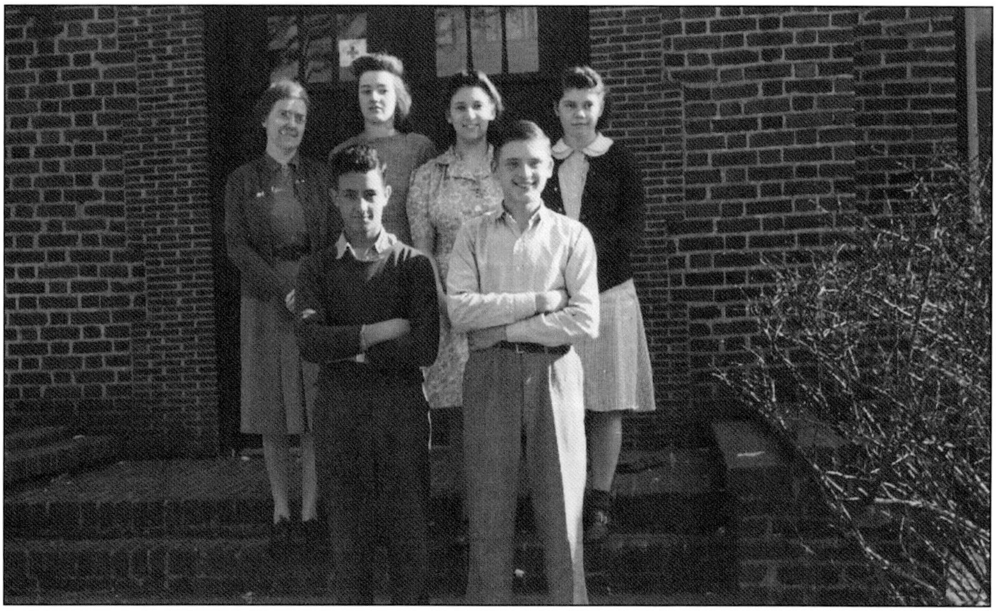

Pictured here is a junior class from the Picture Rocks High School. The next year there was only one person in the senior class—Joan Gansell (second row, far right). (Courtesy of Charley Gansell.)

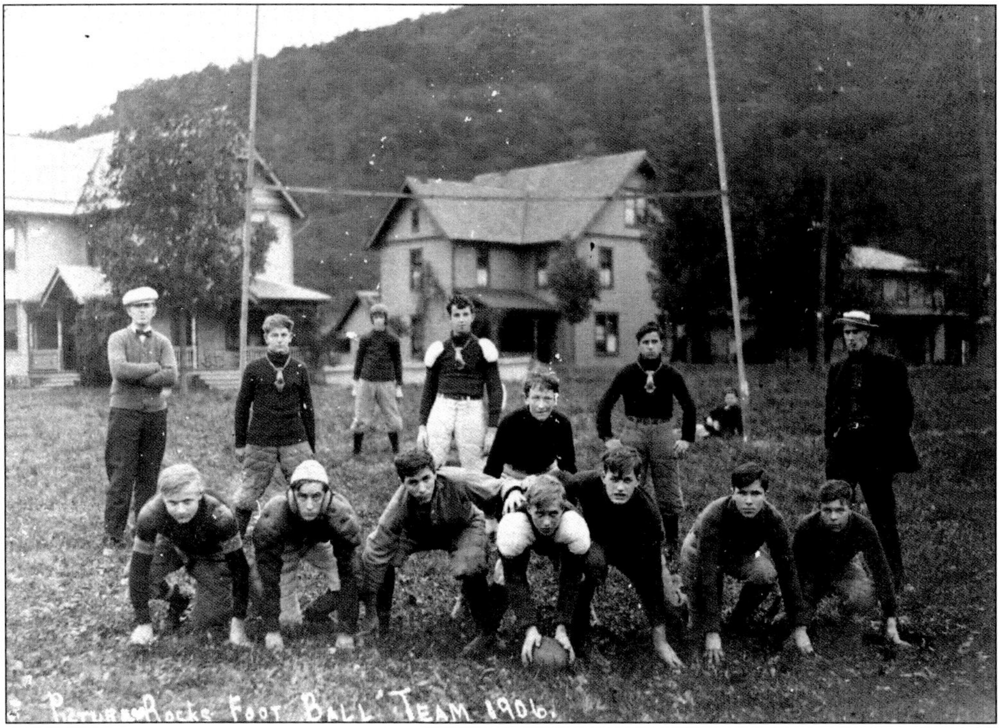

Shown here is the 1906 Picture Rocks football team. (Courtesy of Wes and Pat Sprout.)

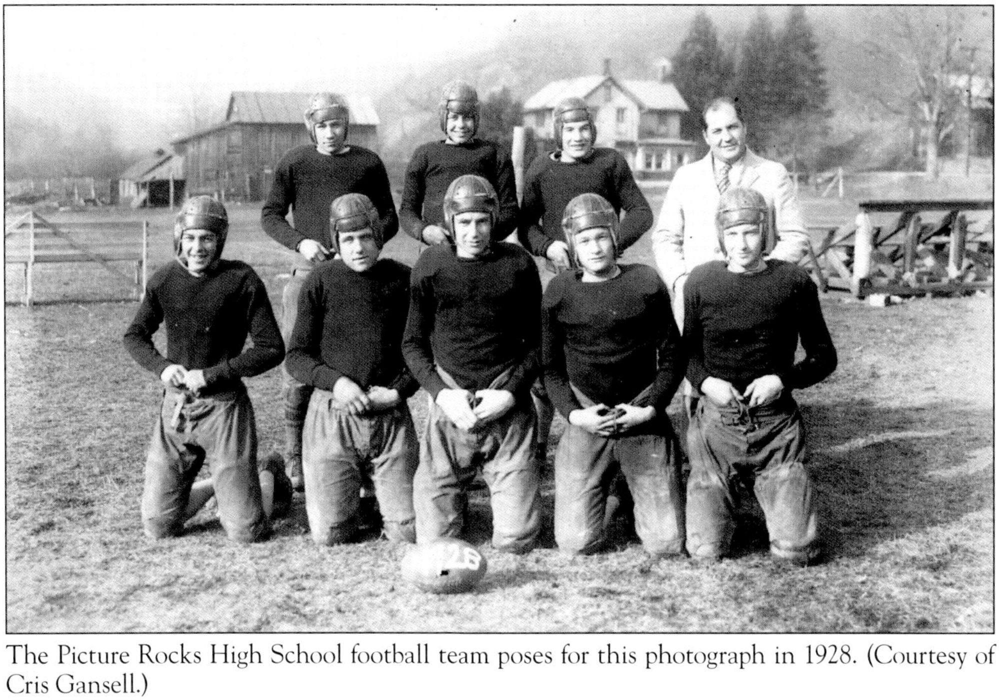

The Picture Rocks High School football team poses for this photograph in 1928. (Courtesy of Cris Gansell.)

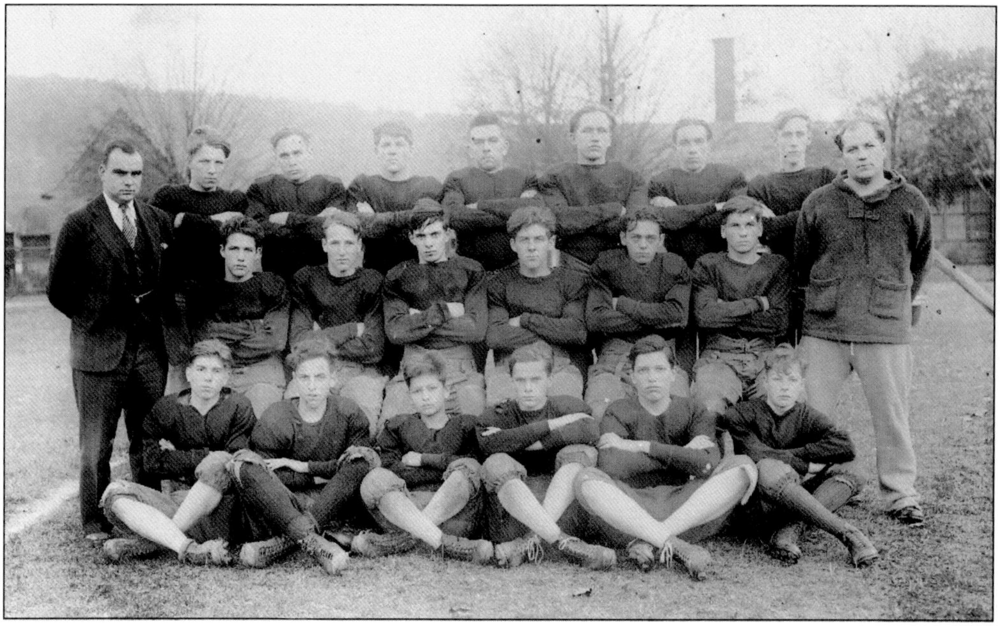

The 1929 Picture Rocks High School football team is pictured here. (Courtesy of Wes and Pat Sprout.)

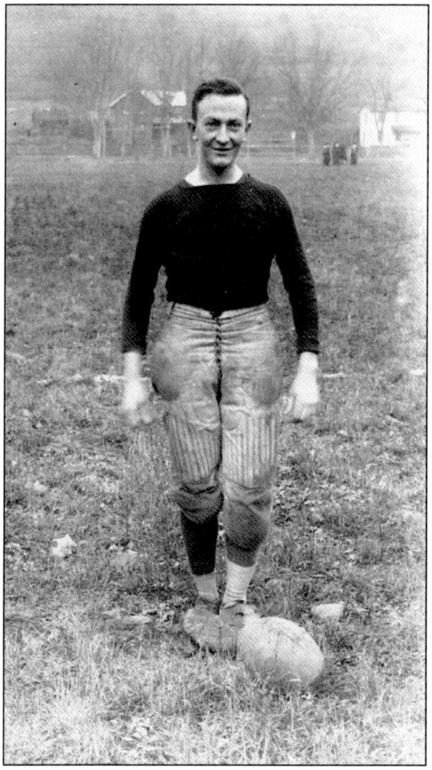

Picture Rocks held some fantastic athletic teams. Many were championship-winning teams. This is Robert Ferrell Sr. when he played for the Picture Rocks High School football team. (Courtesy of the Sandmeyers.)

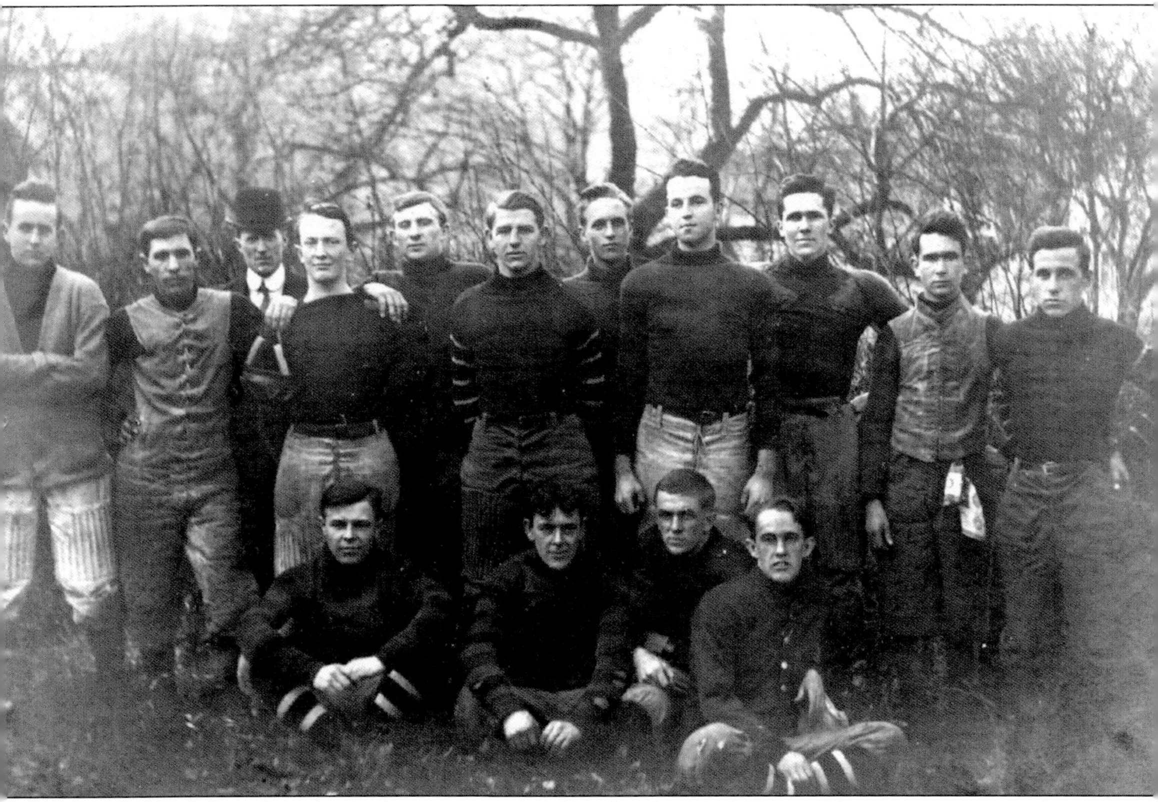

Some of the star athletes at Picture Rocks High School included E. Roller, Don Sprout, Bob Ferrell, and L. Sprout. (Courtesy of Wes and Pat Sprout.)

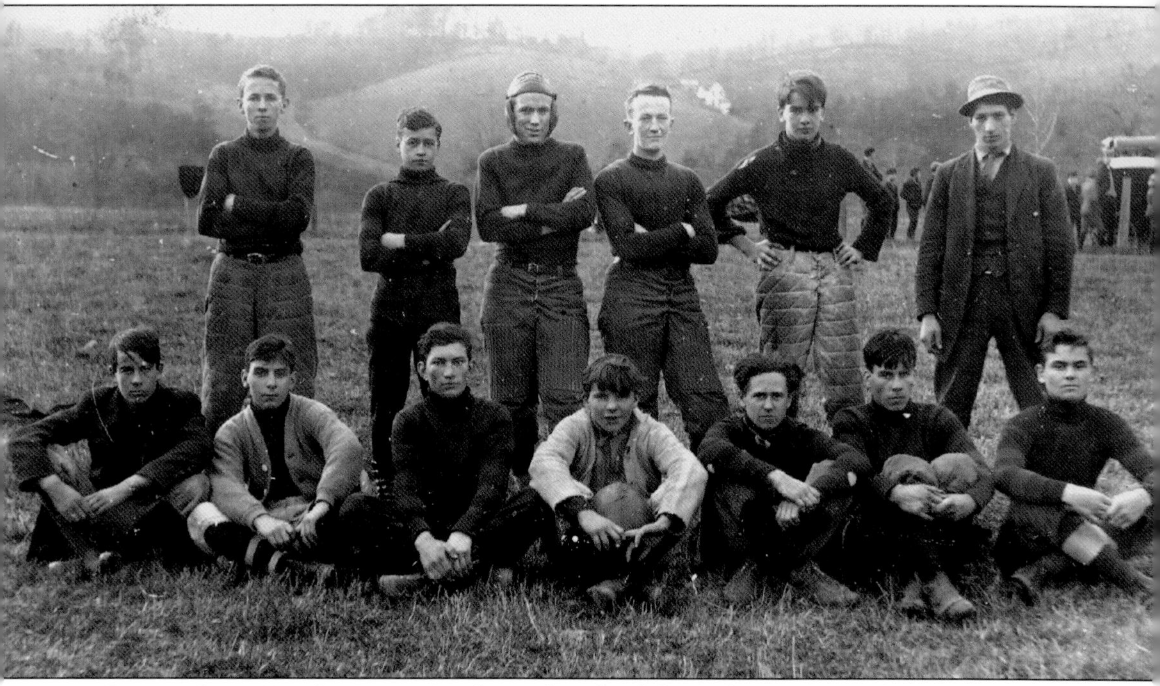

During the 1920s, the Picture Rocks High School football team boasted many wins against rival schools, such as Berwick and Jersey Shore. The team was also known to beat junior college teams like Bucknell and Dickinson Seminary. (Courtesy of Wes and Pat Sprout.)

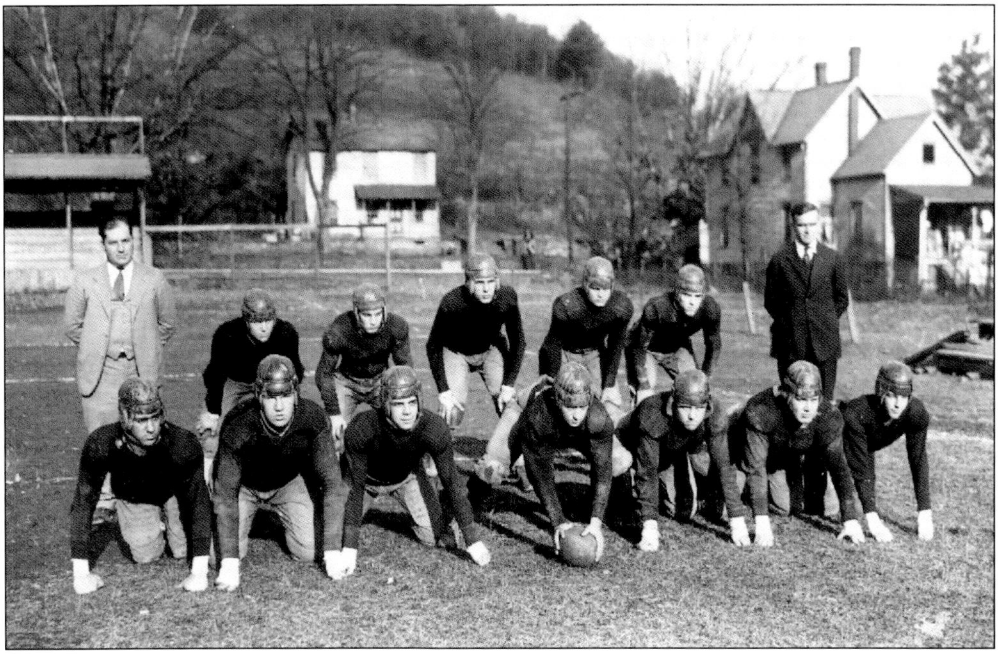

One of the football team's biggest feats was against Shickshinny. Picture Rocks won with a score of 119 to 0. That team was coached by Pat Collins. (Courtesy of Cris Gansell.)

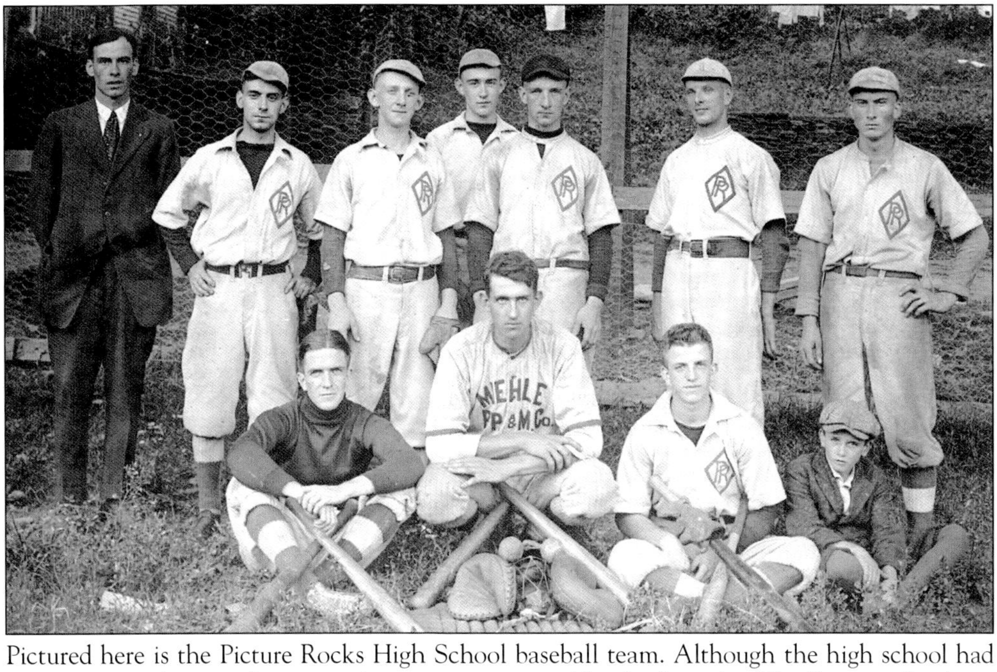

Pictured here is the Picture Rocks High School baseball team. Although the high school had its own team, the very first teams in town were started by the factories. The Burrows Brothers, H and E, and the Ladder Factory all had teams throughout the years. For many years, the teams had to play behind the fire hall until the field at Van Rensselaer Park was created. (Courtesy of Ron Hicks.)

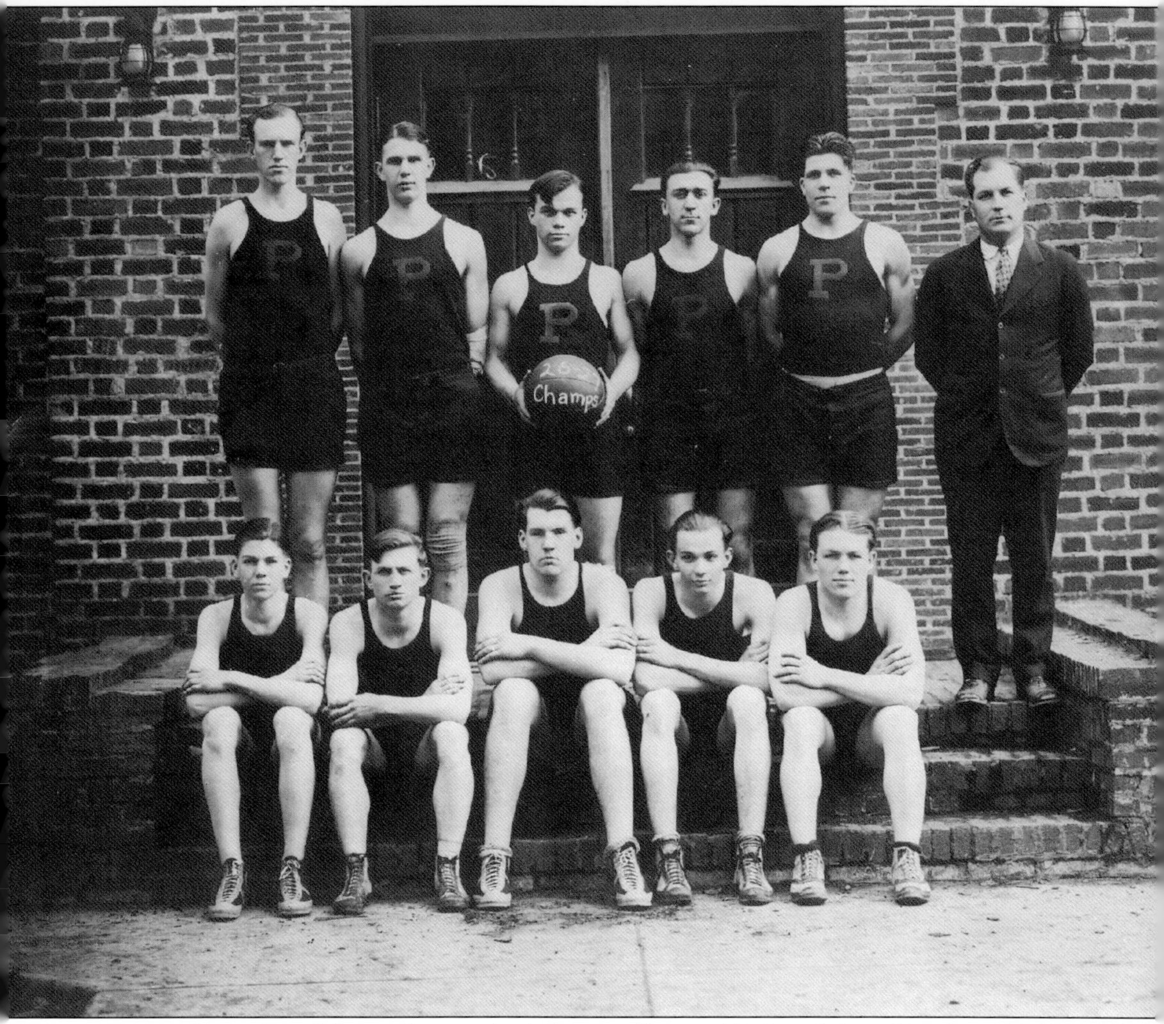

Pictured here, from left to right, are the following: (first row) Robert Pelton, Henderson Robbins, Girton "Tiny" Lenheart, Gerald Nunn, and Bert Miller; (second row) James Smith, Henry Fry, Russell Sprout, Kenneth Mysen, Cleon Boston, and Professor Walp. (Courtesy of Cris Gansell.)

Three

PEOPLE OF PICTURE ROCKS

August 17, 1865
Worked 9 hours for ES, did chores. Self and family took tea at S. H. Burrows practiced singing with others for soliders welcome. Berry Jearty came home, soldiers also.

—Amos Sprout

To know Picture Rocks, one has to know the people. The early settlers held high moral standard and had a work ethic that could turn useless land into a thriving, self-sustaining town. They were Baptist in faith and Republican in politics. Over the years, the spirit of those settlers has carried on.

Factories still exist in this town, and local people still own the businesses here. The town is still a dry town. Alcohol cannot be sold within the limits of Picture Rocks. This is one of the original laws on the books. People still have to go to the post office to get their mail.

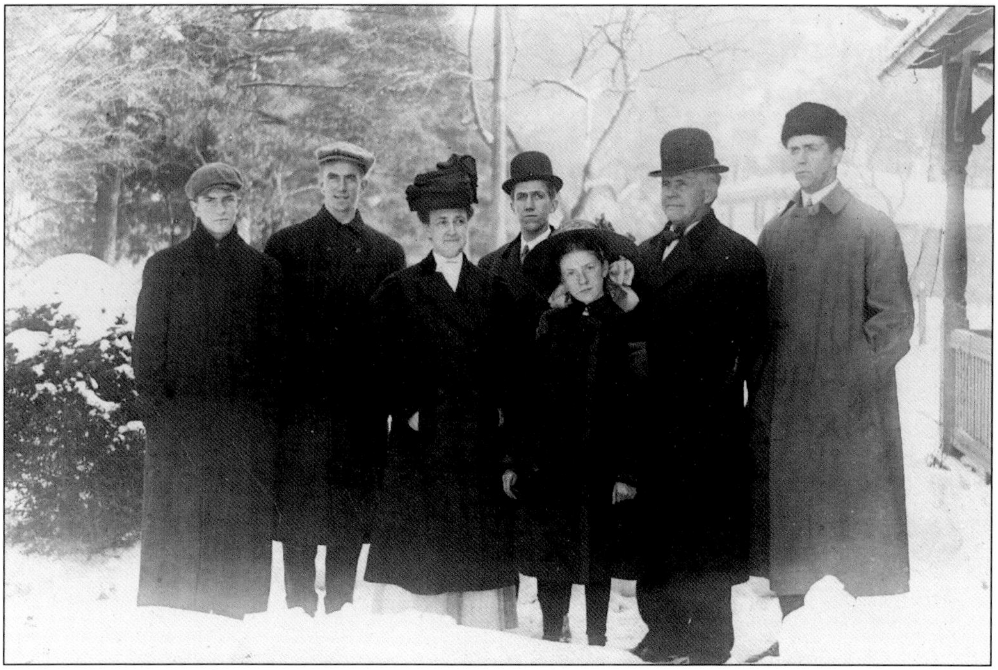

This is the family of Morton I. Sprout. Pictured, from left to right, are Clinton Sprout, Donald Sprout, Lucinda Sprout (mother), Carl Sprout, Marjorie E. Sprout, Morton I. Sprout (father), and W. Lee Sprout. (Courtesy of Evelyn Bryan.)

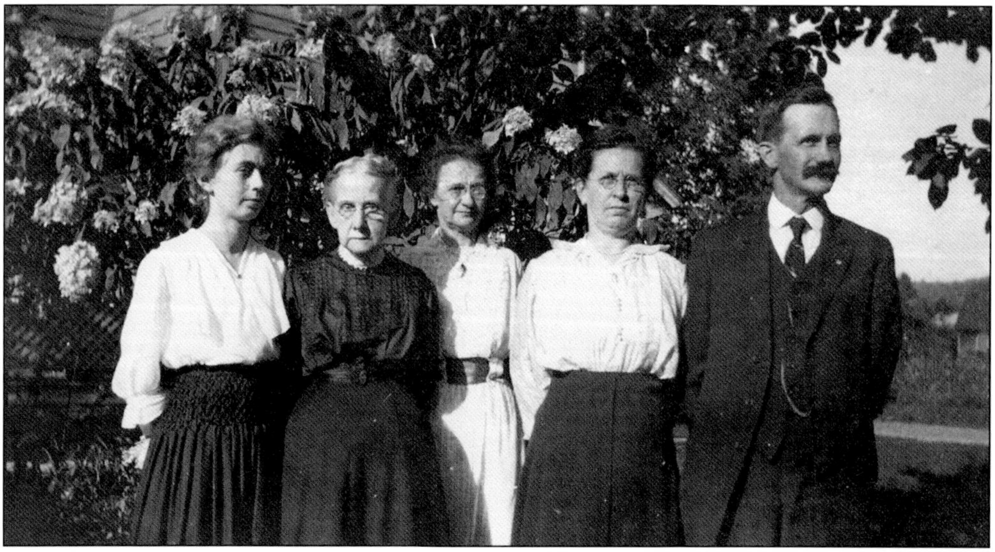

The Melhuish family is pictured here. Family members, from left to right, are Edna Melhuish, Rose Melhuish (grandmother), Jennie Melhuish, Debbie Cruse Melhuish, and Harvey Melhuish. (Courtesy of Evelyn Bryan.)

Edna Melhuish was very active in the Baptist church. Members of the Melhuish family organized the mission band in November 1893 and the Farther Lights Society in June 1897. Edward Melhuish served as a deacon to the church. (Courtesy of Evelyn Bryan.)

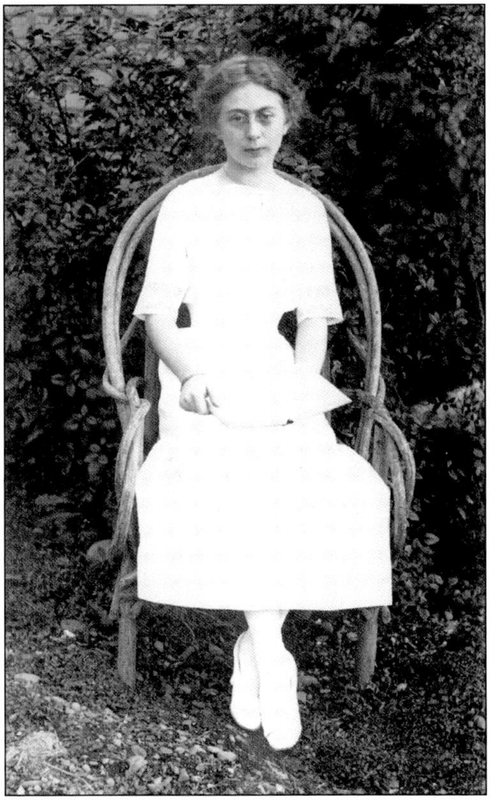

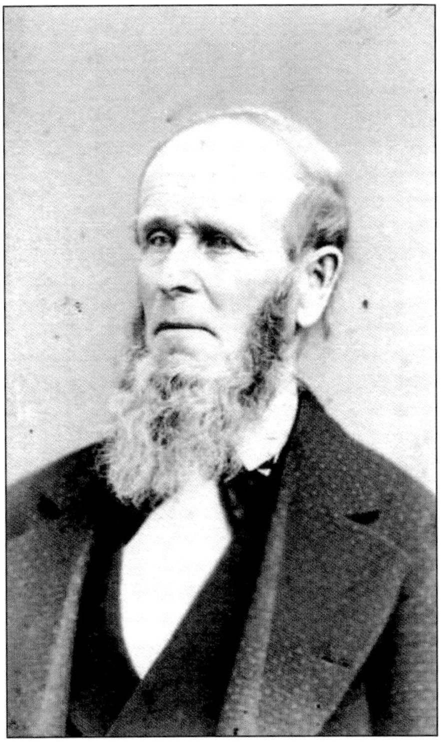

Amos Burrows is one of the town's founding fathers. He is the uncle of Amos Sprout who initially found the land. Amos Sprout, his brother Asa, and (their uncle) Amos Burrows purchased the land and gave the town the foundation of what it is today. (Courtesy of Sherry Gardner.)

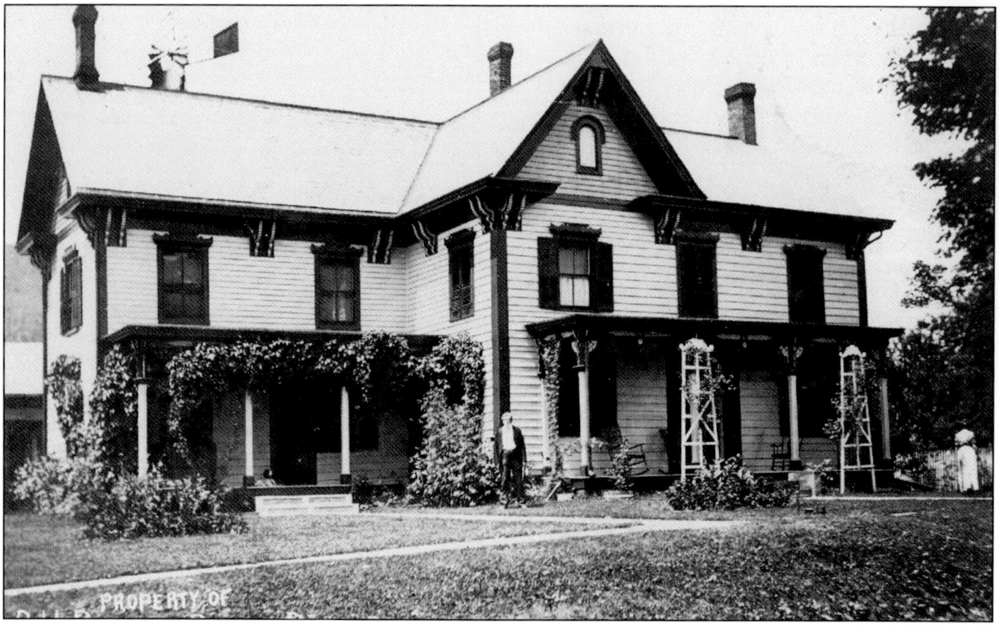

This was the home a Sabin H. Burrows, son of Amos Burrows, who started the Burrows Brothers furniture factory. Sabin also served as the town of Burgess's postmaster and even served under the administration of President Garfield. Sabin also served the Picture Rocks Baptist Church as a deacon for many years. He was considered a staunch Republican. (Courtesy of Wes and Pat Sprout.)

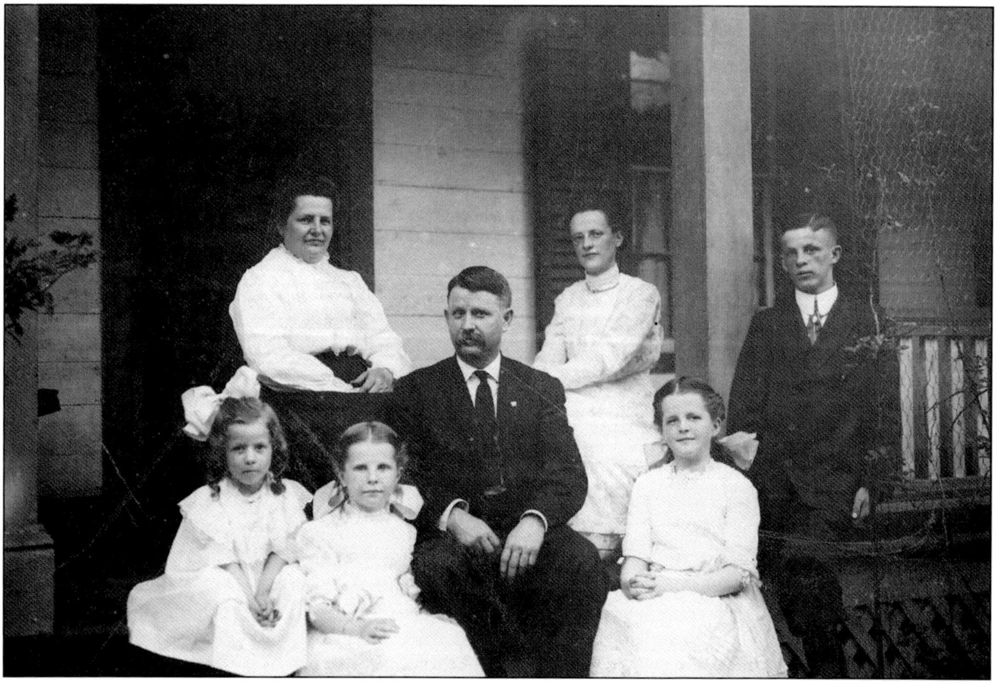

This is Ellis and Orpha Cruse. Orpha is the daughter of Amos and Catherine Sprout, who were among the first settlers of Picture Rocks. (Courtesy of Evelyn Bryan.)

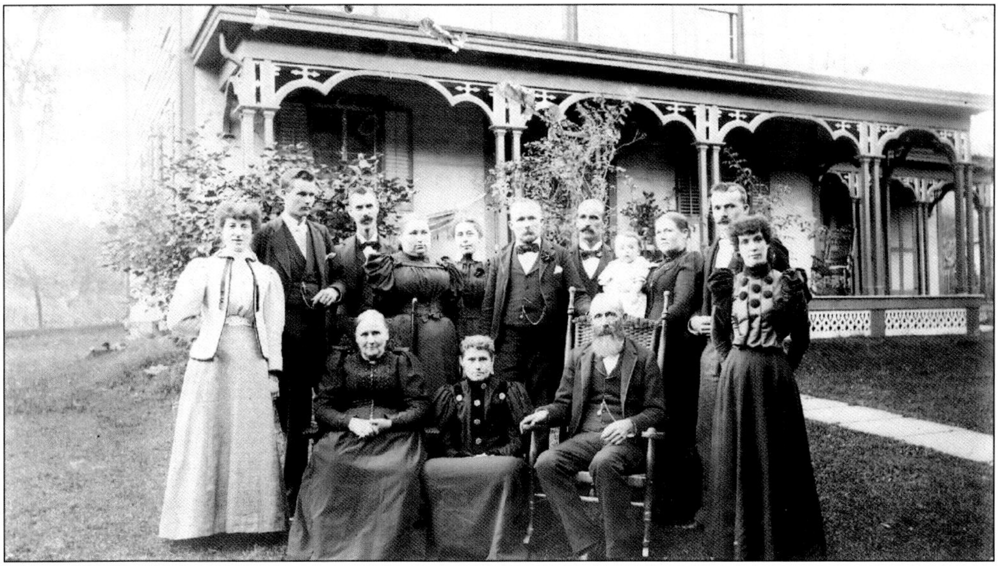

This photograph of the Asa W. Burrows family was taken around 1898. Family members, from left to right, are as follows: (first row) Huldah Hinds Burrows (mother), Fanny Burrows Heath, and Asa W. Burrows (father); (second row) Elizabeth Burrows (wife of Howard), Howard Burrows, Ralph M. Clark, Catherine Burrows (wife of Ralph Clark), Maggie Kahler Burrows (wife of James), James Hinds Burrows, Levi Sherman Weaver, Miriam Burrows Weaver, baby Howard Asa Weaver, Edgar Asa Burrows, and Estella Burrows (wife of Edgar). (Courtesy of Evelyn Bryan.)

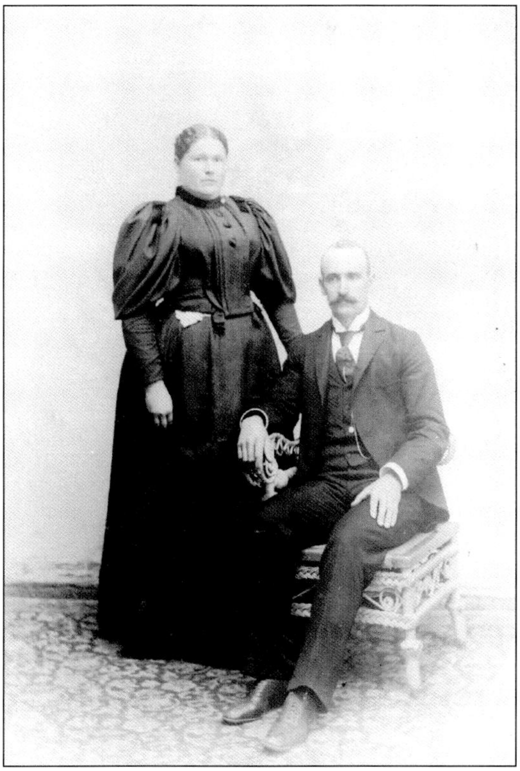

Miriam Weaver is the daughter of Sabin Burrows. Levi Weaver was a mason. (Courtesy of Evelyn Bryan.)

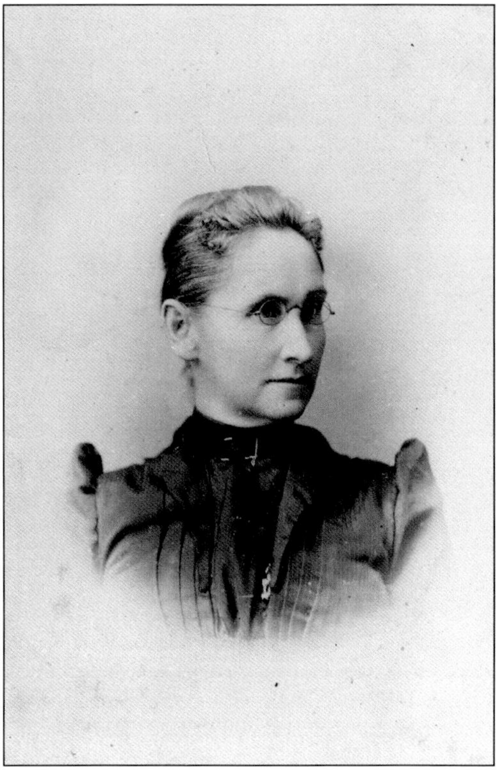

Mrs. Henry C. Munro is pictured here in 1885. (Courtesy of Evelyn Bryan.)

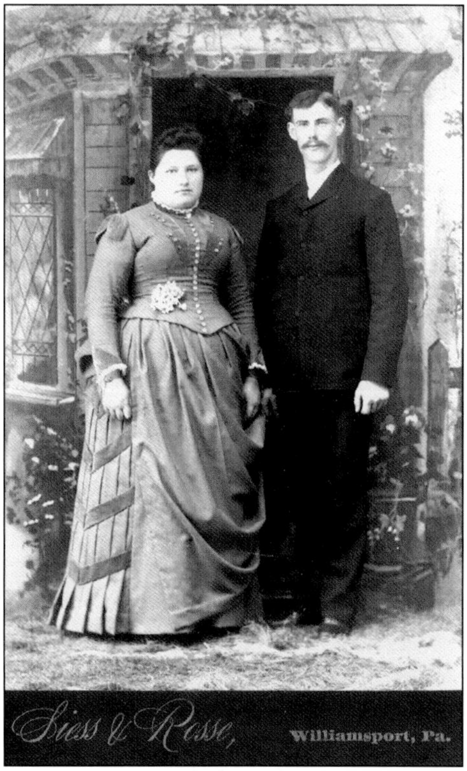

Ralph and Catherine Clark are pictured here. Catherine is the daughter of Sabin Burrows. (Courtesy of Evelyn Bryan.)

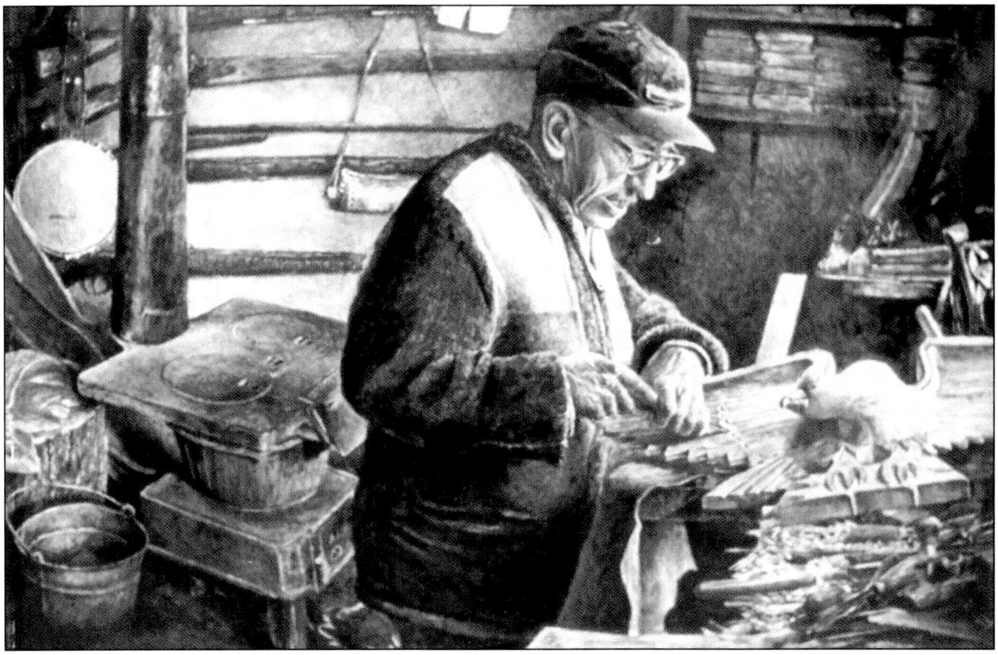

Louis E. Gansell was the town gunsmith and woodcarver. This is the painting that artist David Armstrong did in the 1970s. The picture never went to print, so the original painting is the only one in existence and it is currently on display at Bucknell University. (Courtesy of Cris Gansell.)

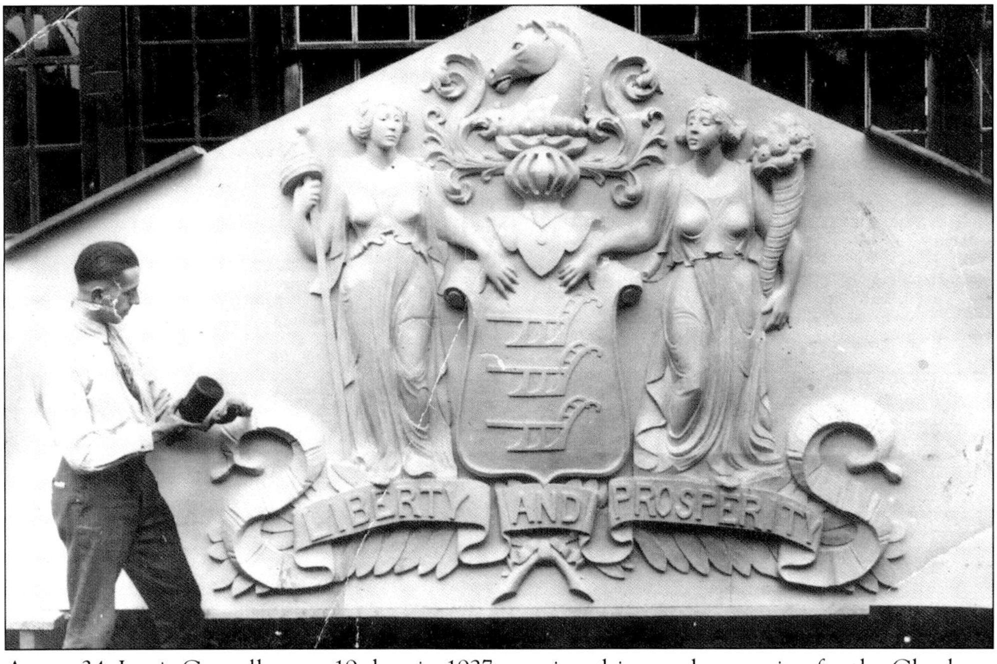

At age 34, Louis Gansell spent 19 days in 1927 creating this wooden carving for the Glassboro Normal School in Glassboro, New Jersey, now Rowan University. It was created at the Williamsport Planning Mill Company where Gansell worked at the time. The woman in the carving was modeled after a living person. (Courtesy of Charley Gansell.)

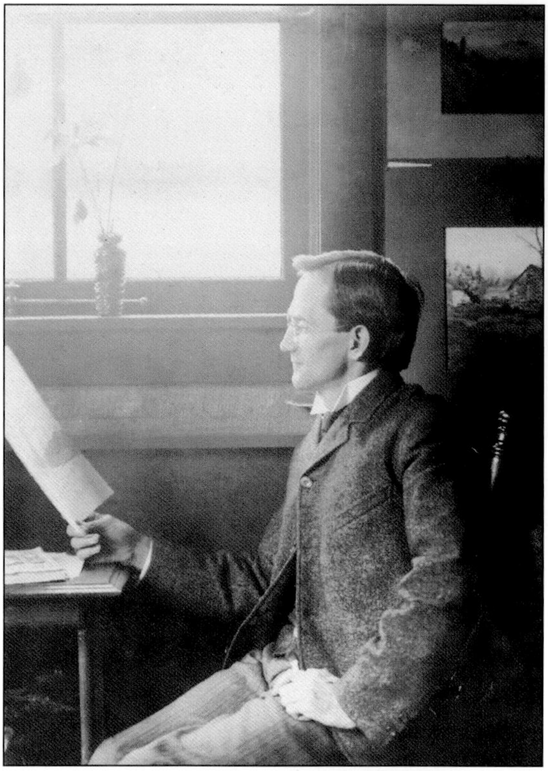

J. Wesley Little moved to Picture Rocks from Forksville at a very early age. At the age of 21, he studied at the National Academy of Design in New York. For further study and painting, Little made trips to Europe. (Courtesy of Dot and Bill Sandmeyer.)

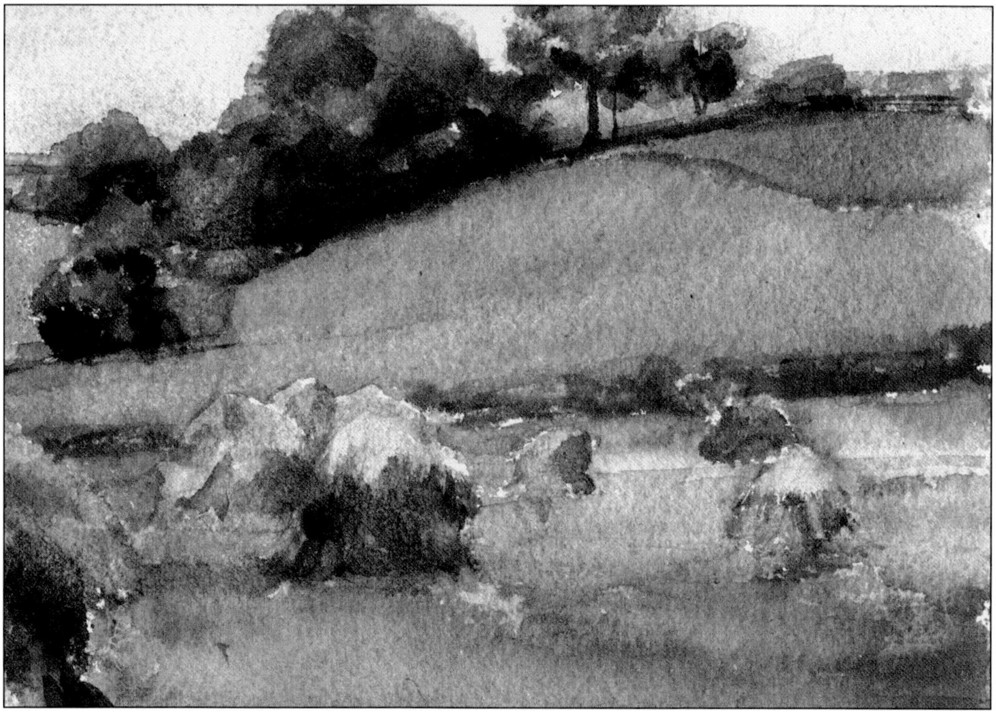

One story of J. Wesley Little is that he would easily walk 16 miles a day to look for inspiration for his next piece of work. (Courtesy of Dot and Bill Sandmeyer.)

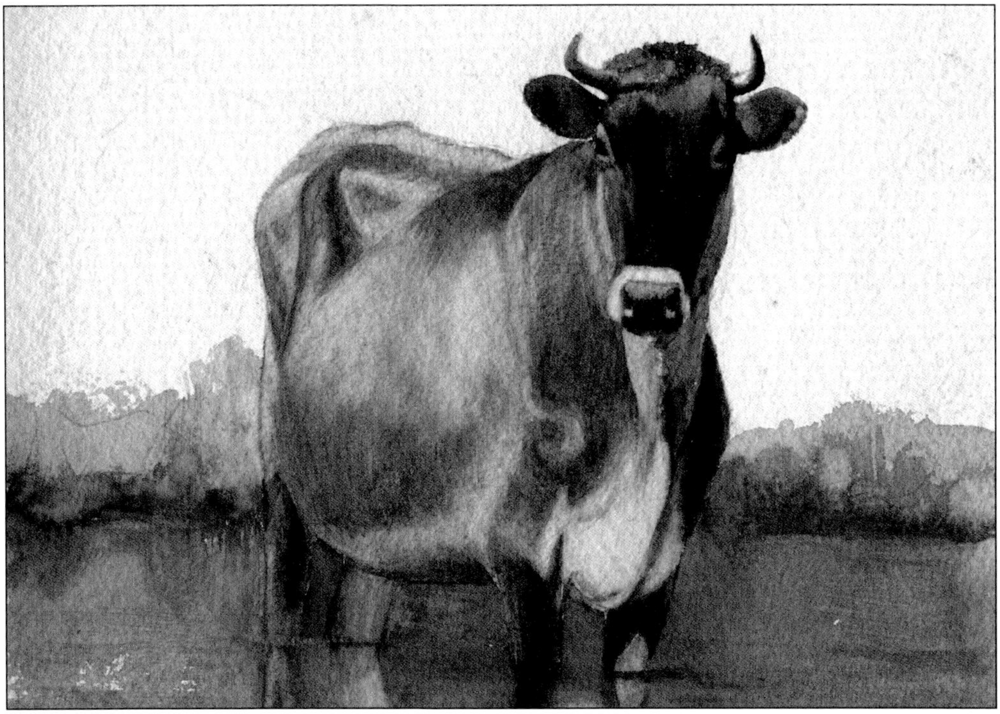

J. Wesley Little was known for his depictions of nature. (Courtesy of Dot and Bill Sandmeyer.)

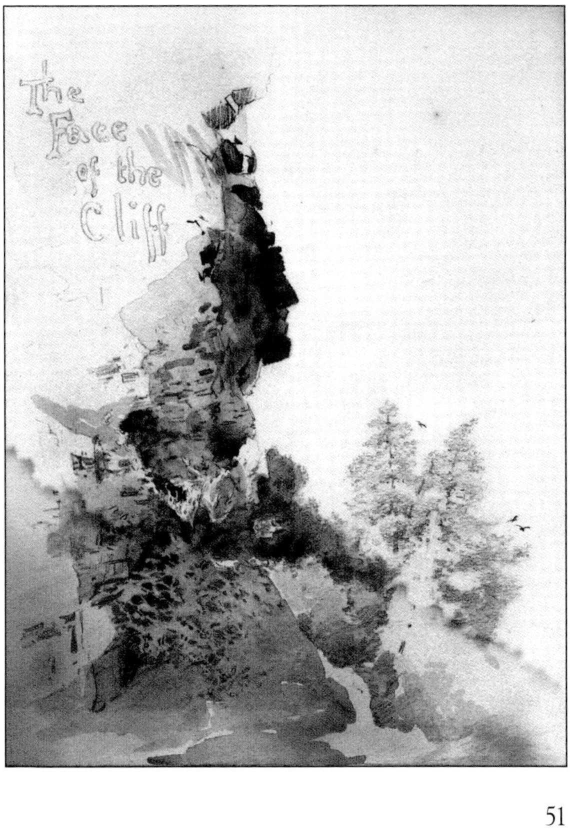

Pictured here is local artist J. Wesley Little's famed piece *The Face on the Cliff*. (Courtesy of Dot and Bill Sandmeyer.)

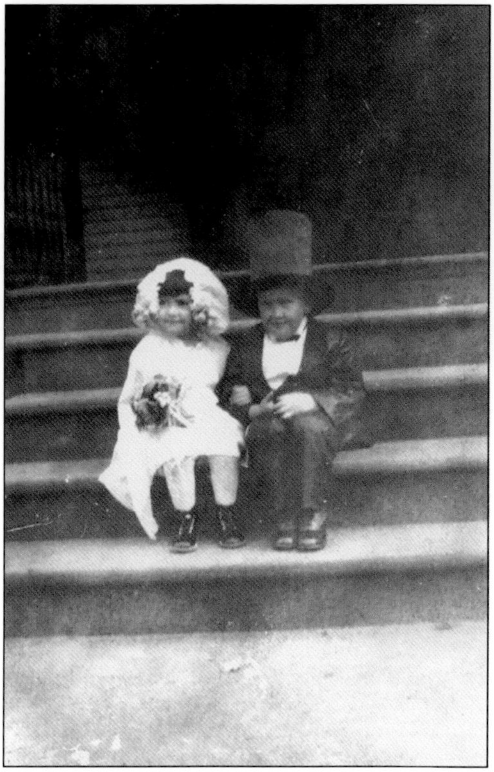

Dot Ferrell and Bud Gillmore are seen here hanging around town. (Courtesy of Dot and Bill Sandmeyer.)

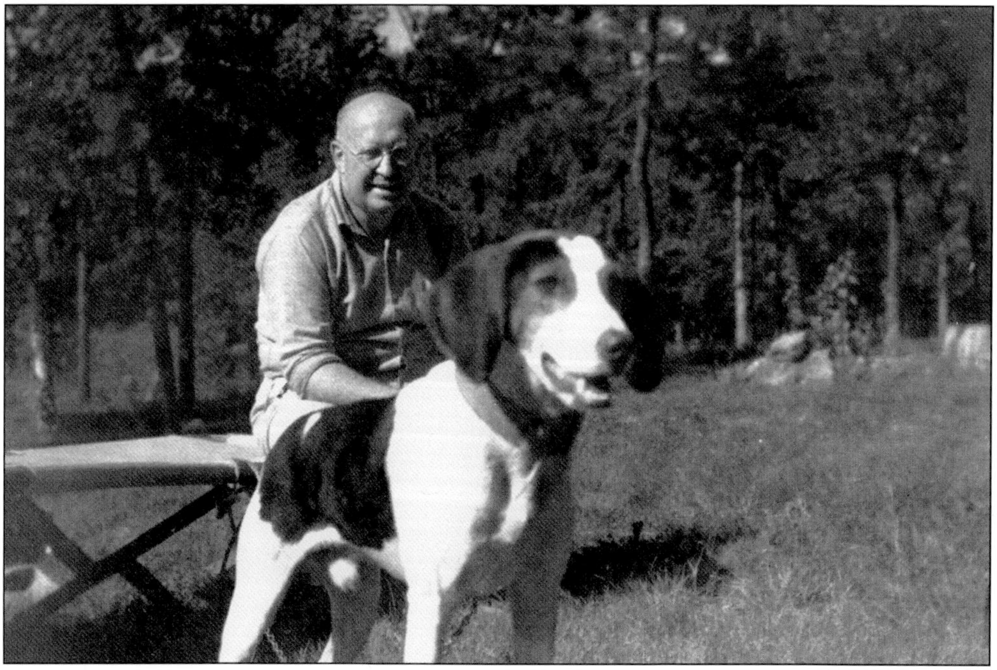

Doc Gilmore and his dog are shown here. It was said that if a door-to-door salesperson came to his house and did not make a fuss over his dog, he would not buy a thing from him. (Courtesy of Dot and Bill Sandmeyer.)

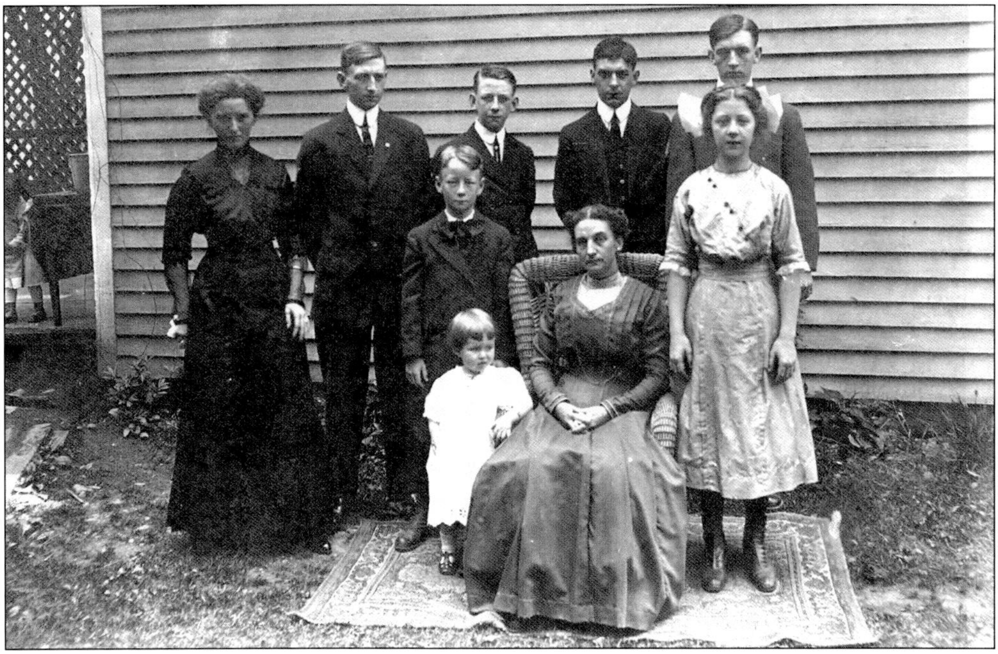

The McClain family is pictured here. Family members, from left to right, are as follows: (first row) Bucky McClain, Margaret (Dorman) McClain, Ella (Collins) McClain, and Sarah (Haynes) McClain; (second row) Blanch Collins, Willie McClain, Jake McClain, Jake McClain, and Frank McClain. (Courtesy of Ron Hicks.)

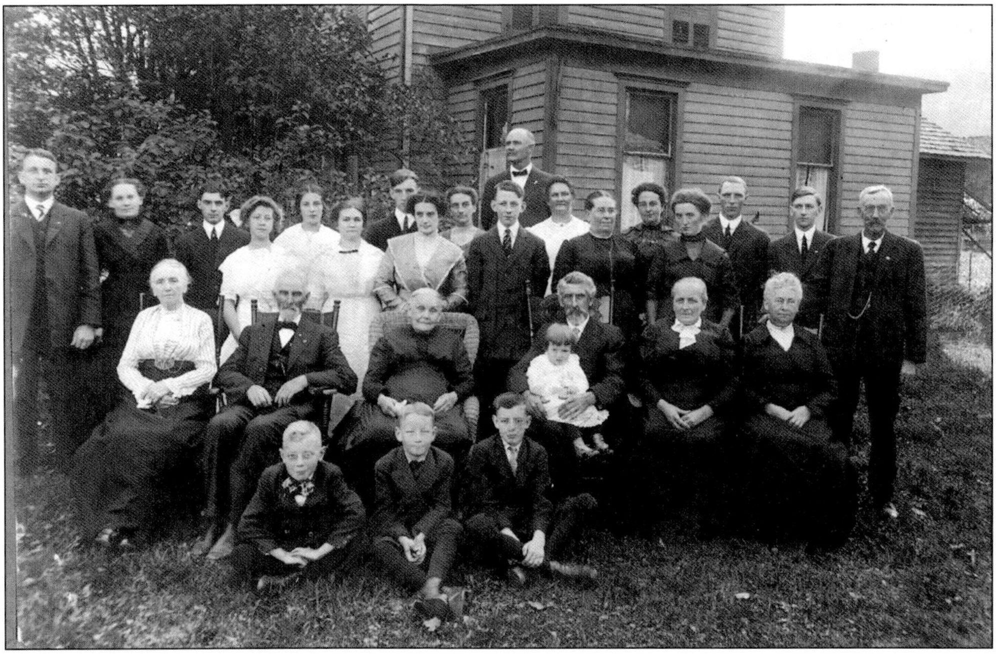

The Collins family is pictured here. Family members, from left to right, are as follows: (first row) Milton Collins, Bucky Collins, and Leon Collins; (second row) Charlie and Emma May Collins, Jack McClain, Blanch Brink Collins, Sarah Haynes McClain, Willie McClain, Ella Collins McClain, Jake McClain, and Frank McClain. (Courtesy of Ron Hicks.)

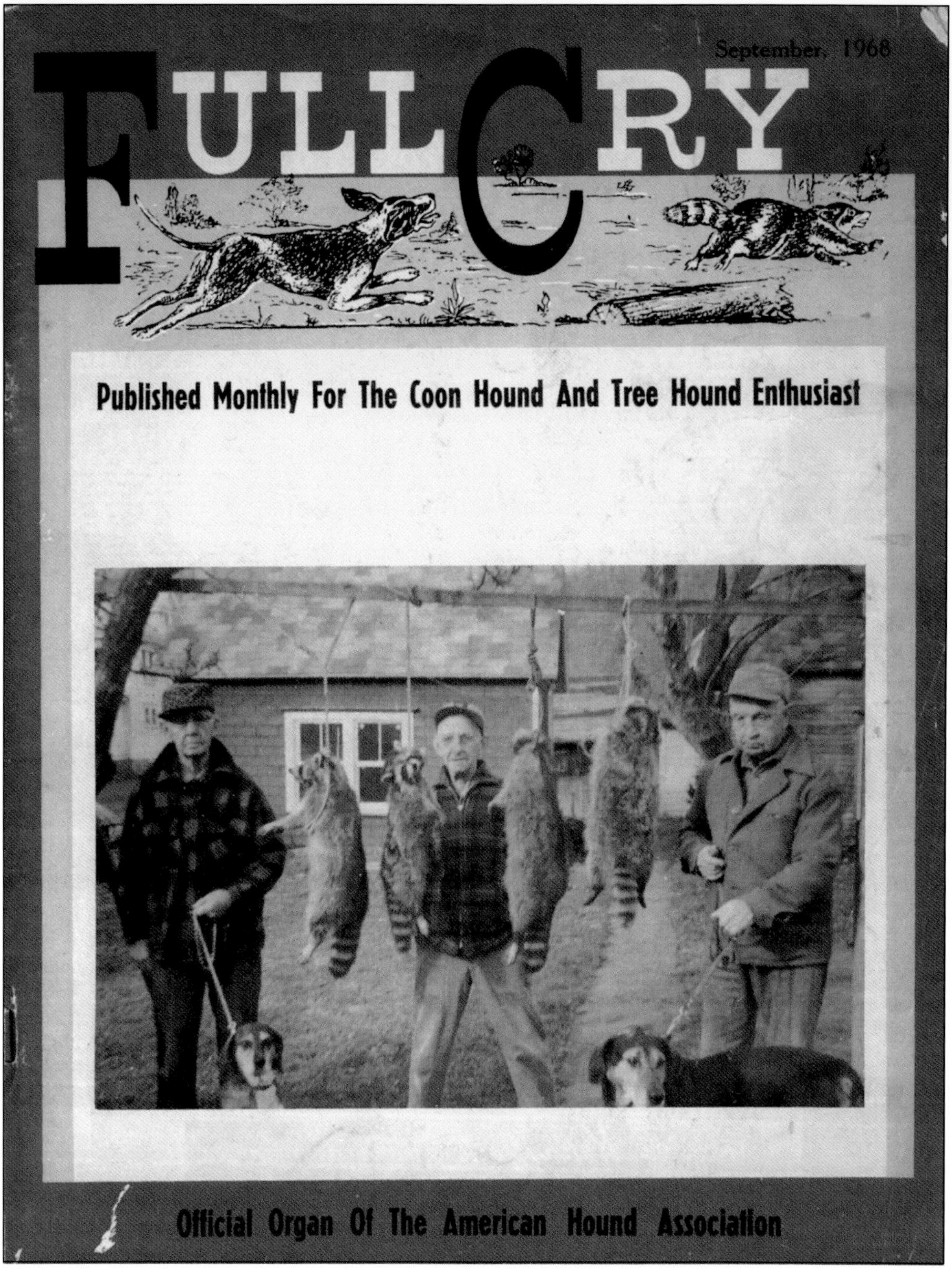

Shown here is the cover from *Full Cry* magazine from 1968. Pictured are Jack McClain, Jake McClain, and Frank McClain. (Courtesy of Ron Hicks.)

Four

CHURCHES

October 25, 1884
Prepared to go to Moreland to deliver a lecture on morals and get subscriptions for the (Baptist) church. Lewis called and took dinner with us and started home at 2 and ½ hours. I started at same time and arrived at maddisons at 5pm took supper and walked 1 and ¼ ms to church, talked ¾ hour got sub(scriptions) but col(lected) $1,30 (one hundred thirty dollars) from about 100 persons present. S. Farr and Nilson Derr paid the sub(scription) $7.00. Stay at M tonight.

—Amos Sprout

Religion was of the utmost importance to the early settlers. When the Baptists of town were tired of worshiping in a schoolhouse, they built their own chapel in eight days in 1851. It was 25 years until the Picture Rocks Baptist Church was built.

The Methodist built their first church on Water Street in 1869. It is said that the stonework that made up its foundation had carvings and paintings from the Monsie Indians.

The two churches were known to hold joint services and revivals together over the years. Guest choirs and other organizations would also visit the churches.

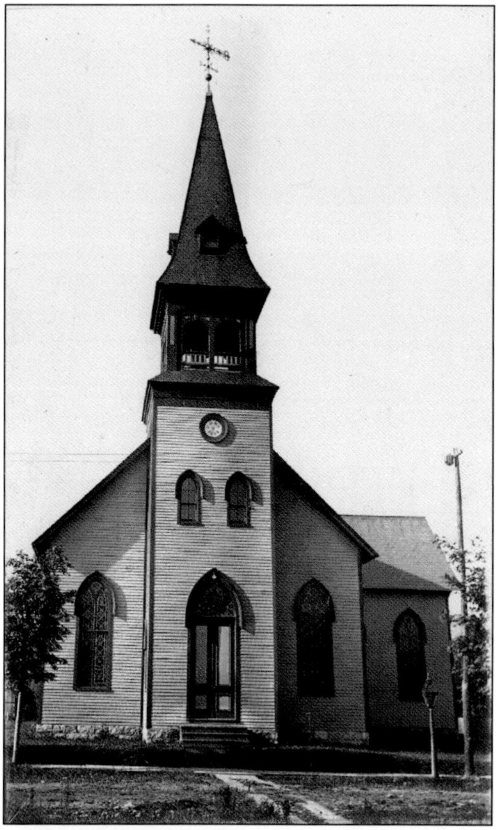

Both the Burrows and the Sprout families had high Christian morals. This was the first church built in town. The church as it is today was built between 1884 and 1885. The land was donated by Asa R. Sprout. When the church was officially dedicated in June 28, 1885, it was free of all debt. (Courtesy of Evelyn Bryan.)

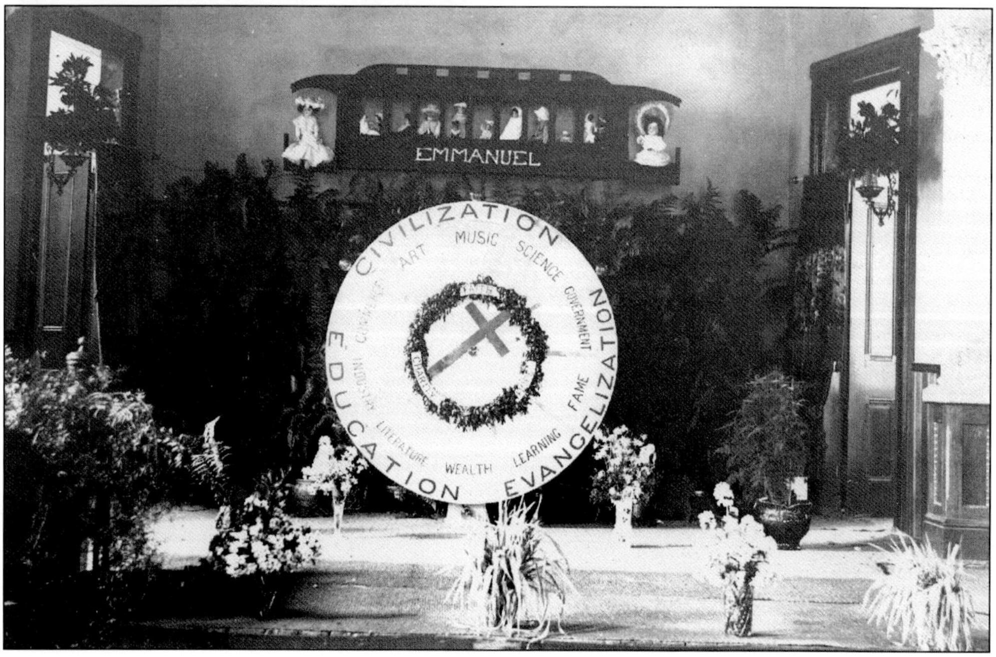

The first service was held at the Baptist church on February 22, 1885, under Rev. H. G. Munro. (Courtesy of Evelyn Bryan.)

With the Methodist church right down the street, the two organizations worked together many times holding joint services and revivals. (Courtesy of Evelyn Bryan.)

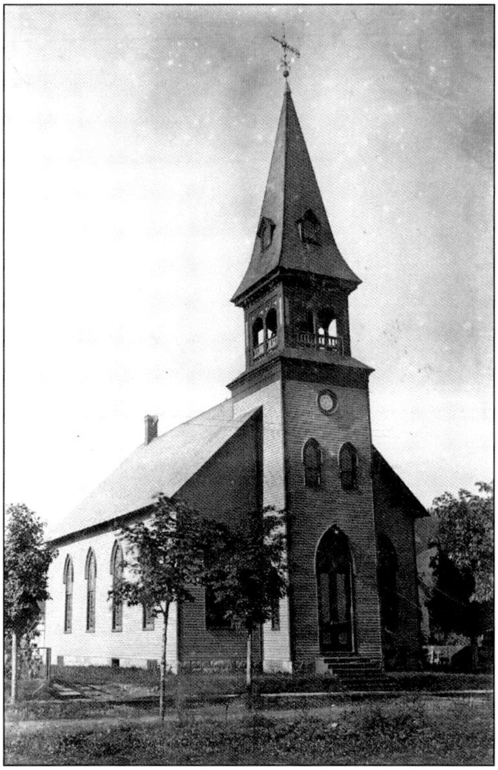

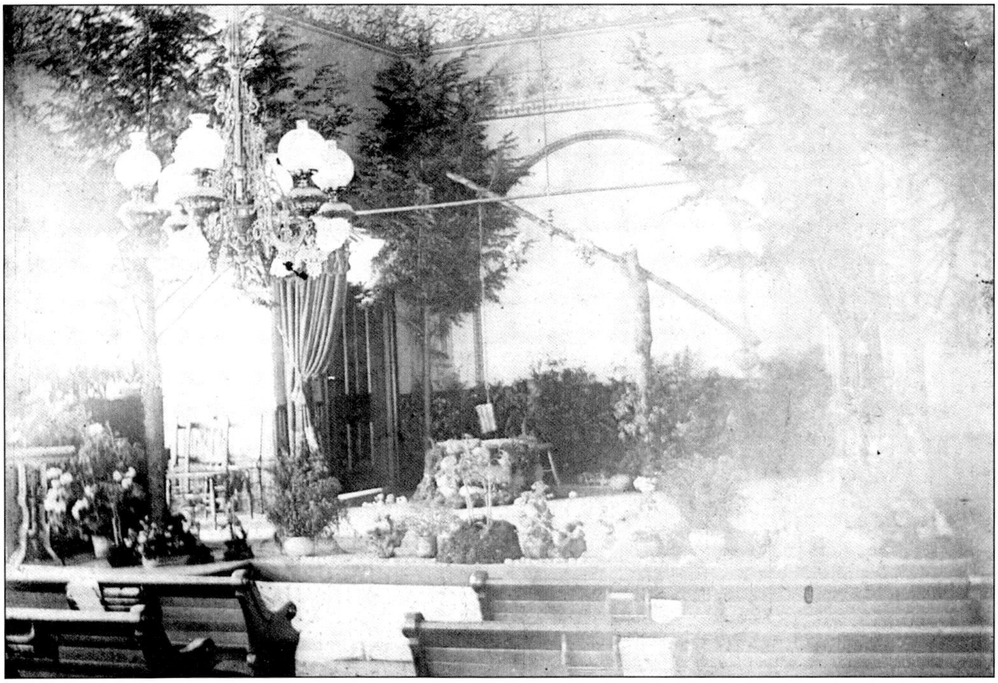

Many of the features in the church, such as the stone fireplace, furniture for the junior Baptist and pulpit furniture were give to the church by its own members, all of whom lived in Picture Rocks. (Courtesy of Evelyn Bryan.)

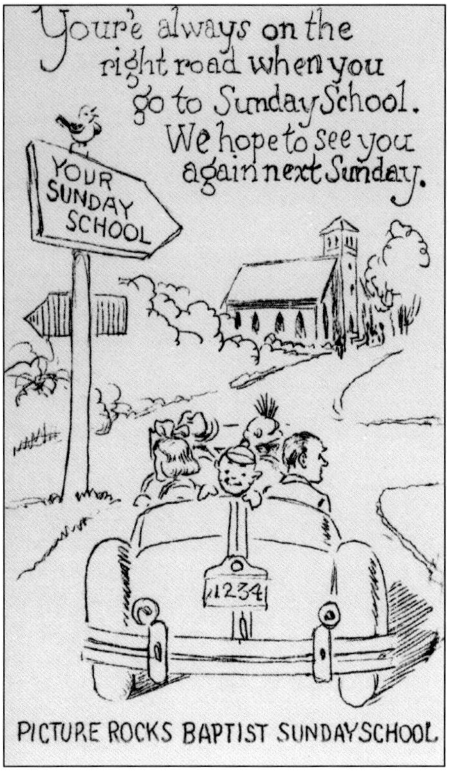

This is one of the postcards children might have received if they attended Sunday school. There was also a postcard those would receive if they missed Sunday school. (Courtesy of Evelyn Bryan.)

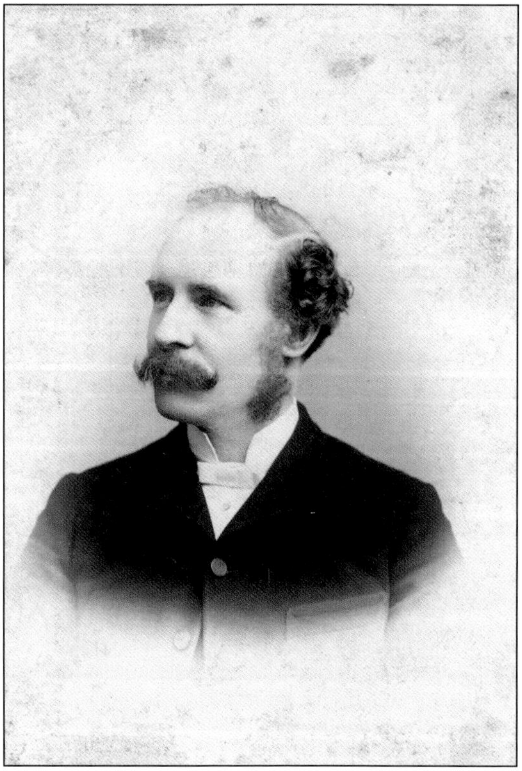

Pastor J. A. Aldred poses for this photograph in 1893. (Courtesy of Evelyn Bryan.)

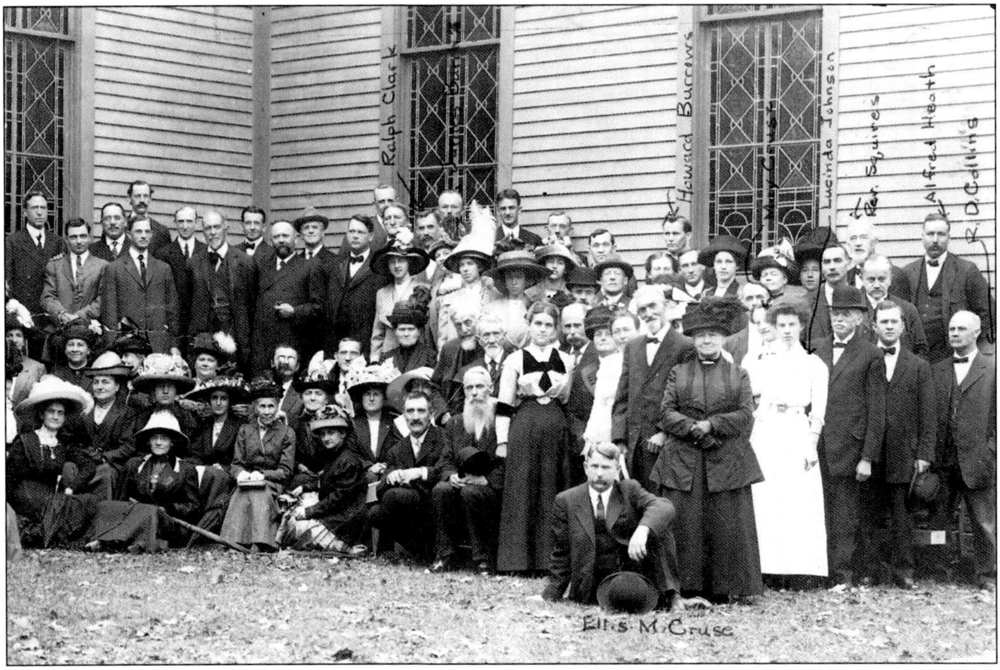

Here is the Northumberland Baptist Association. In July 1927, the church decided to invite Rev. J. B. Adams to the church for the month of August promising to pay $15 for every Sunday. (Courtesy of Evelyn Bryan.)

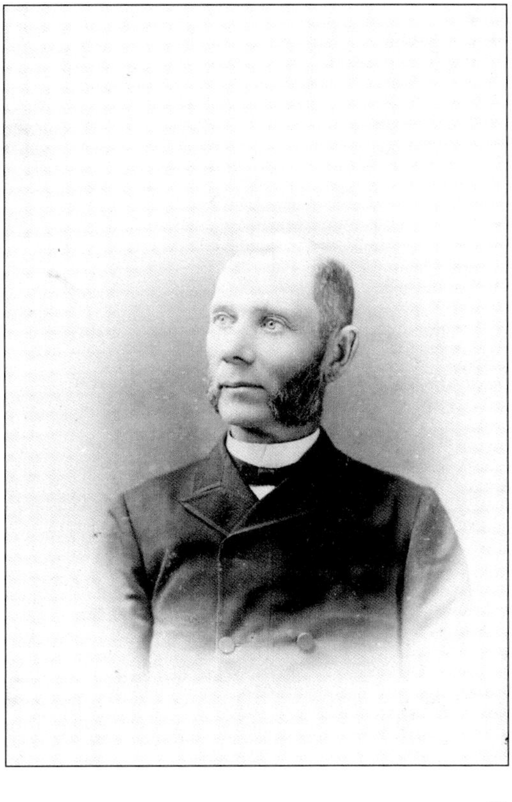

Rev. Dr. Henry Munro, pictured here in 1885, was the first pastor of the Picture Rocks Baptist Church. (Courtesy of Evelyn Bryan.)

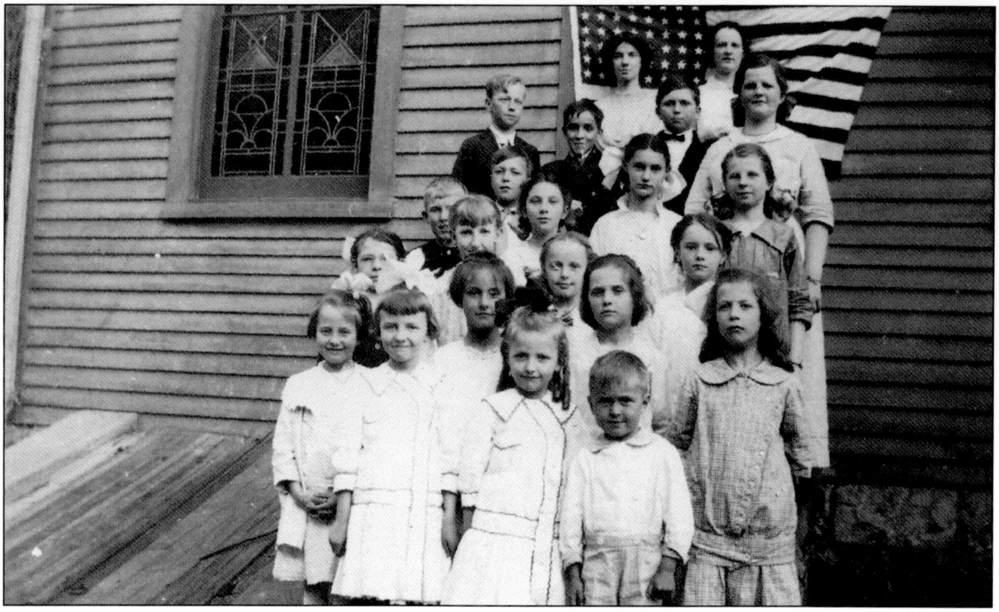

Junior Baptists pose for a photograph at Picture Rocks Baptist Church. (Courtesy of Evelyn Bryan.)

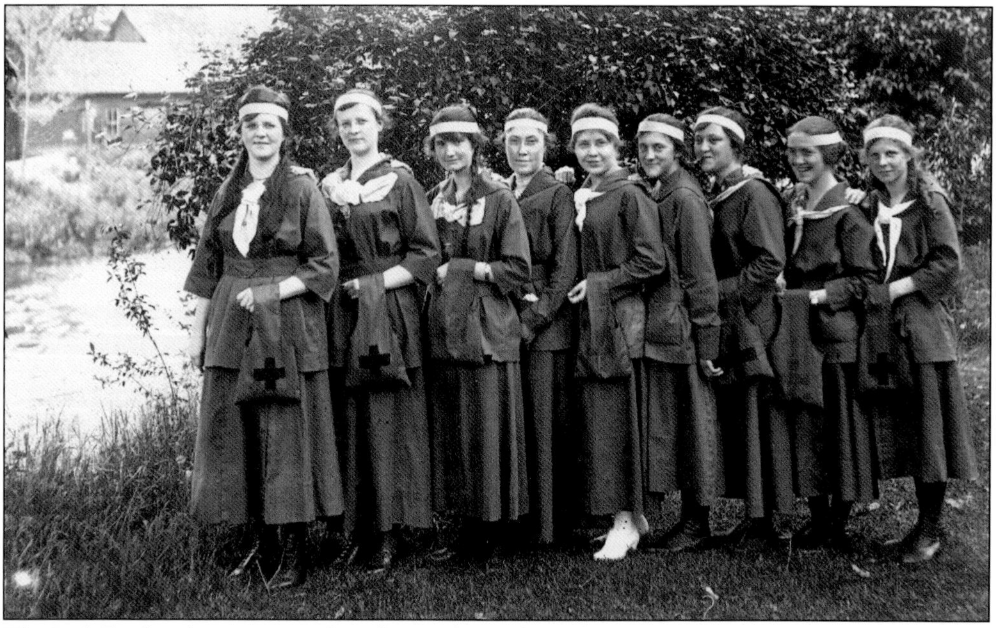

The Path Finders (sometimes referred to as the Faith Finders) was a woman's church organization run by Mrs. Harold Thompson, the wife of the pastor. Pictured, from left to right, are Lois Cruse, May Cruse, Edna Johnson, Mrs. Thompson, Edith Emery, Eleanor Little, Eva Gumble, Marjorie Sprout, and Elva Cruse. (Courtesy of Evelyn Bryan.)

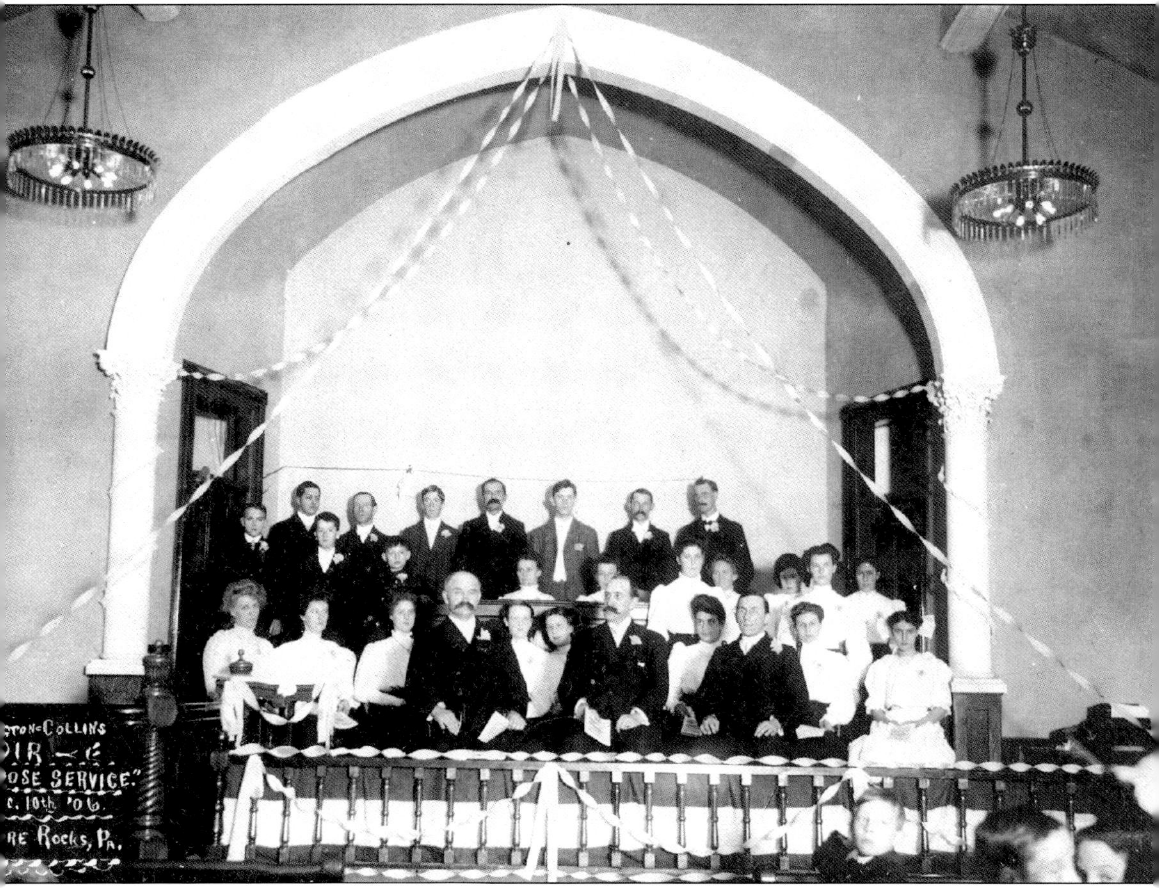

The Harrington Collins Choir visited the Picture Rocks Baptist Church in 1906. (Courtesy of Evelyn Bryan.)

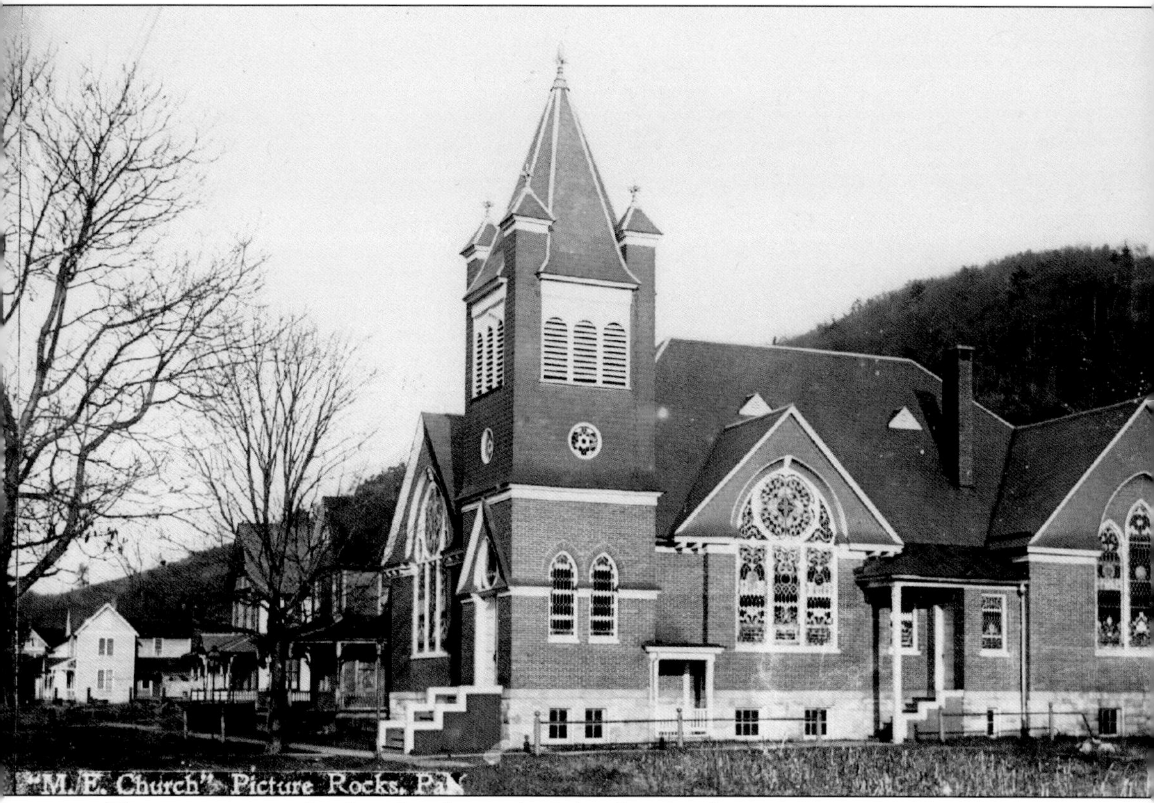

The corner stone for this church was laid the first Sunday in May 1901. A pipe organ was installed in 1903 with Andrew Carnegie paying half the cost. (Courtesy of Cris Gansell.)

Five

PROTECT AND SERVE

August 17, 1865
Worked 9 hours for ES, did chores. Self and family took tea at S. H. Burrows practiced singing with others for soldiers welcome. Berry Jearty came home, soldiers also.

April 19, 1865
Attended soldiers welcome, about 100 soldiers present about 500 took dinner. Wife and self attended ice cream party at Eraestus in evening.

—Amos Sprout

Picture Rocks had many services in town that where there to protect or provide a service too. There was the volunteer fire company, the Lions Club, and even the boy scouts. One thing the town never had was police officers. Perhaps because one was never needed, the law in town was upheld by its people. More notably Picture Rocks was also a town that served its country. During the Civil War, Franklin J. Krause was a prisoner of war and imprisoned in the infamous Andersonville Prison. Thankfully, Krause came home at the end of the war. During World War II, the town sent 20 percent of its people to war, compared to the national average of only a mere six percent. Picture Rocks represented every branch of the military. The highest position in the military was held by Malcom Elder who had become the commander of the navy. Picture Rocks also represented almost every theater of the war. During the war, the following people from town paid the ultimate sacrifice with their lives: Howard Clark, Roy Charles, Donald Falls, Frank Frantz, Ralph Miller, Harold Stead, Irvin Smith, and Clair Taylor.

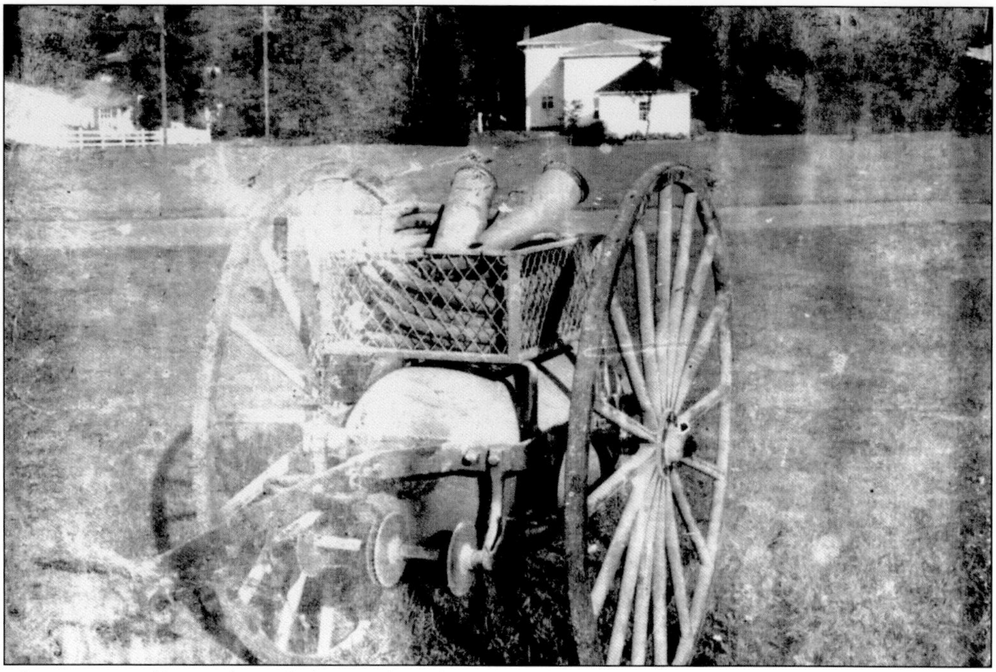

This is a 30-gallon soda acid chemical tank used by the Picture Rocks Volunteer Fire Company. The company started out with many hand-drawn pieces of equipment. They also used a hand-pulled wagon that carried about 100 fire buckets. (Courtesy of Picture Rocks Volunteer Fire Company.)

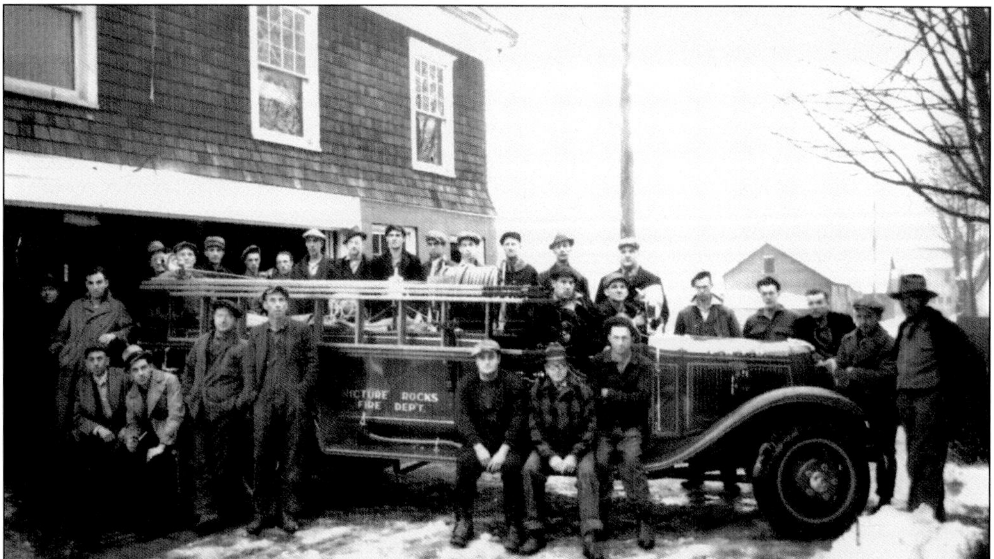

The Picture Rocks Fire Volunteer Company reorganized in 1932. Within a year, they received their first truck. Doc Gilmore lost his home to a fire only a block away from the fire station in 1933. It was lost because the fire company only had hand-drawn wagons that had to be filled at the creek, taking far too long to get to the burning home. After that incident, Gilmore was a prime motivator in getting the Picture Rocks Fire Company a drivable truck. (Courtesy of Picture Rocks Volunteer Fire Company.)

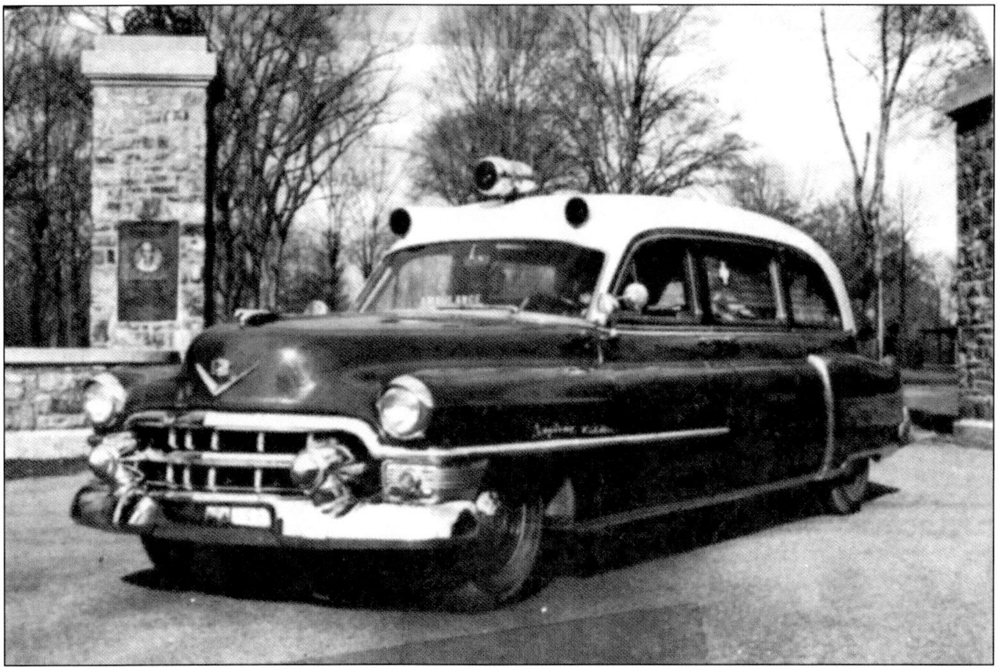

This is the first ambulance that the Picture Rocks Volunteer Fire Company commissioned. (Courtesy of Picture Rocks Volunteer Fire Company.)

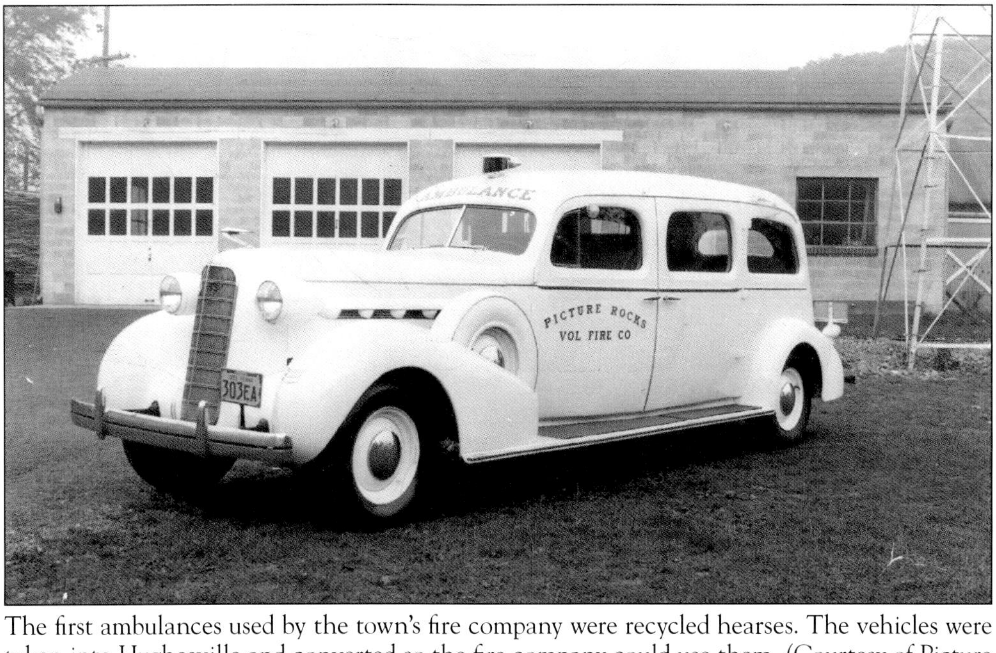

The first ambulances used by the town's fire company were recycled hearses. The vehicles were taken into Hughesville and converted so the fire company could use them. (Courtesy of Picture Rocks Volunteer Fire Company.)

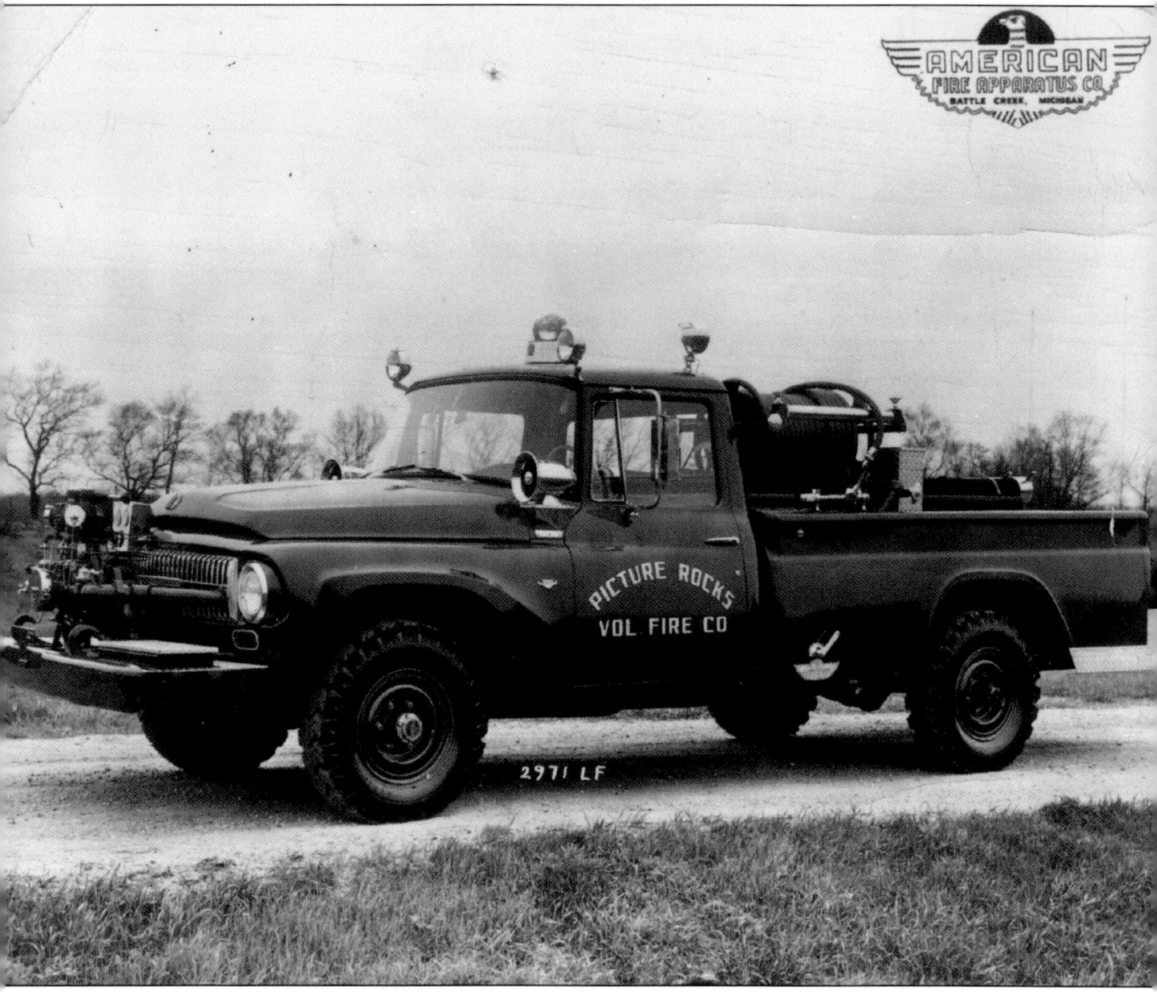

This is a brush truck used by the Picture Rocks Volunteer Fire Company. (Courtesy of Picture Rocks Fire Hall.)

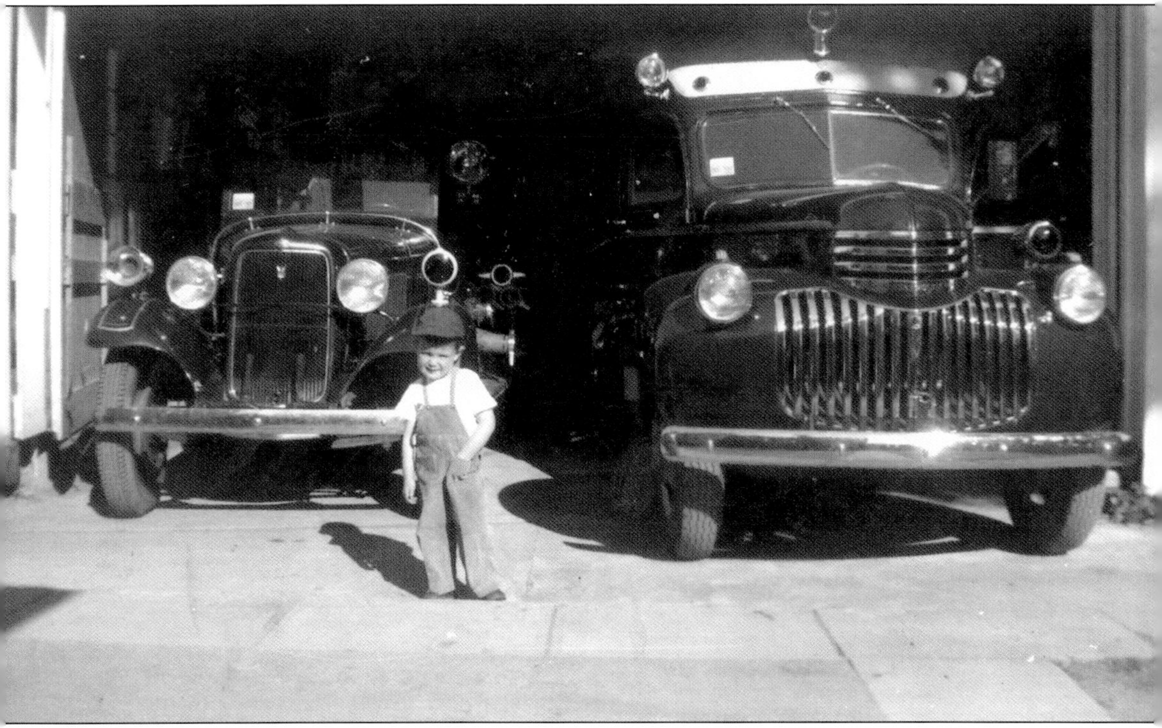

The Picture Rocks Volunteer Fire Company started out next to the Picture Rocks Baptist Church. Today it is located on Main and Factory Streets, and it is still a volunteer company. Here is a little boy posing in front of some of the company's fire trucks. (Courtesy of Picture Rocks Volunteer Fire Company.)

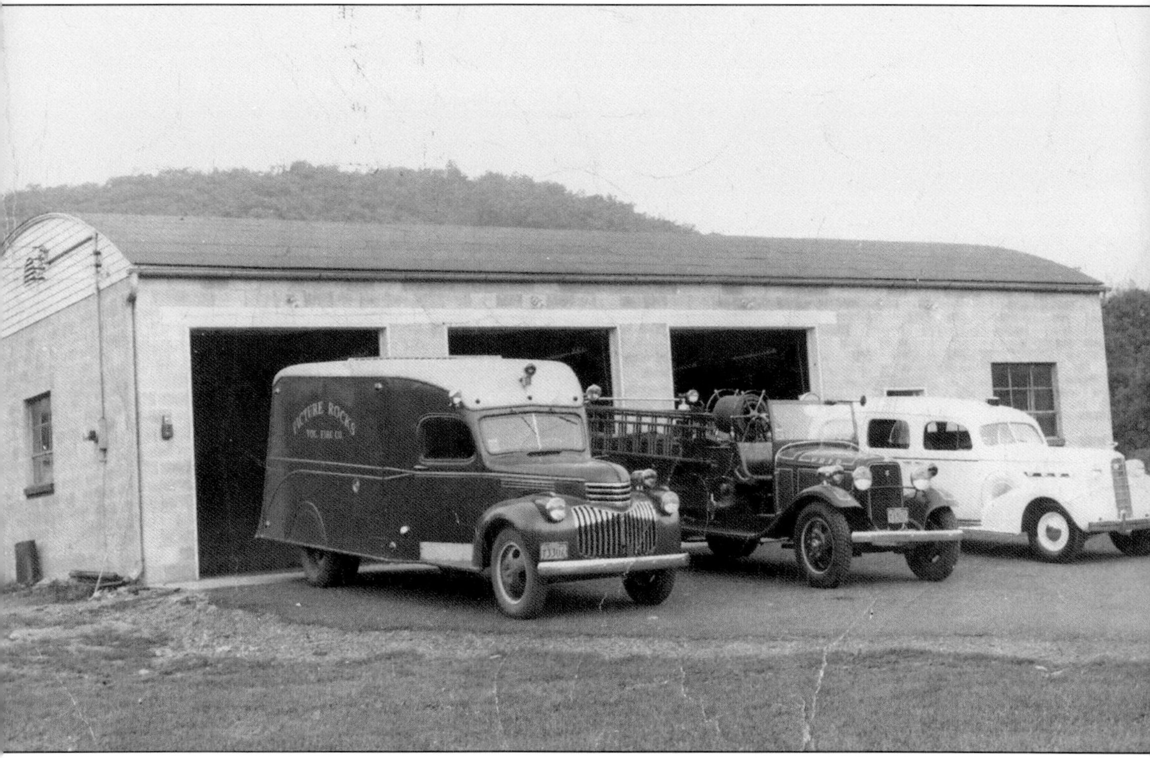

The company's fire trucks are seen here in the 1940s. (Courtesy of Picture Rocks Volunteer Fire Company.)

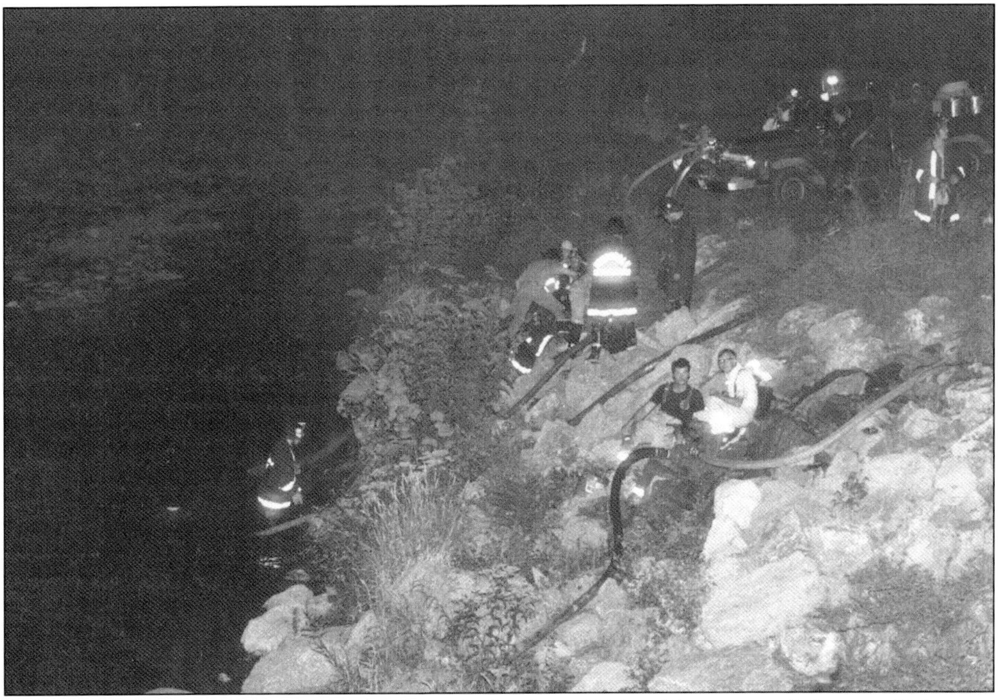

The rescue trucks used this method until the late 1980s. (Courtesy of Picture Volunteer Fire Company.)

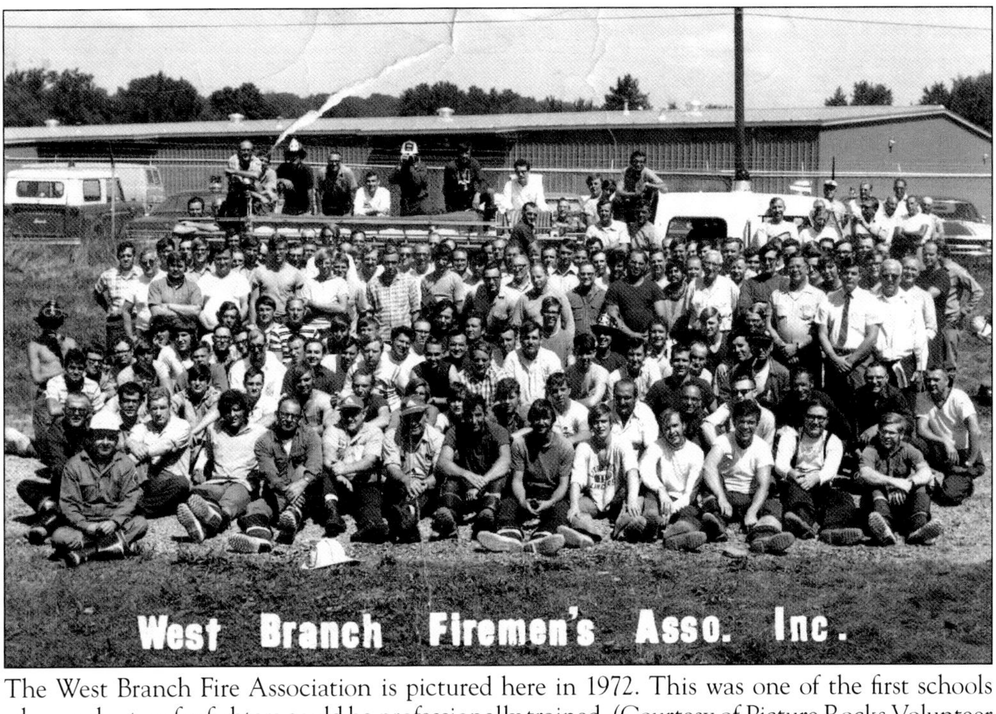

The West Branch Fire Association is pictured here in 1972. This was one of the first schools where volunteer firefighters could be professionally trained. (Courtesy of Picture Rocks Volunteer Fire Company.)

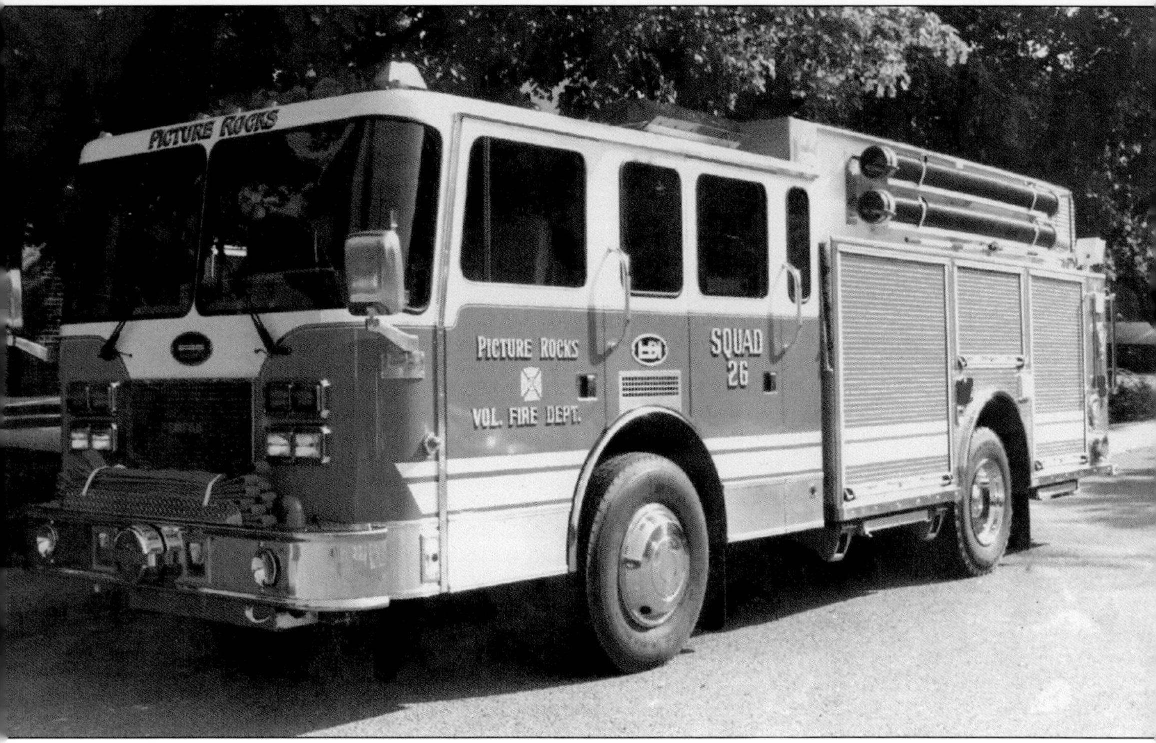

The fire squad is pictured here in 1993. (Courtesy of Picture Rocks Volunteer Fire Company.)

Robert Ferrell Sr. served the United States during Word War I. (Courtesy of Dot and Bill Sandmeyer.)

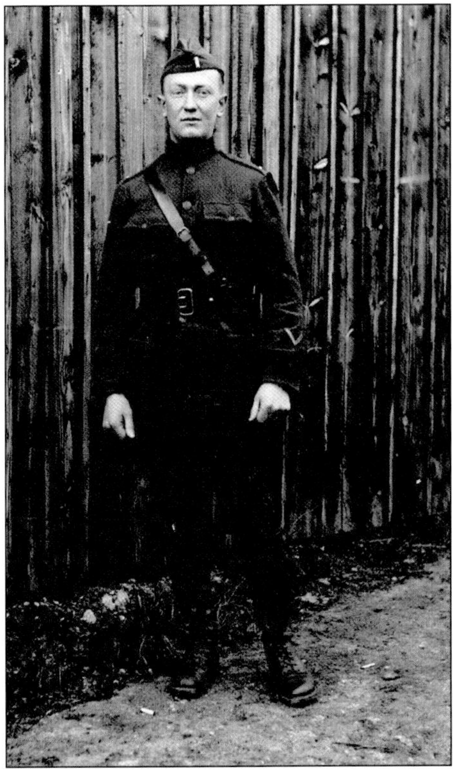

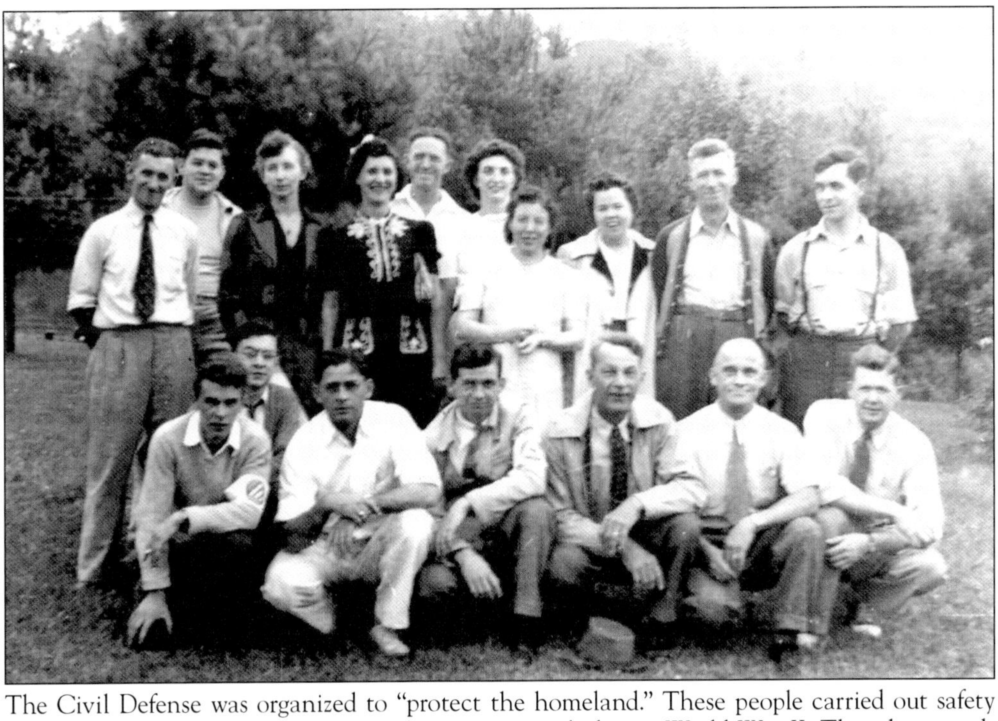

The Civil Defense was organized to "protect the homeland." These people carried out safety measures if the town was to come under enemy attack during World War II. This photograph was taken in 1943. (Courtesy of Wes and Pat Sprout.)

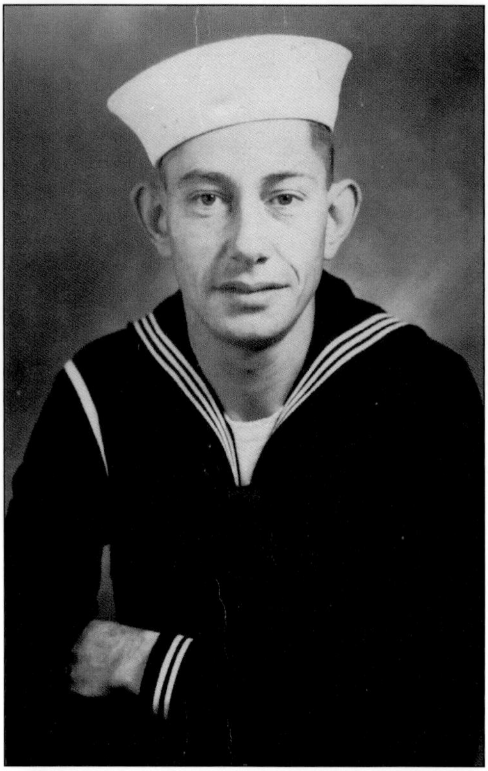

Eugene Daye of Picture Rocks served the country in the U.S. Navy during World War II. (Courtesy of Cap Daye.)

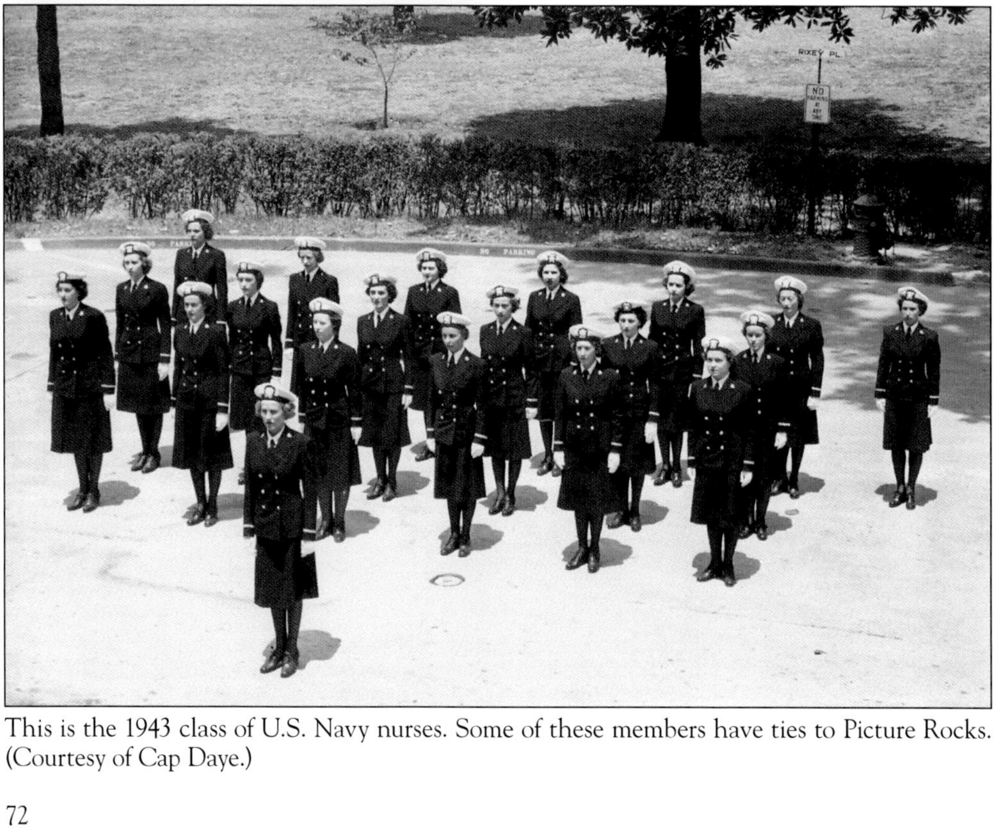

This is the 1943 class of U.S. Navy nurses. Some of these members have ties to Picture Rocks. (Courtesy of Cap Daye.)

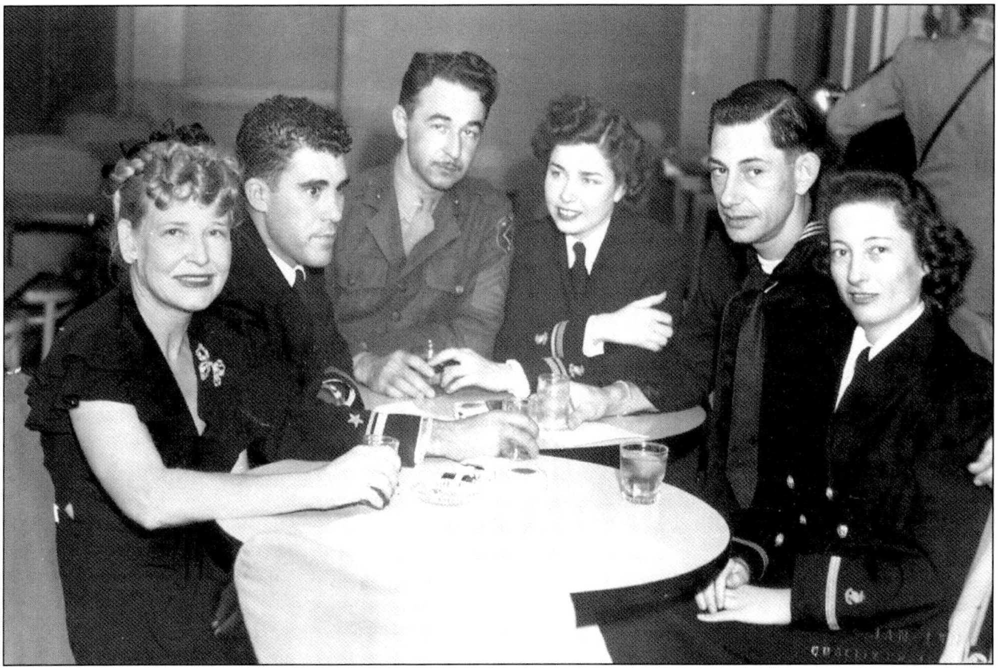

Some military friends relax at the Continental Room in 1945. Second from the right is Eugene Daye, a Picture Rocks resident. (Courtesy of Cap Daye.)

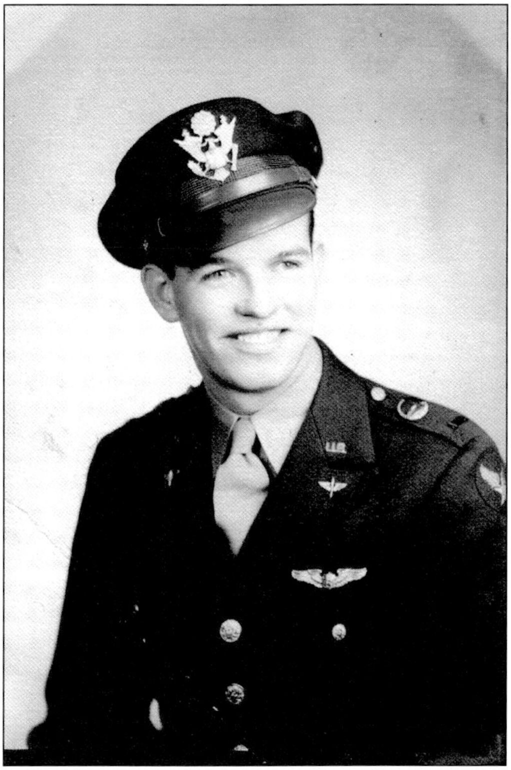

Byrton Winder was in the U.S. Army during World War II. He flew 96 missions over "The Hump." Winder has flown 23,000 flights as an aviator, all accident-free. (Courtesy of Bert and Margi Winder.)

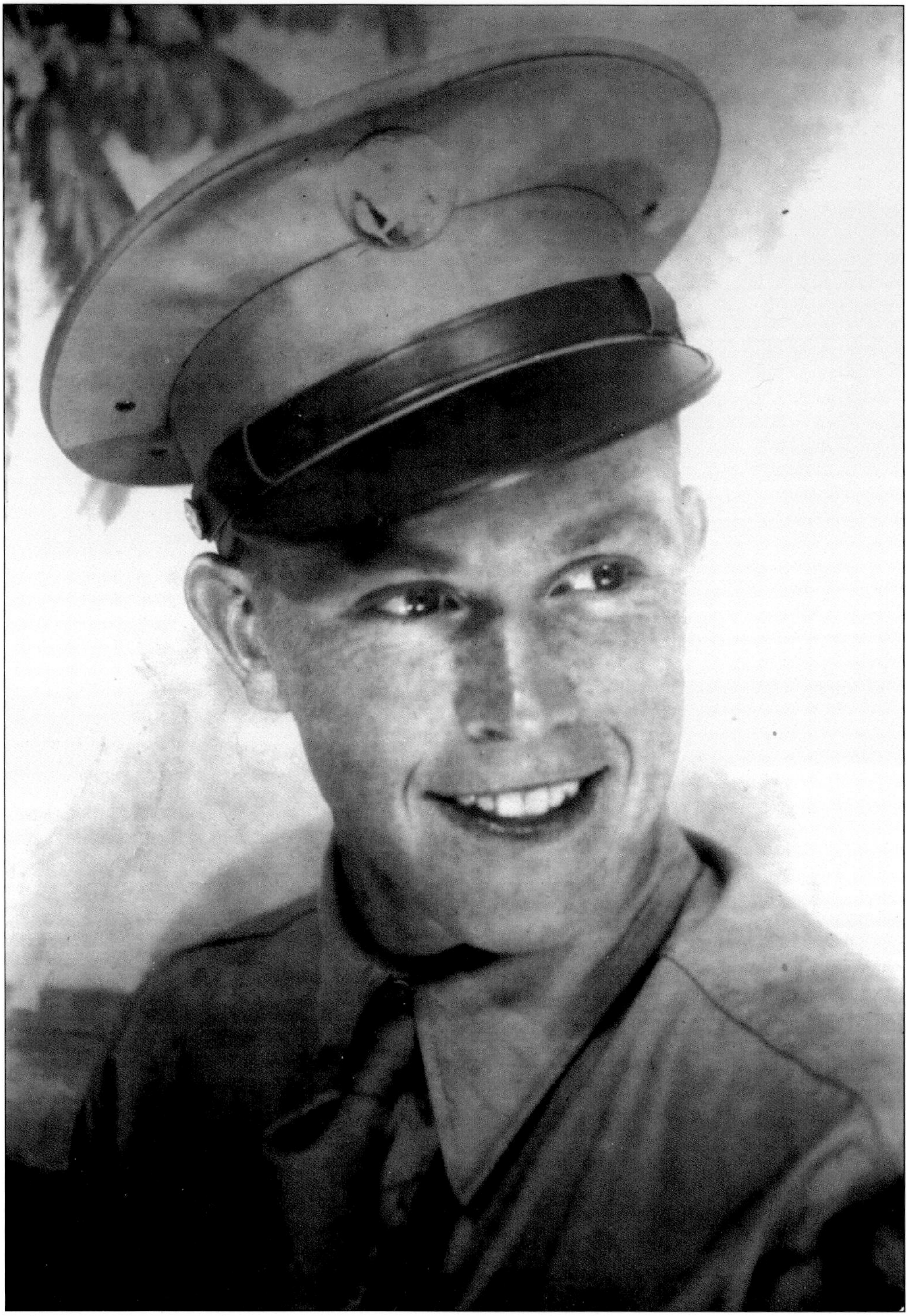

Luke Gansell served the United States in World War II with the U.S. Army. (Courtesy of Charley Gansell.)

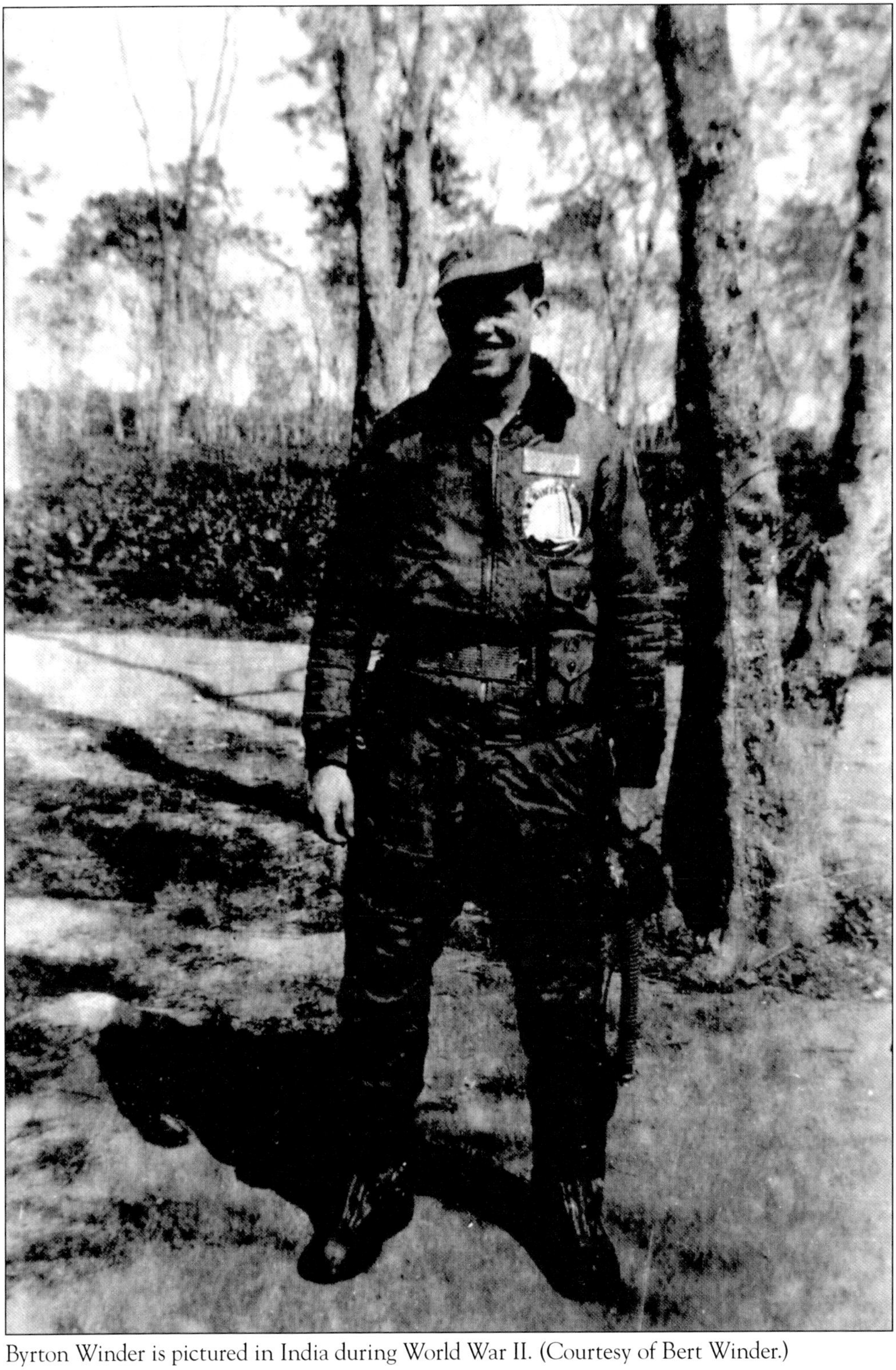

Byrton Winder is pictured in India during World War II. (Courtesy of Bert Winder.)

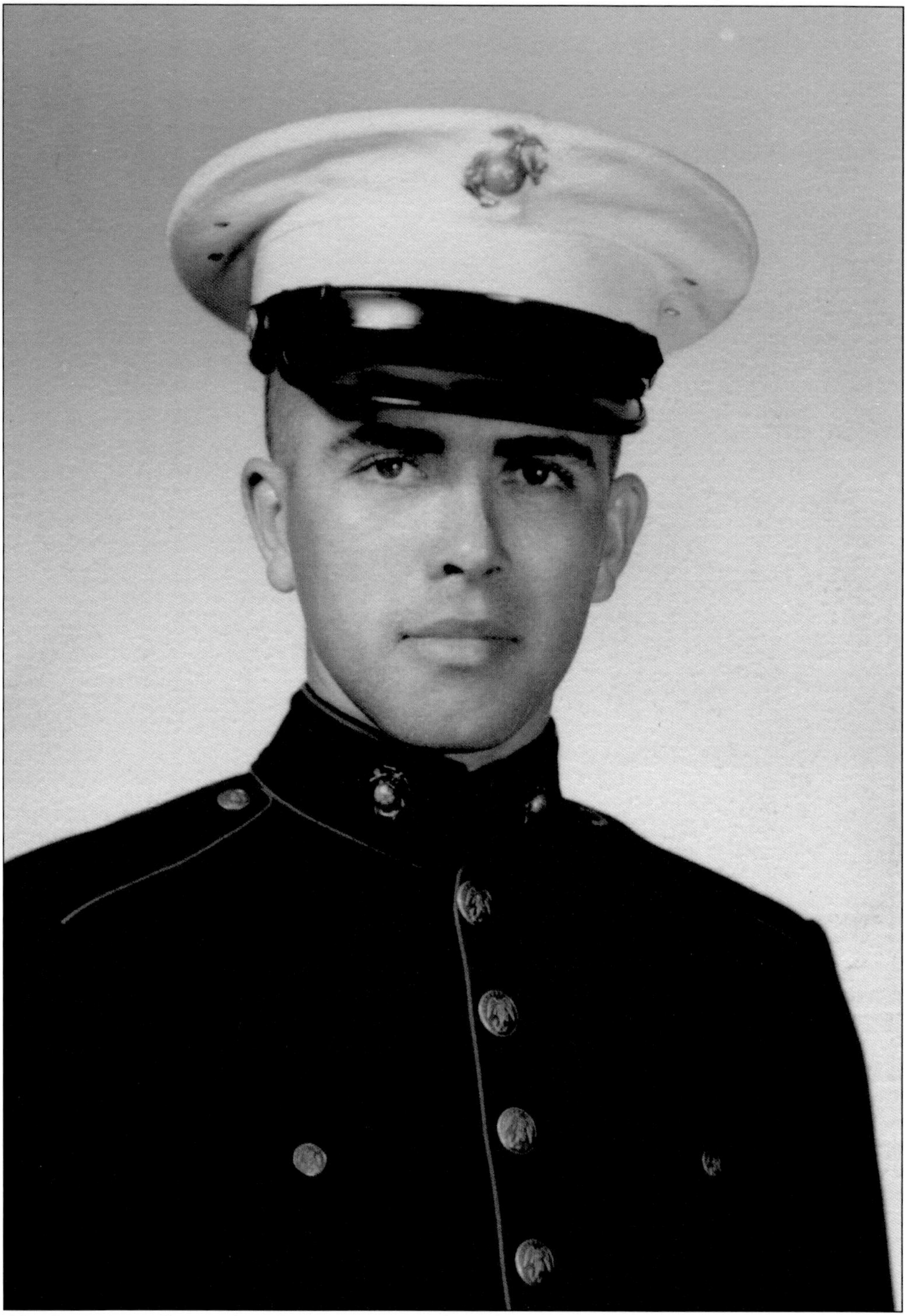

Charles I. Gansell served in the U.S. Marines from December 4, 1951, to December 4, 1953. He served in the Korean Conflict. (Courtesy of Cris Gansell.)

Clair Taylor is shown here in 1942.
(Courtesy of Ron Hicks.)

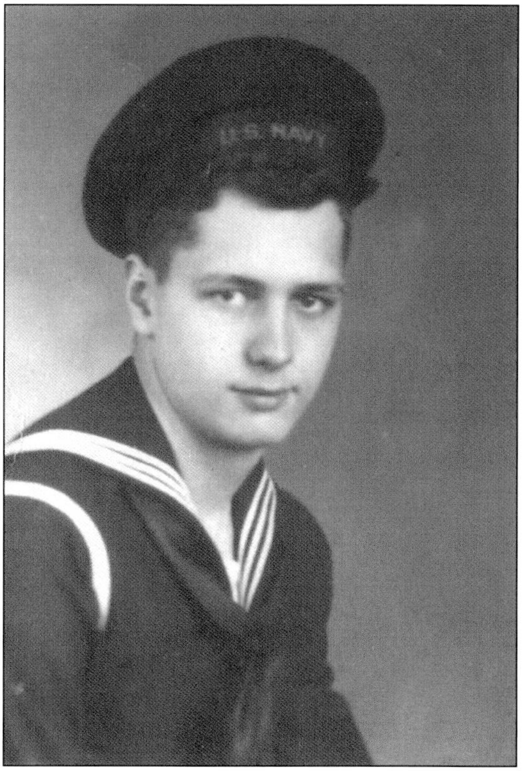

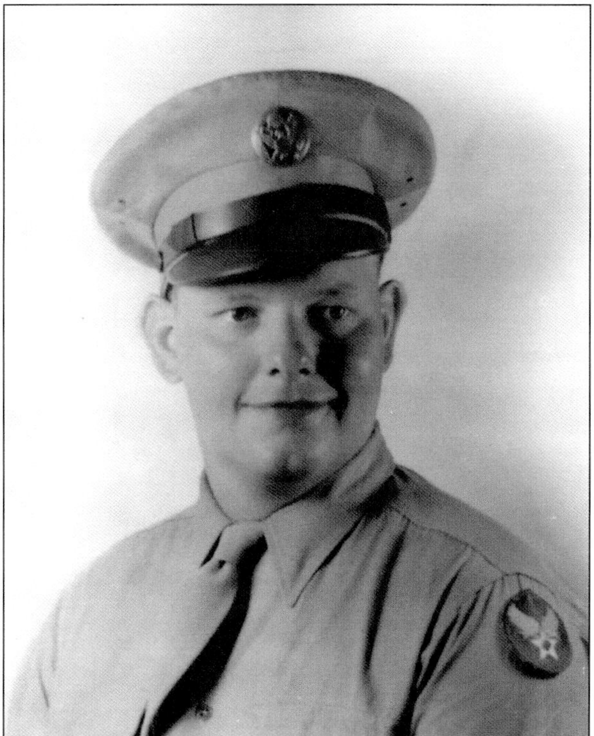

Pictured here is Arnold Hicks.
(Courtesy of Ron Hicks.)

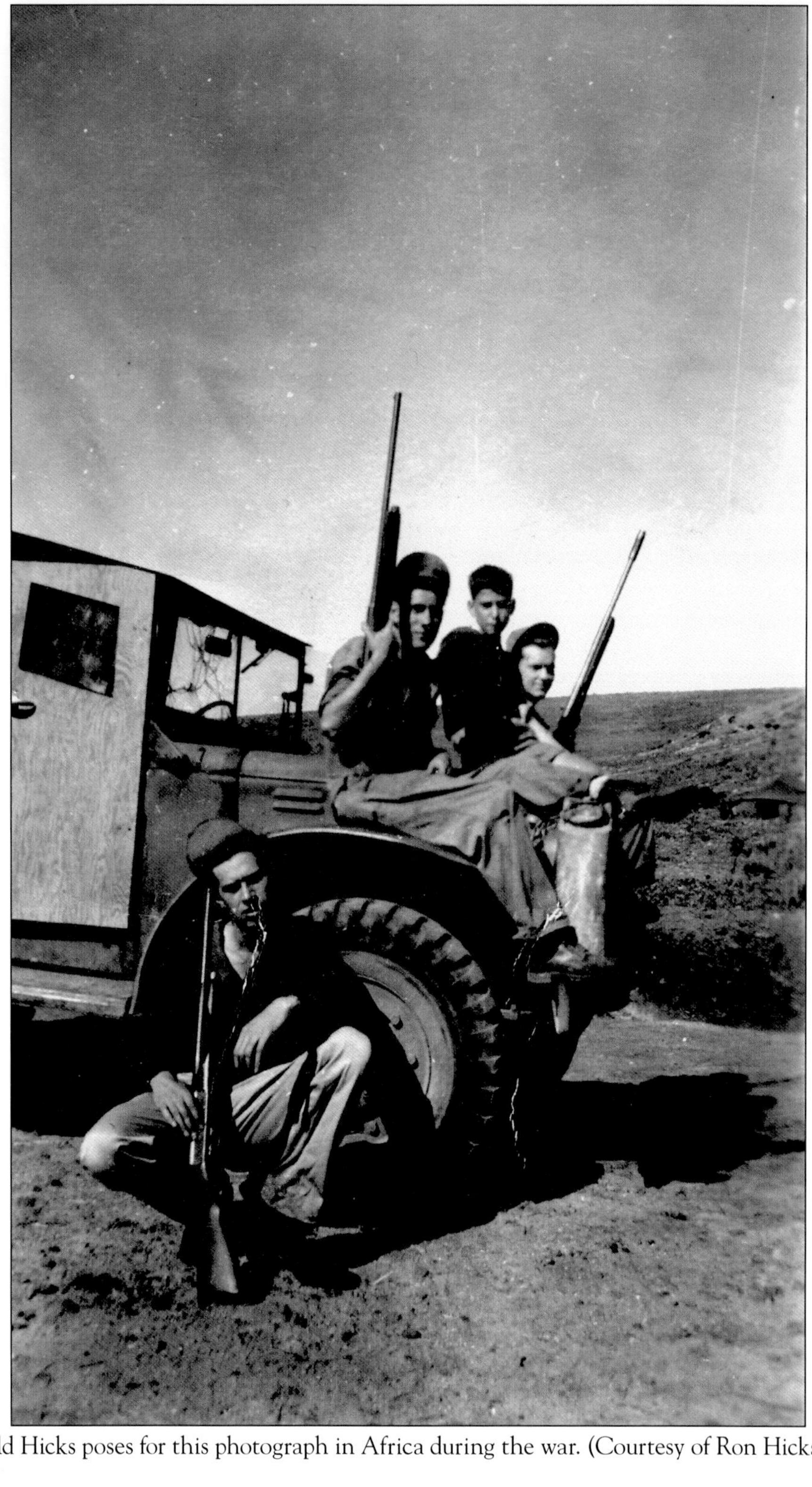

Arnold Hicks poses for this photograph in Africa during the war. (Courtesy of Ron Hicks.)

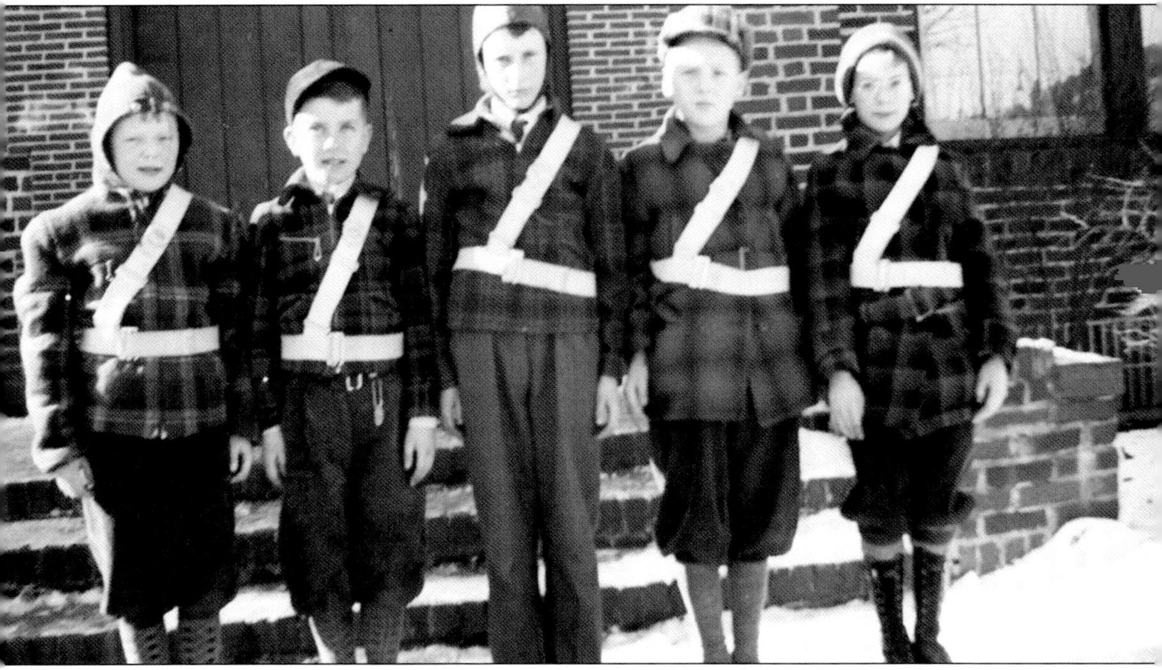

Shown here, from left to right, are Dean Barrett, Charley Gansell, Bob Overdorf, Dan Little, and Fred Hunter Jr. (Courtesy of Cris Gansell.)

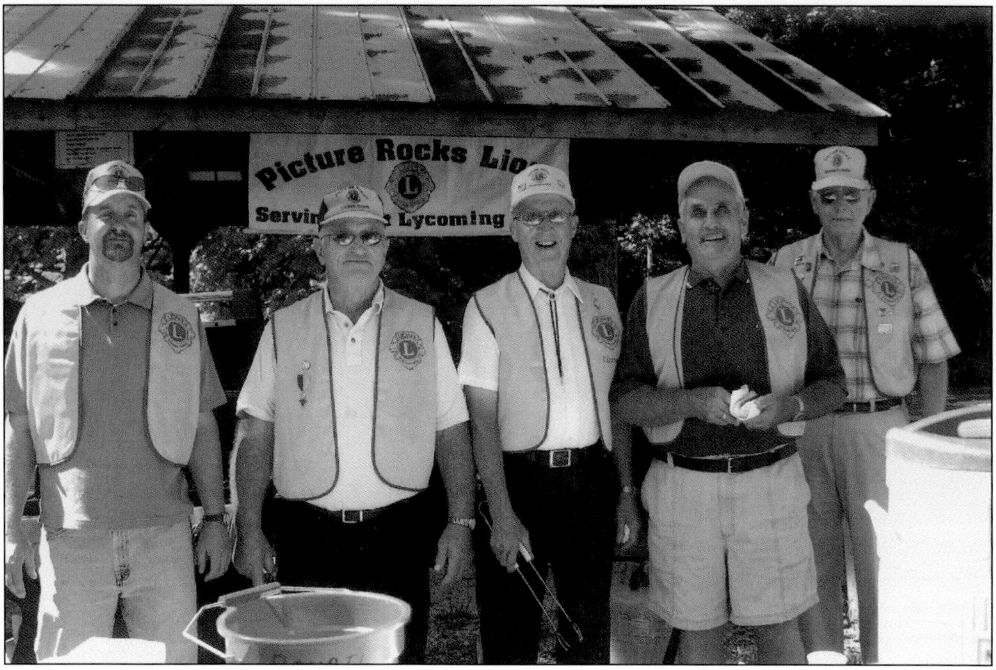

One thing that the Picture Rocks Lions Club is famous for is their homemade sauerkraut. It should be tried at least once in a lifetime. (Courtesy of Cris Gansell.)

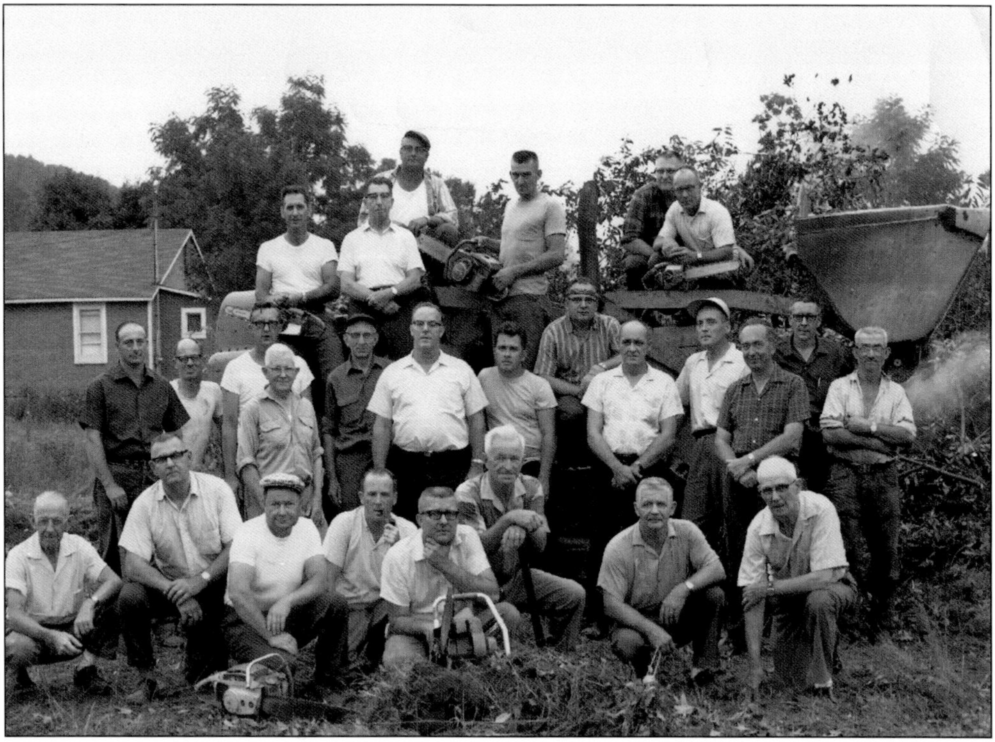

The Picture Rocks Lions Club is shown here in 1966. (Courtesy of Charley Gansell.)

The Picture Rocks Lions Club members hand make the sauerkraut from scratch and sell it in the end of December, just in time for the new year. (Courtesy of Charley Gansell.)

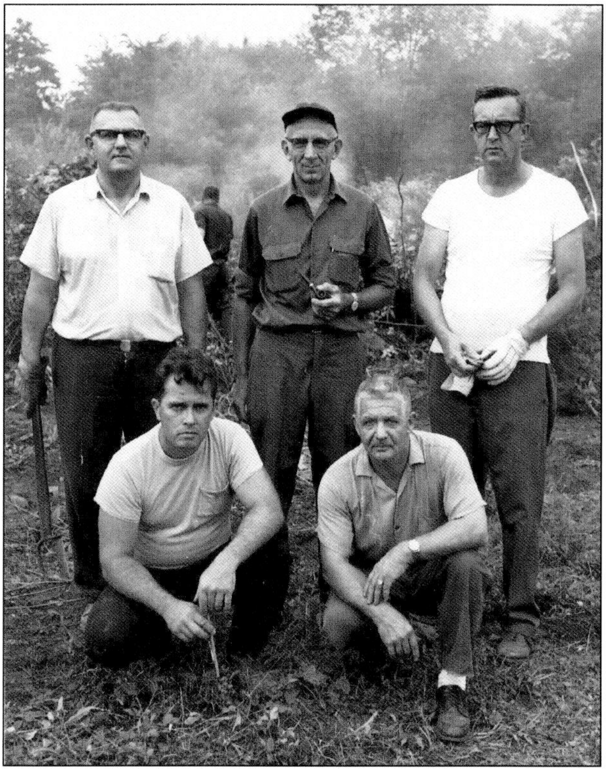

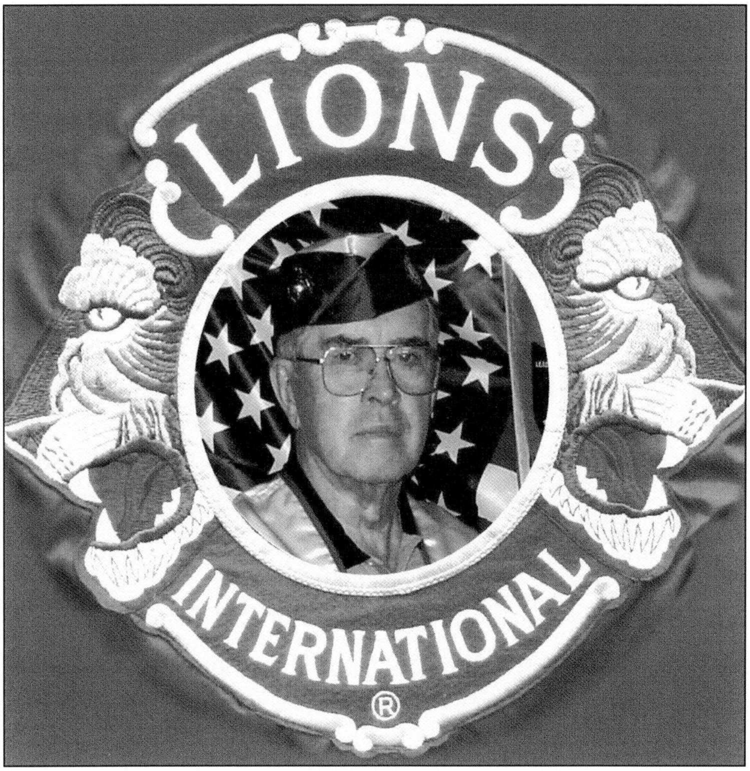

Charles Gansell is the last charter member of the Picture Rocks Lions Club, which was organized in 1955. (Courtesy of Cris Gansell.)

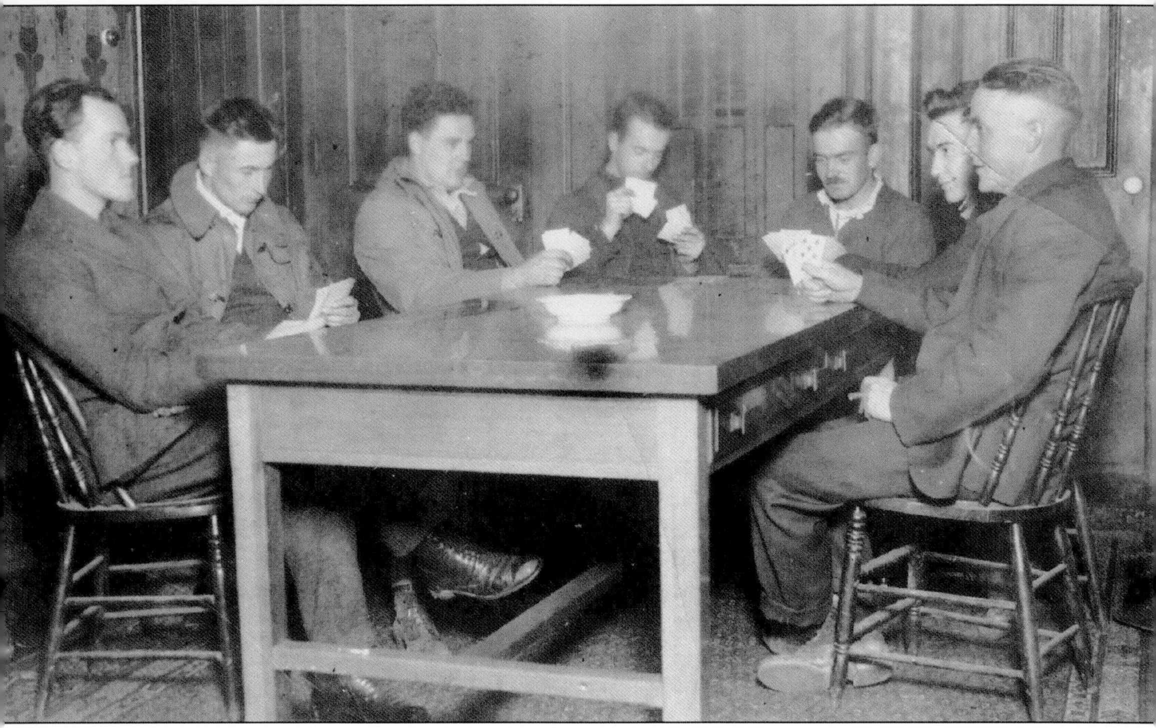

Pictured here is the Picture Rocks American Legion. Unfortunately, not much is known about this organization. However, this photograph proves that it did exist at one time. (Courtesy of Dot and Bill Sandmeyer.)

This is a bankbook from the American legion. This item, along with a logbook, was found in the attic of Jake McClain's home. The book remains in the family. (Courtesy of Ron Hicks.)

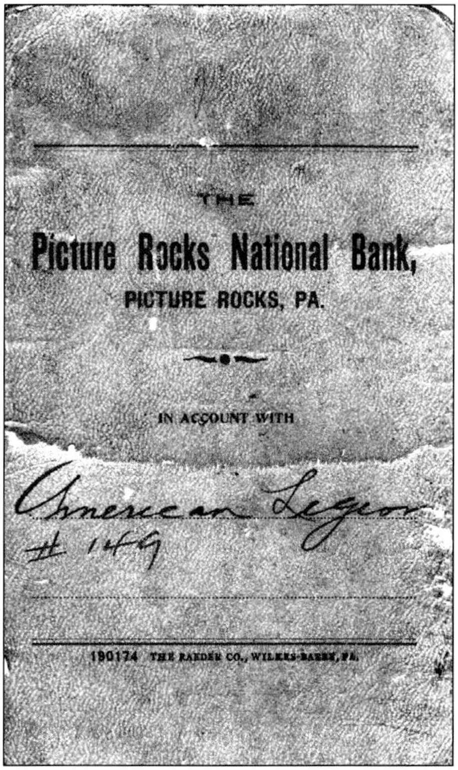

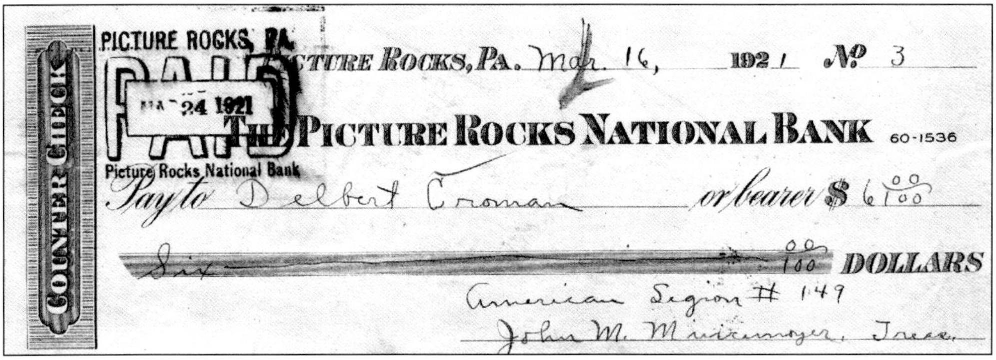

Seen here is a check from the legion. (Courtesy of Ron Hicks.)

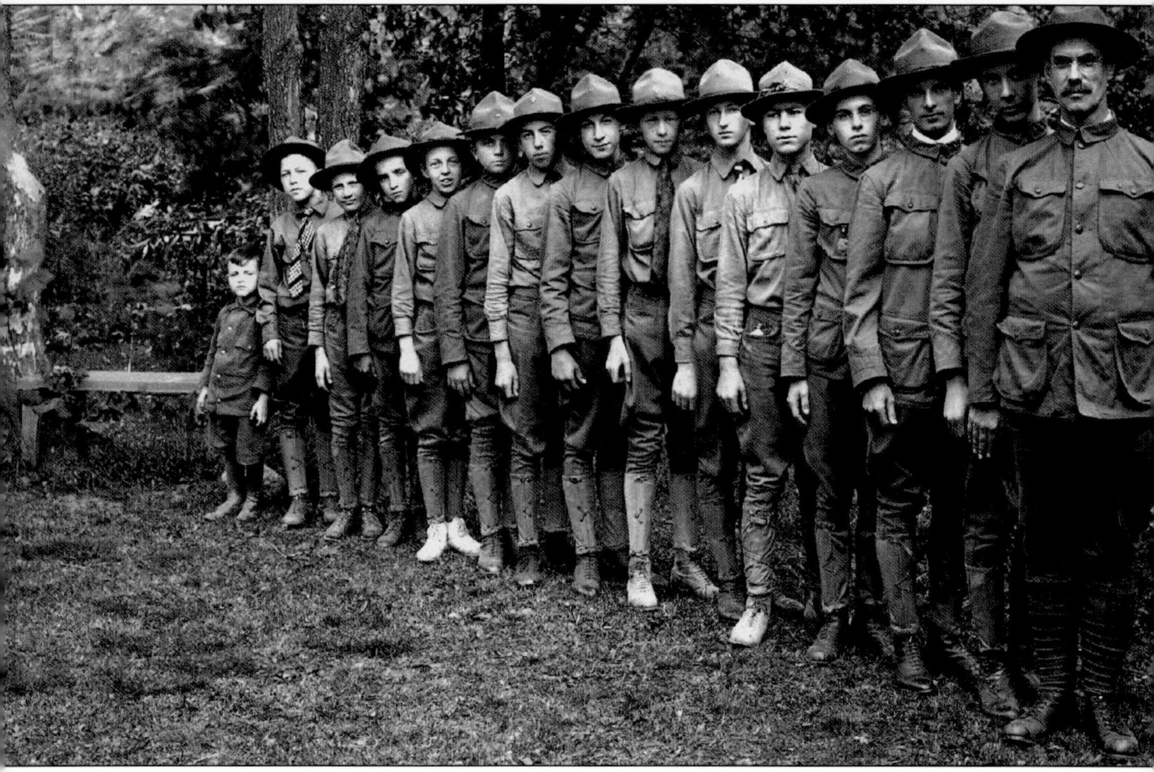

The Picture Rocks Boy Scouts pose for this photograph in 1920. The scouts, from left to right, are Gene Steckle, Clyde Roller, Eldon Parsons, Ralph Eddy, Howard Crawley, Otto Parsons, Otto Taylor, Paul Reeser, George Roller, Elmer Barbour, Howard Wertman, Ralph Emery, Roscoe Burrows, Nile Little, and troop leader Ralph Clark. (Courtesy of Wes and Pat Sprout.)

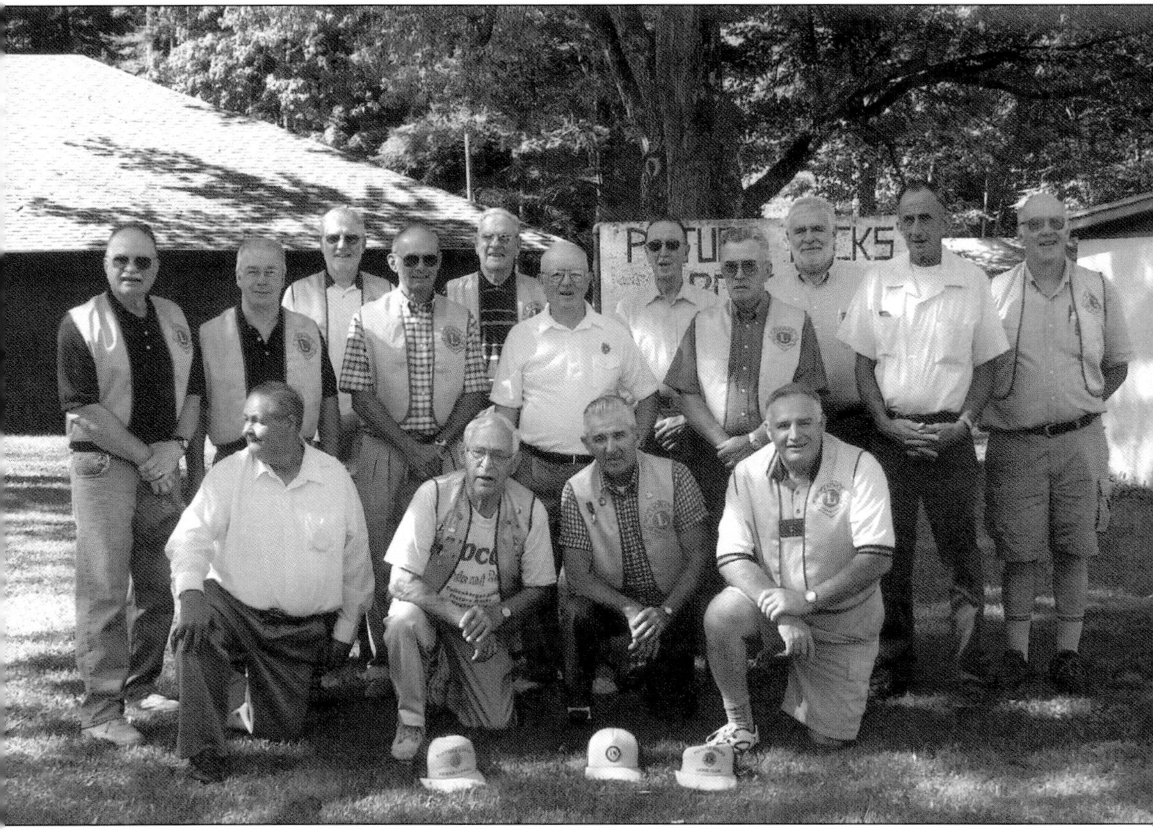

In 2005, the Picture Rocks Lions Club celebrated 50 years of serving the community. (Courtesy of Cris Gansell.)

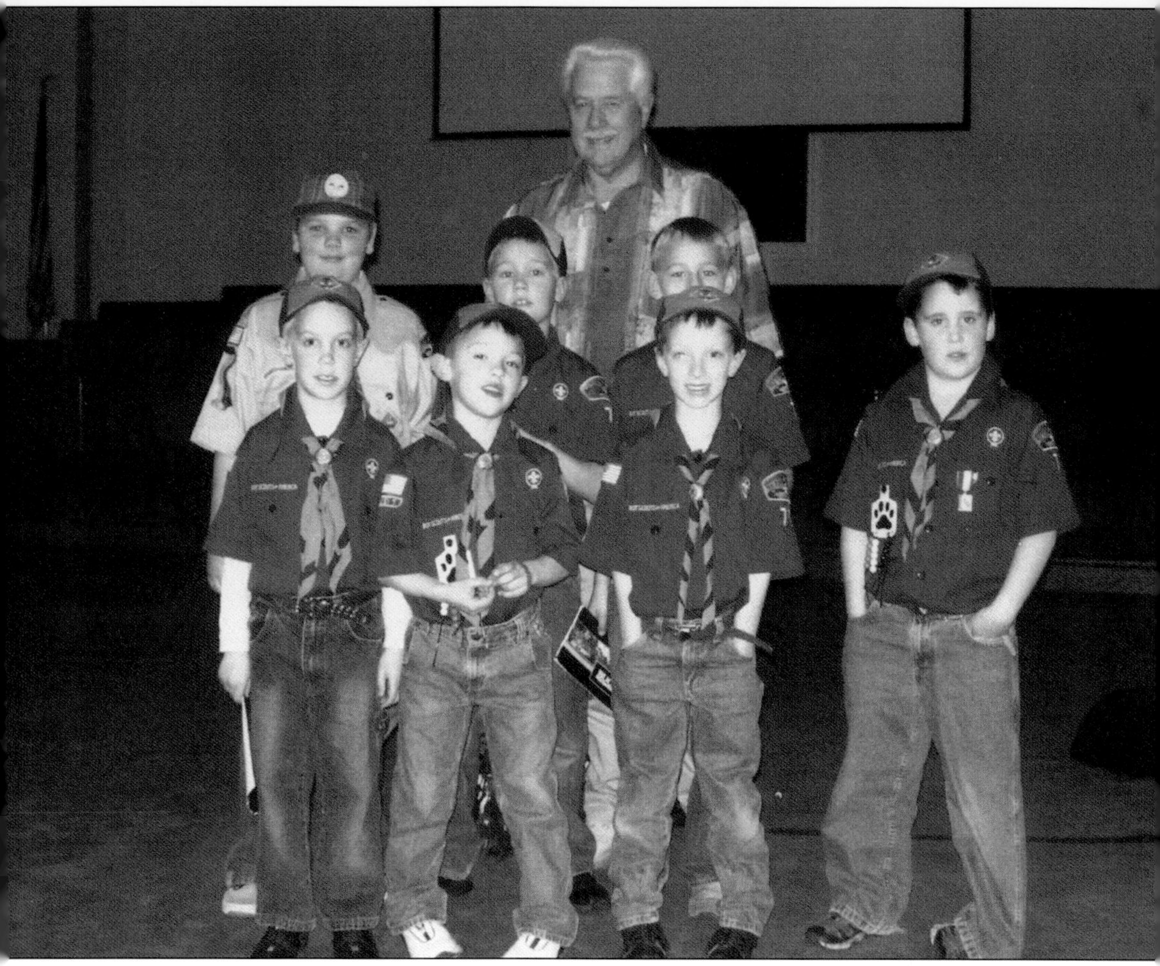

A group of Cub Scouts poses for a photograph. (Courtesy of Ron Hicks.)

Six

A Tour of Picture Rocks

Friday March 17, 1865
Worked for Sprout and Bros 8 hours. Fair and Heavy rain last night. Creek and river very high. Immence damage to done. Bridges, houses and other property destroyed. River 35ft above low water mark.

—Amos Sprout

Even though Mother Nature has thrown Picture Rocks a curve ball or two, there are still many wonderful sights to see. Walking through the town today is very much like walking in town 100 years ago. Many homes and structures still exist. Although some buildings have come down, there are still remnants of them. Walking around town, one can see the hitching posts that were used to tie up horses. The original structures in town were built by the people of the town.

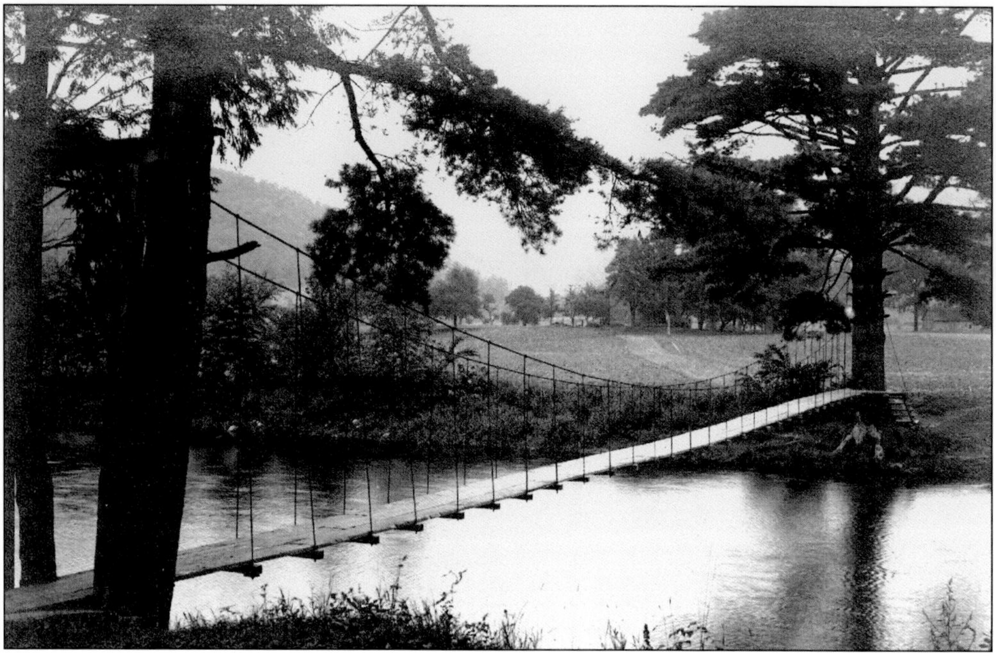

This footbridge was built between 1908 and 1909. The day that it was completed, town leaders crossed it and chose a piece of land that would become the town's cemetery. The tombstones of Asa and Amos Sprout and the Burrows cannot be found in the cemetery. Many of the town's originators passed away before 1909. (Courtesy of Wes and Pat Sprout.)

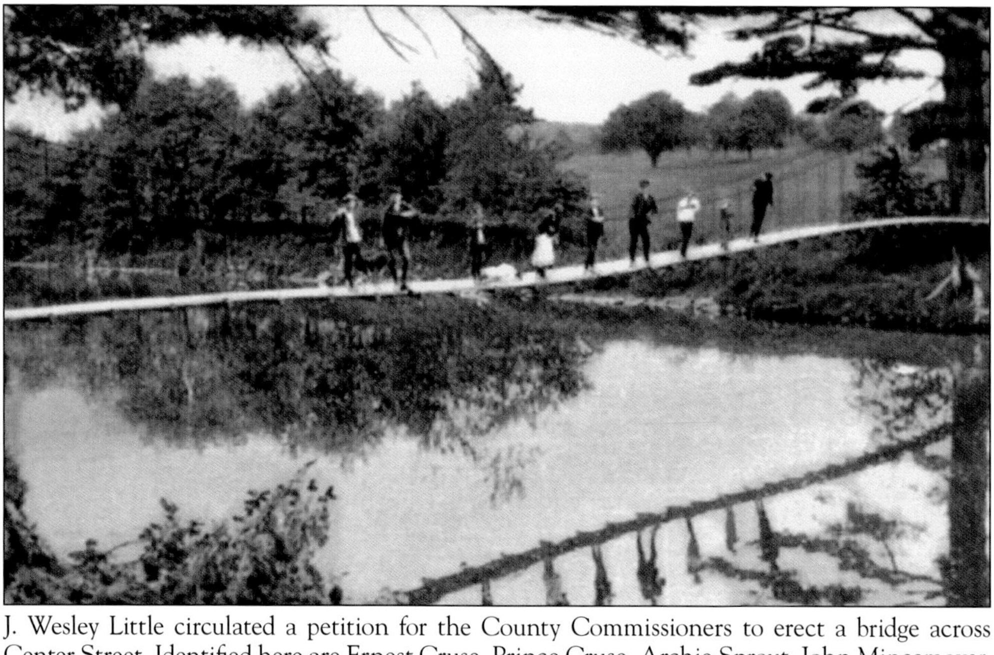

J. Wesley Little circulated a petition for the County Commissioners to erect a bridge across Center Street. Identified here are Ernest Cruse, Prince Cruse, Archie Sprout, John Mincemoyer, Frances Fry, Matt Fry, Bruce Fry, Frank McClain, Dick Stratton, Scott Williams, and Carl Fry. (Courtesy of Stewart Hill.)

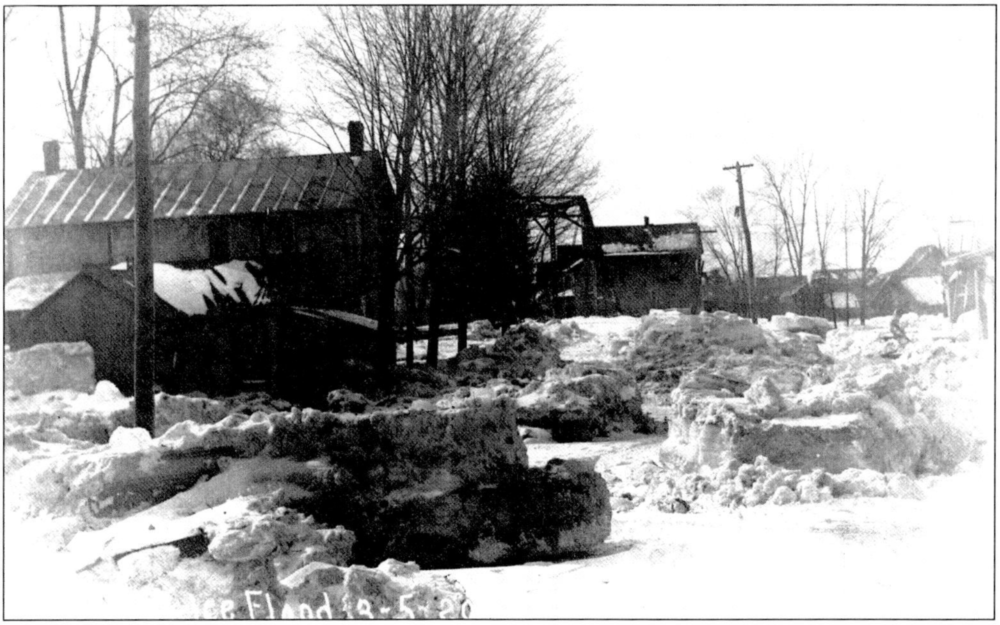

An ice jam was captured in this photograph taken on March 5, 1920. (Courtesy of Ron Hicks.)

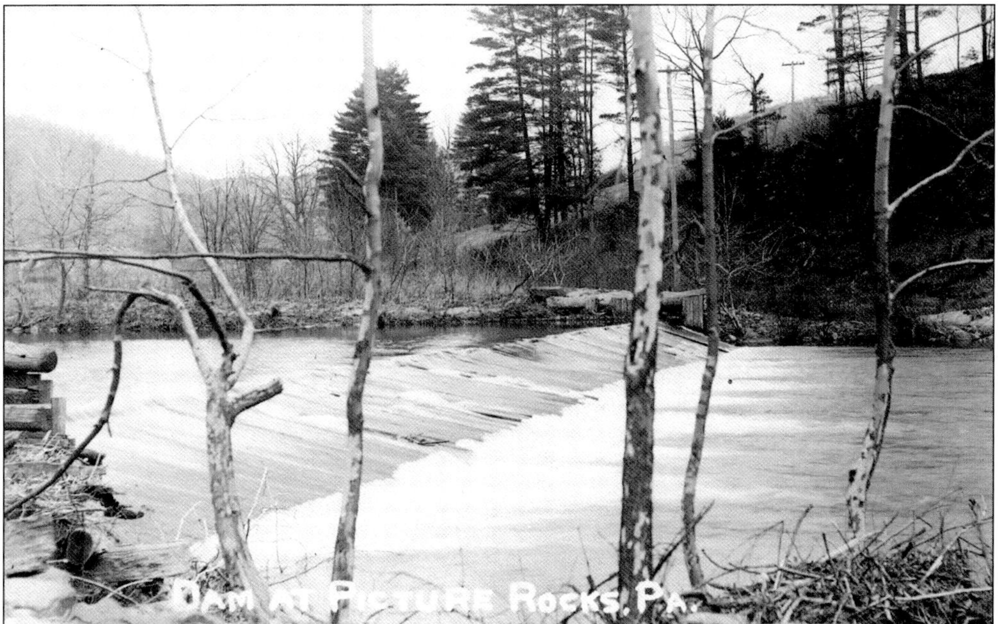

The dam was built for the sawmill that sat along the creek. That mill was powered by energy from a water wheel. However, the creek was too low, so the wheel was built to turn in the opposite direction. This unique water wheel was a one-of-a-kind invention. (Courtesy of Wes and Pat Sprout.)

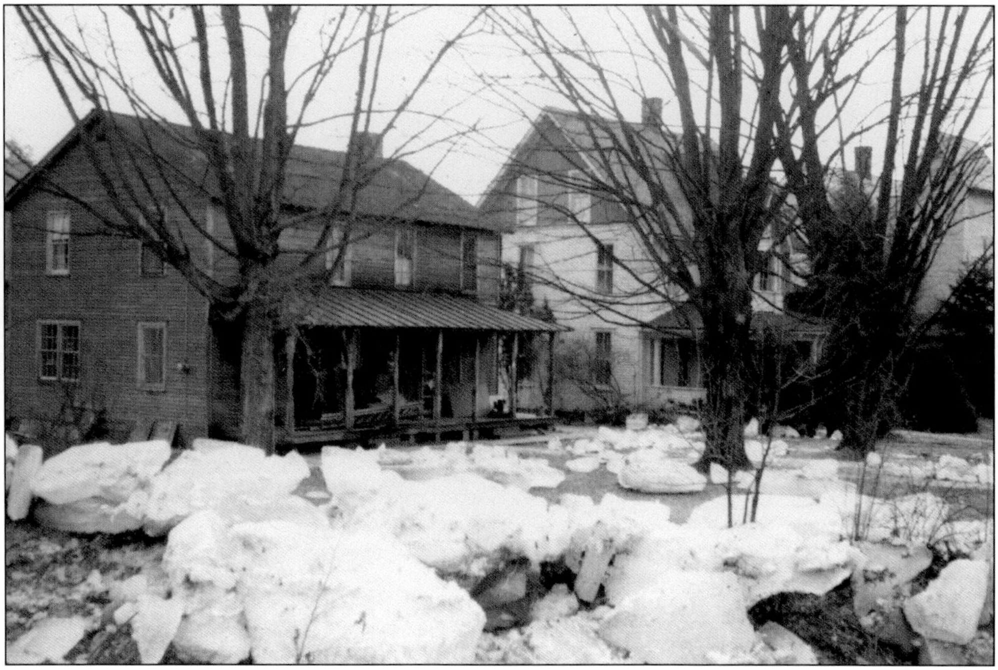

The 1959 ice jam was declared a state emergency by the federal government. The jam caused the Muncy Creek to overflow, pouring water and massive chucks of ice up onto land. The state governor at the time, David Lawrence, came to inspect the damage himself. In all, 30 homes and the town's two biggest businesses received major damage. (Courtesy of Mary Artley.)

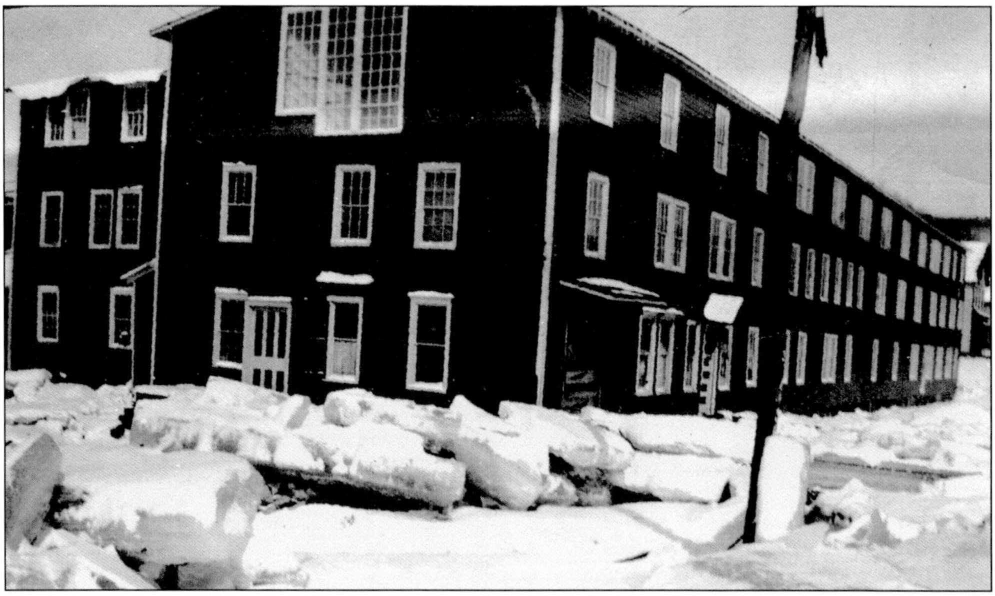

Picture Rocks experienced major ice jams in its history. The jams caused extensive damage to the Burrows Brothers Furniture Company factory and many homes near the Muncy Creek. (Courtesy of Bob Roller.)

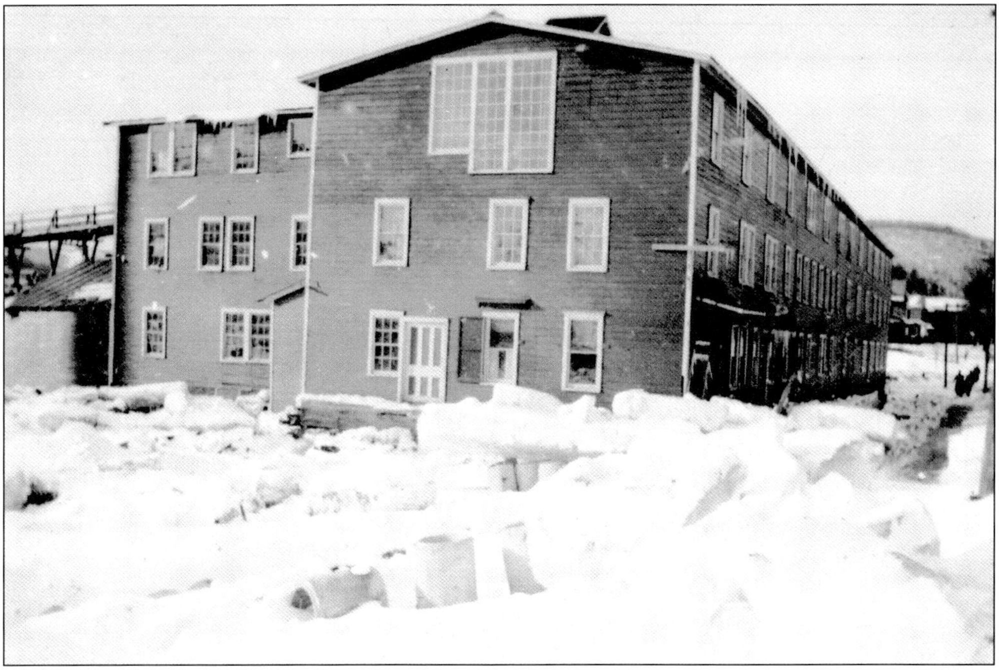

The Burrows Brothers Furniture Company factory is shown here after an ice jam. (Courtesy of Bob Roller.)

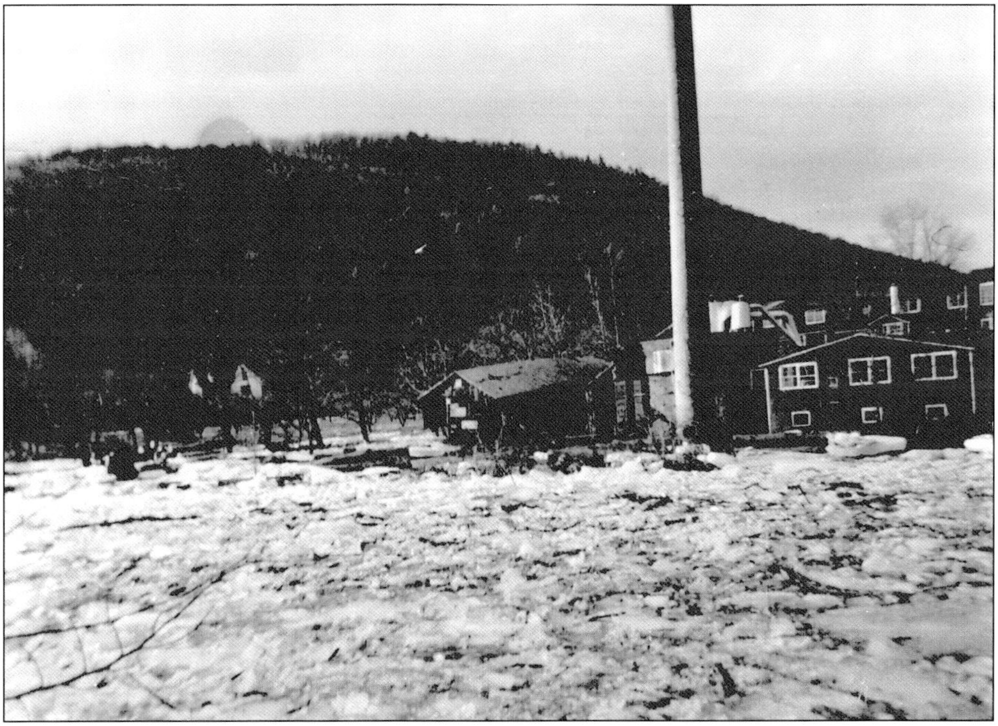

Residents were fed up by the slow moving process set fourth by the government in removing the ice. A couple men from town took matters into their own hands and used a little dynamite. (Courtesy of Cris Gansell.)

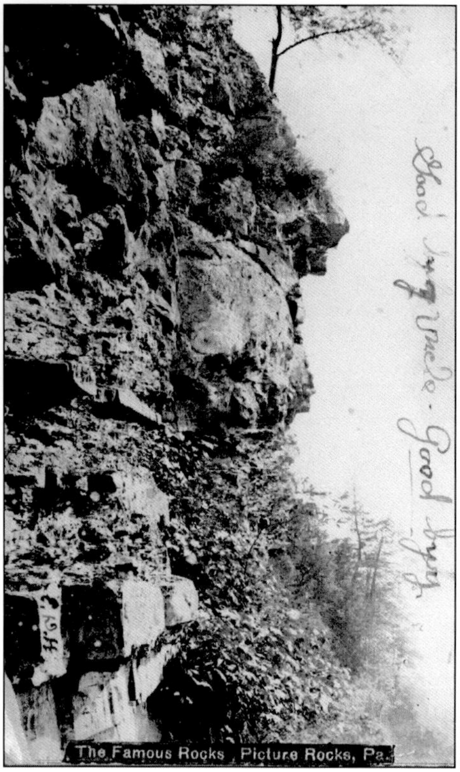

Before being settled by the Sprout and Burrows families, the land of Picture Rocks was occupied by the Monsie Indians. The rock wall along the Muncy Creek boasted massive carvings and paintings. Unfortunately, no one was ever able to translate the meanings of the pictures. This is a picture of the beloved Indian head, which is still visible today. (Courtesy of Wes and Pat Sprout.)

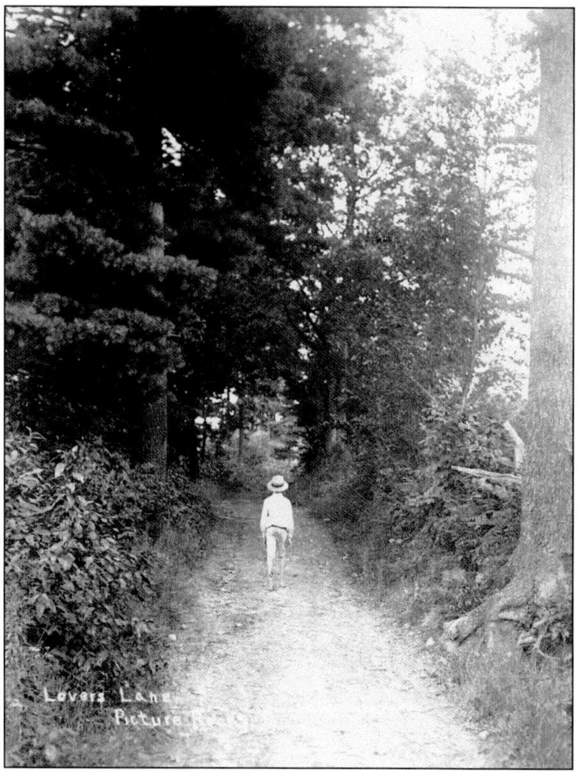

To get to Lover's Lane, one would have to cross the bridge at Center Street and it would be off to the left. Lover's Lane was located along the Muncy Creek, where there were many places for youngsters to swim and hang out. (Courtesy of Wes and Pat Sprout.)

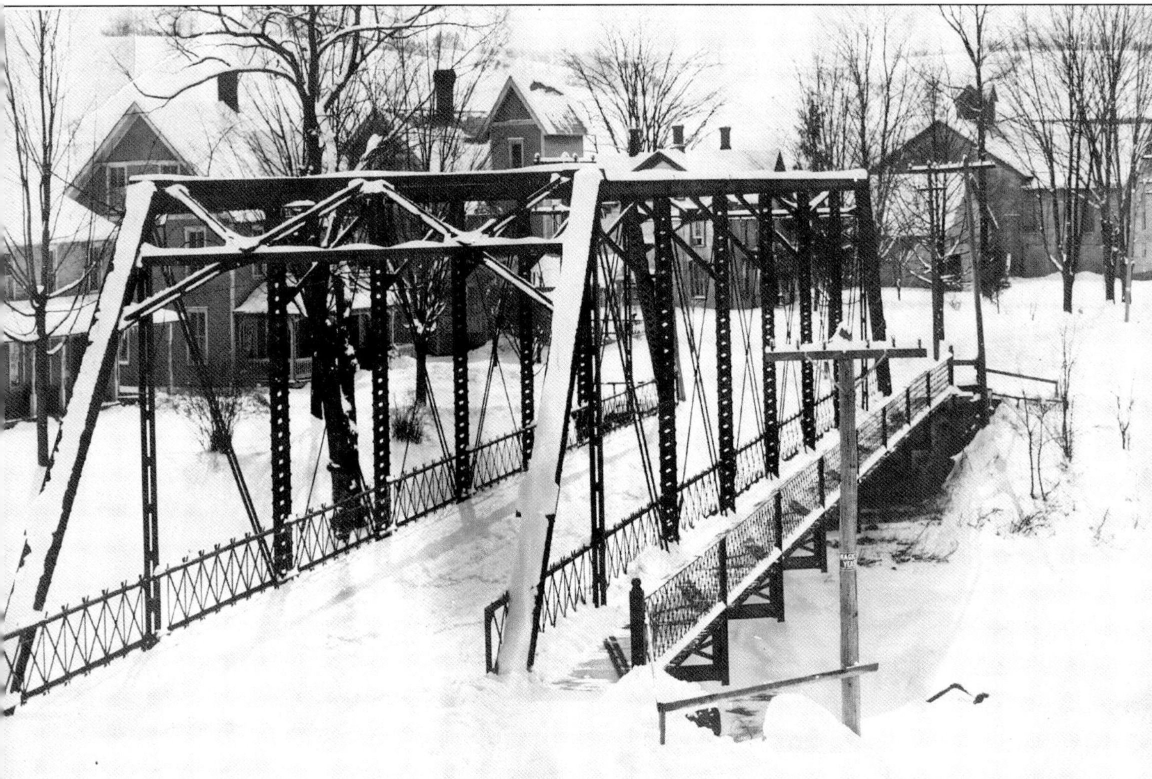

Here is a snowy day in Picture Rocks. This was the bridge that replaced the original wooden bridge as one crossed the Muncy Creek. (Courtesy of Bob Roller.)

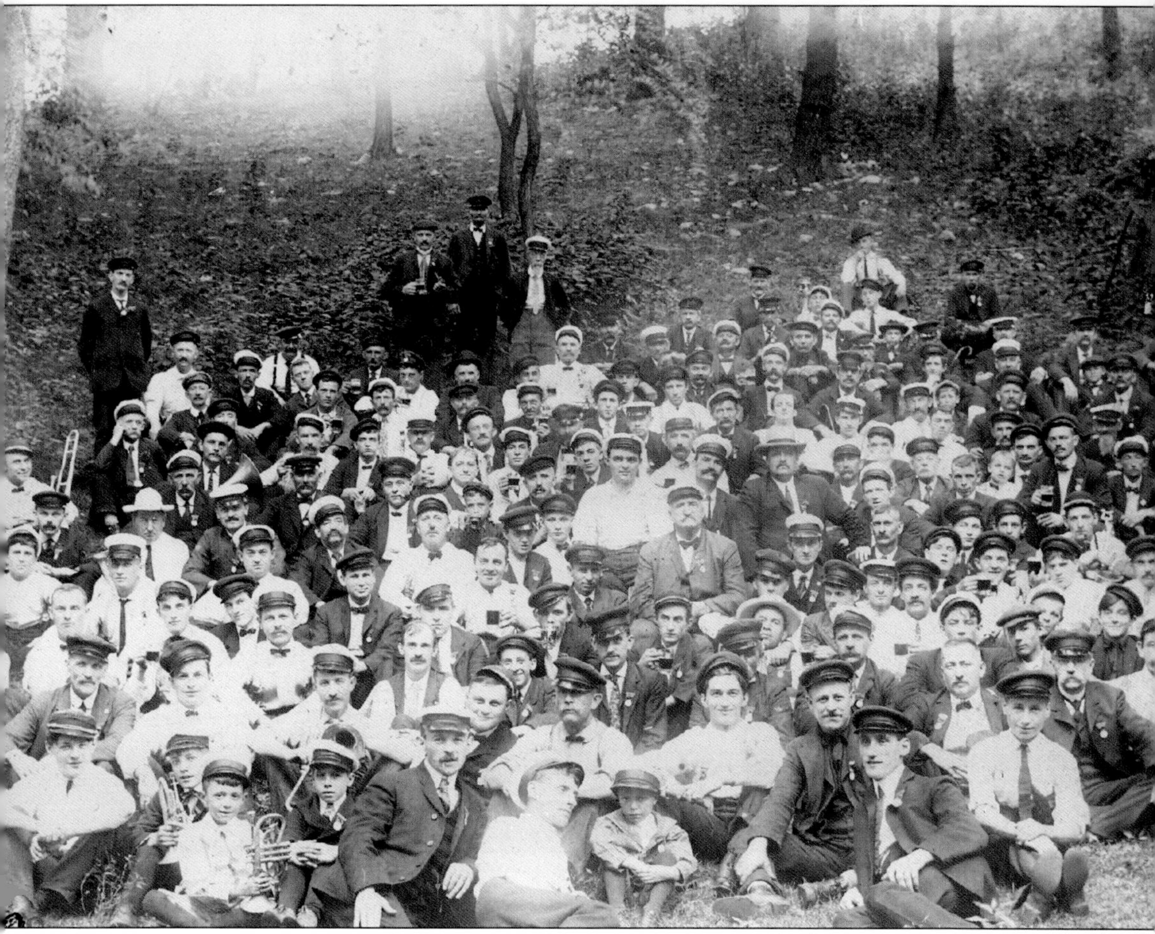

When performers came in for Chautauqua, they slept in railcars that were parked along Railroad Street. They housed their equipment in another car. The men and boys from town would help the performers carry the items to the park. (Courtesy of Bob Roller.)

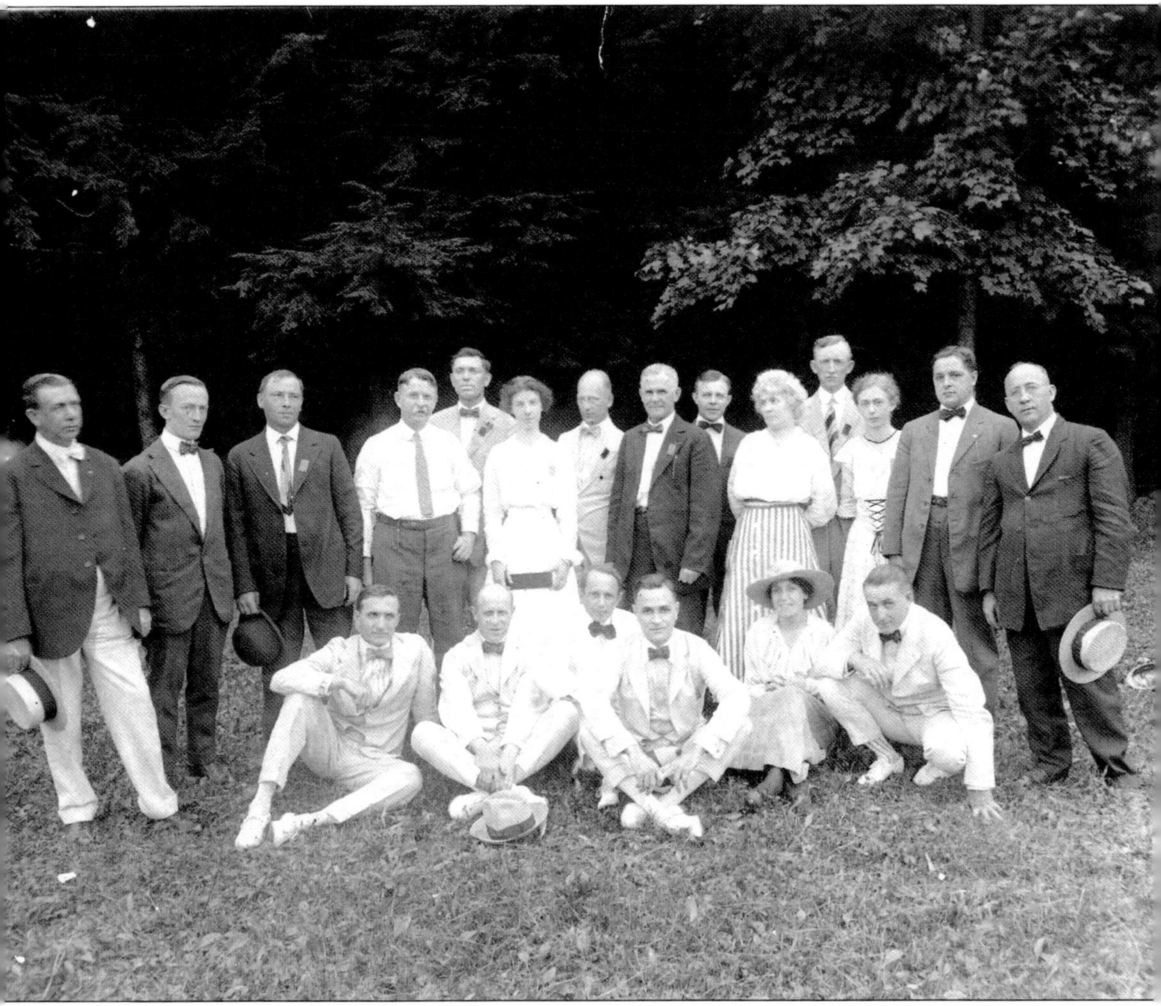

These men and women help financially to make Chautauqua possible as guarantors. Standing, from left to right, are Walter Burrows, Robert Ferrell, Lou Gumble, E. M. Cruse, Ernest Burrows, Lucinda Johnson, Charles Sypher, M. I. Sprout, Ernest Roller, Stella Burrows, D. B. Little, Edna Melhuish, Ray Fry, and Reverend Ruth. Sitting are a group of Chautauqua entertainers.

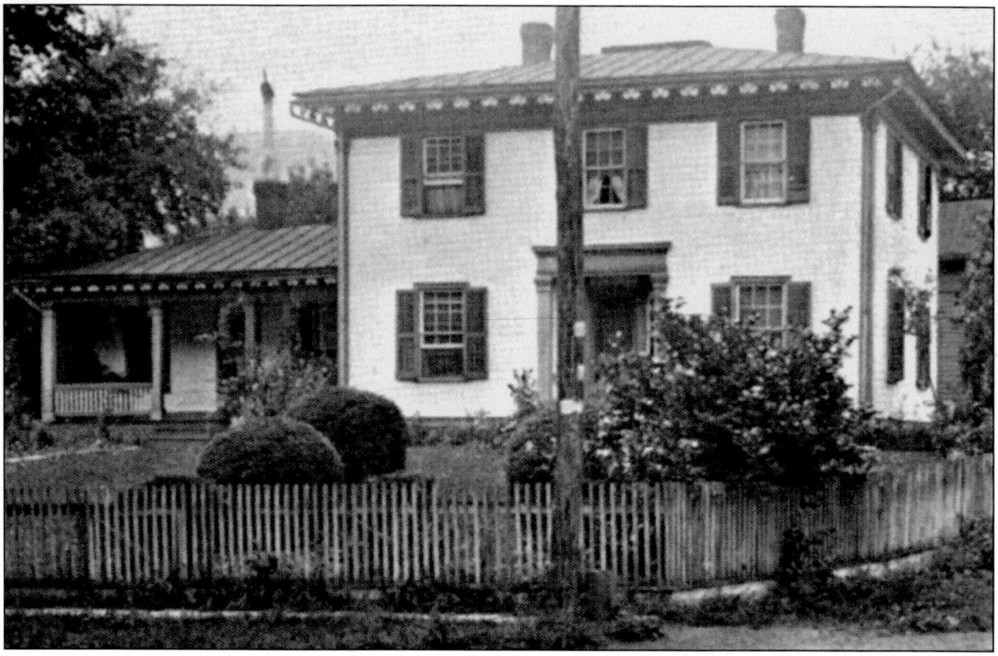

The Orpha Dell was the home of Amos B. Sprout and his family, and it was named for his only daughter, Orpha. Located at 229 Center Street, the home remained in the family until 2005. (Courtesy of *History and Pictures of Picture Rocks* by Ethel Cruse.)

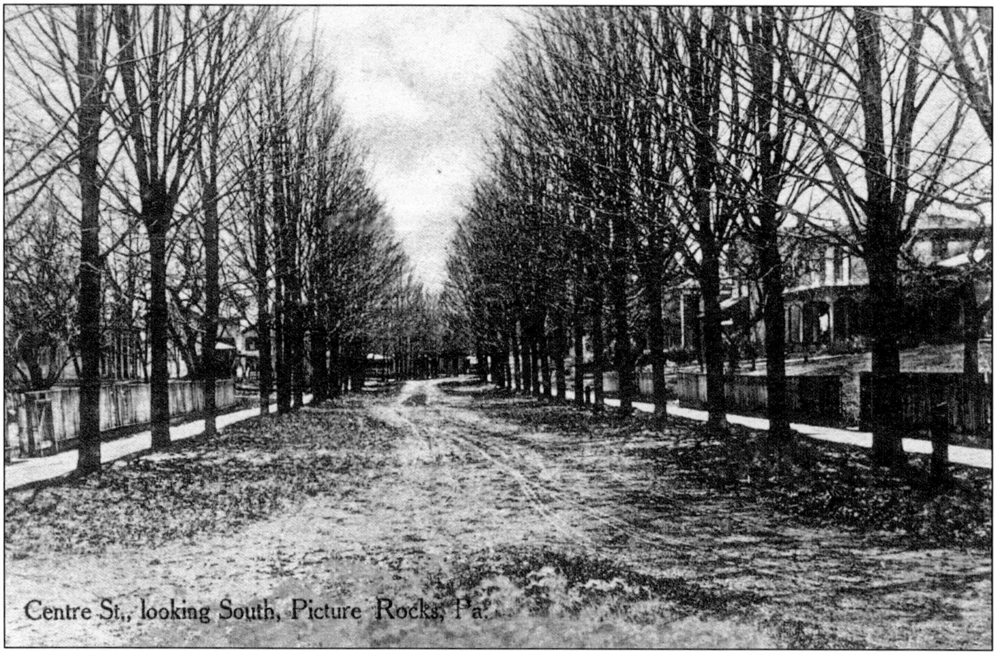

Center Street was originally known as Cottage Street. Some of the most famous homes in town are on this street. The Orpha Dell, the home of Amos Sprout, and the home of Asa Sprout are both located on this street. All are still standing today. (Courtesy of Cris Gansell.)

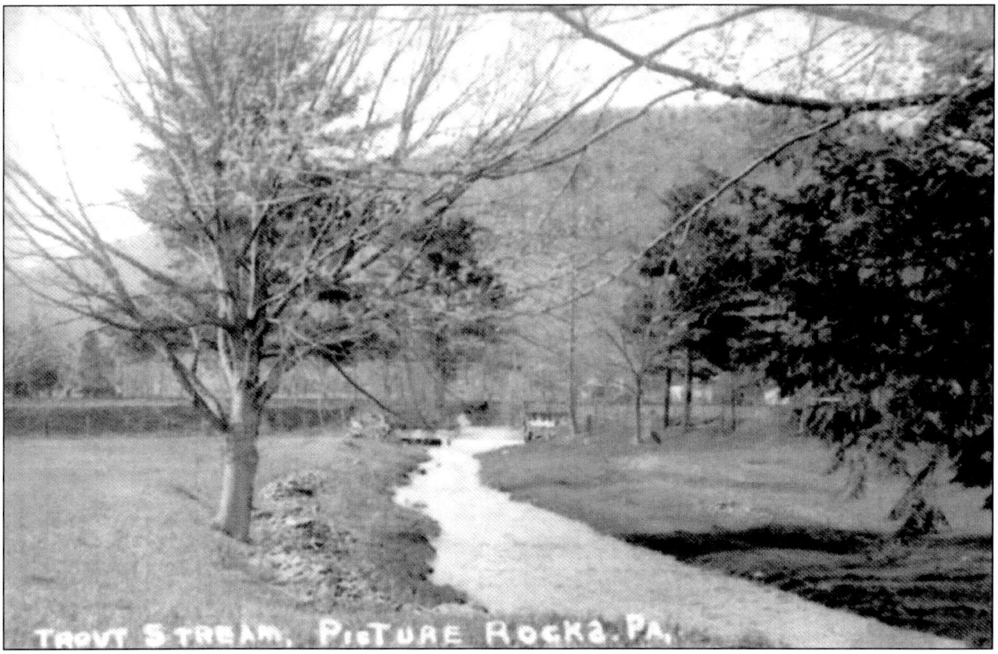

Trout Stream in Picture Rocks is shown here. (Courtesy of Stewart Hill.)

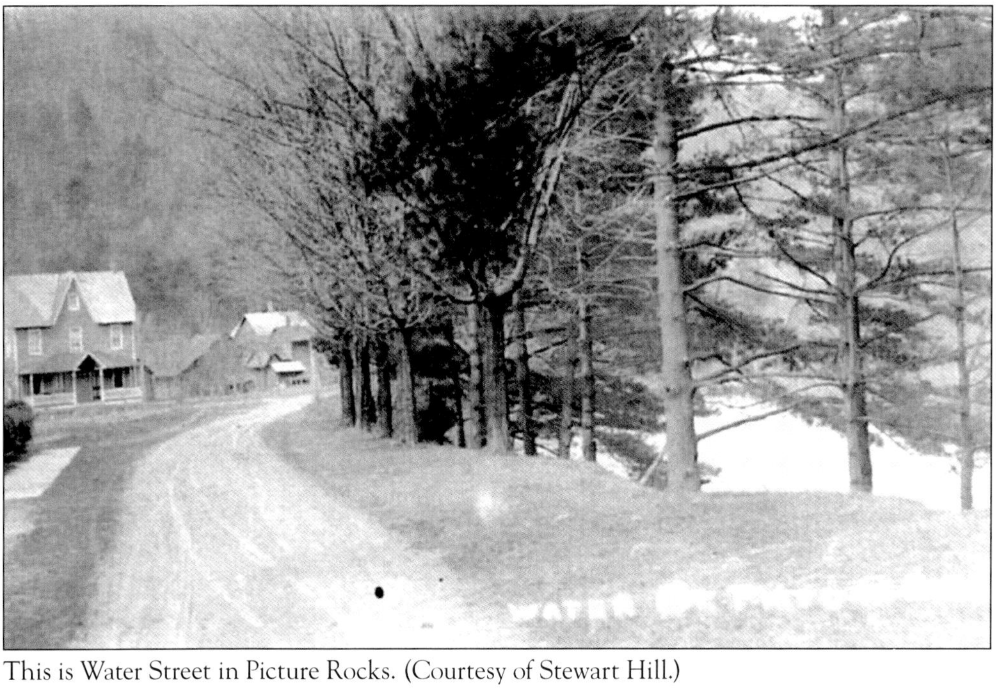

This is Water Street in Picture Rocks. (Courtesy of Stewart Hill.)

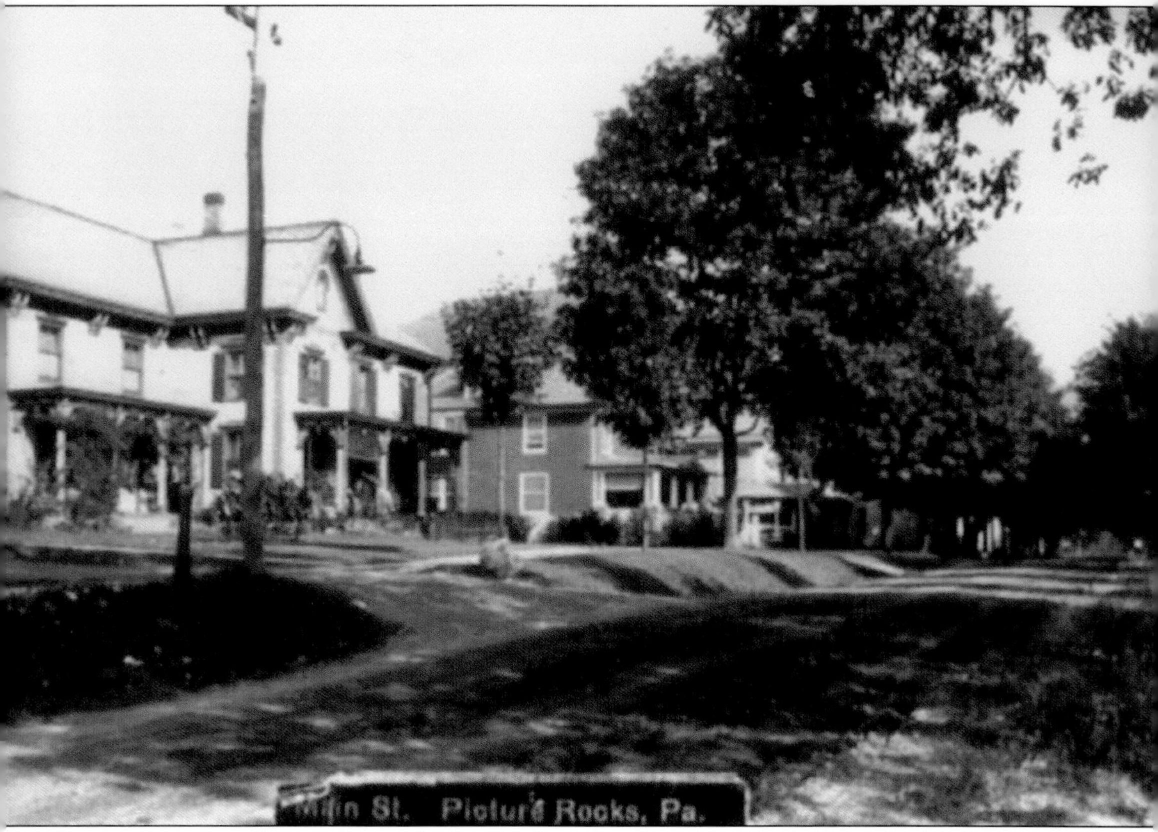

In this view of Main Street, the home of Sabin Burrows can be seen on the left. (Courtesy of Stewart Hill.)

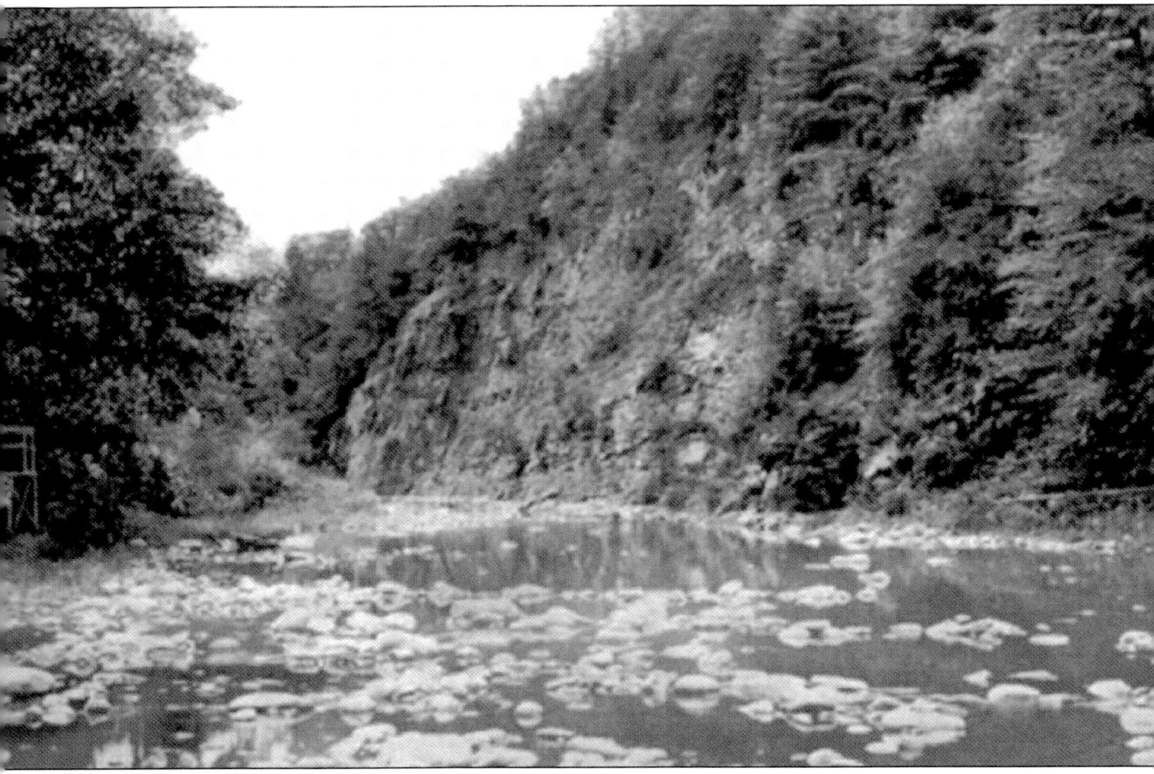

There were many paintings and carvings on this rock wall when the town was settled. Unfortunately, no one knew the meaning behind them. To this day, their meanings are unknown. (Courtesy of Stewart Hill.)

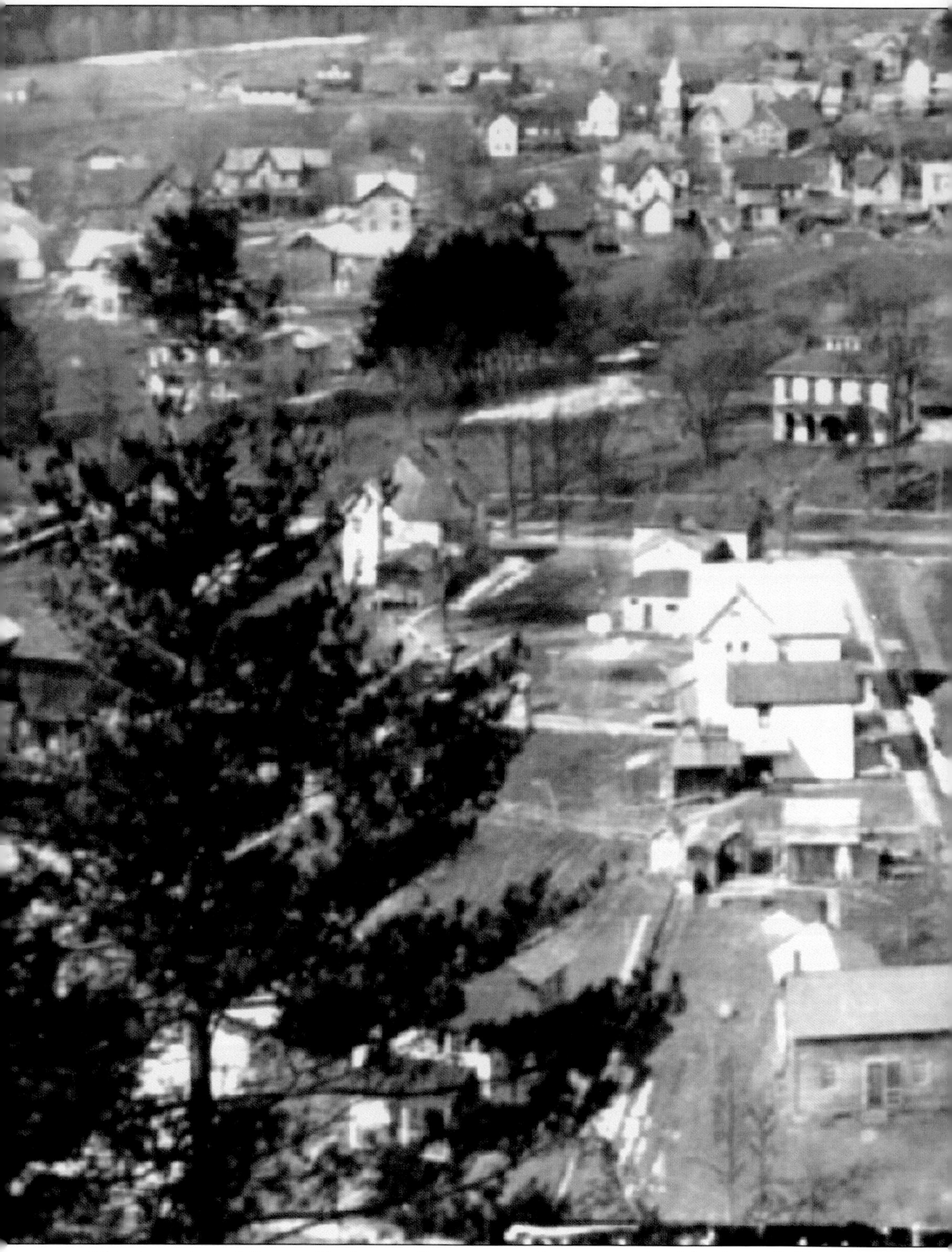

This is a view of Picture Rocks standing on top of its namesake "the Rocks." (Courtesy of

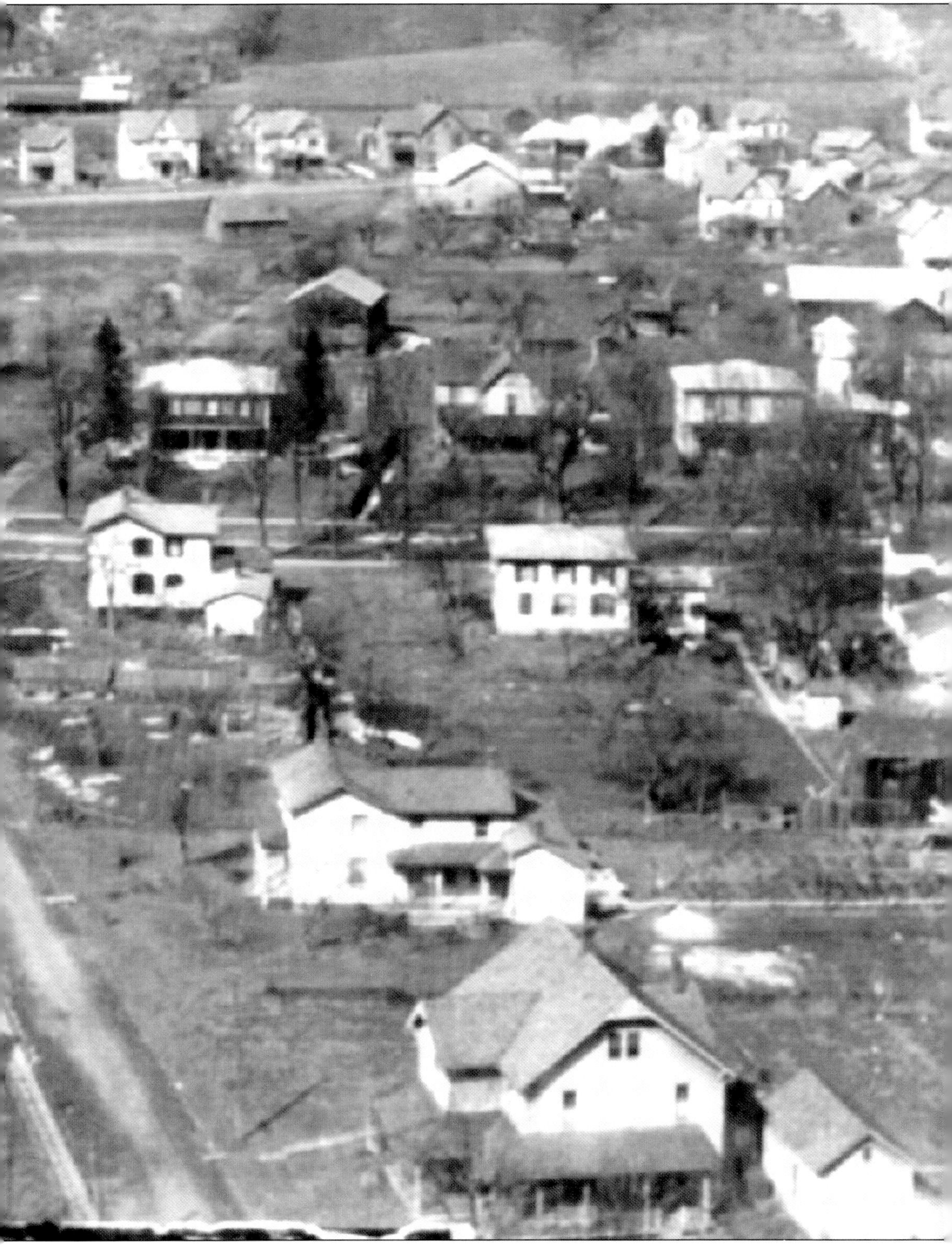

Stewart Hill.)

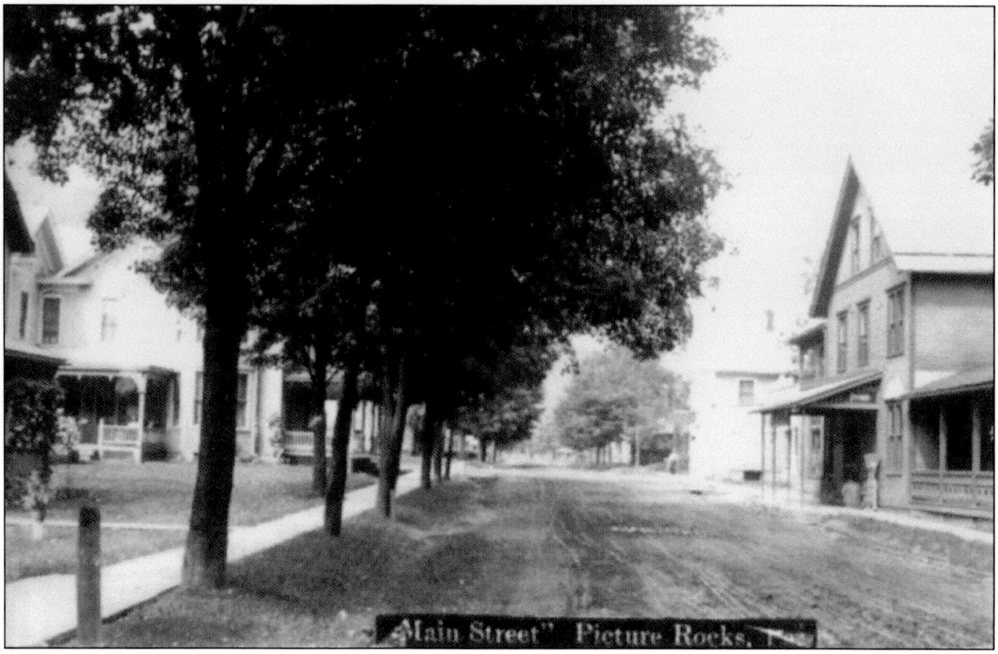

Main Street is located right in the heart of Picture Rocks. To the right is the general store that was operated by Edward Bayley Sr. The porch of his hotel can be seen. That same hotel was known to house schoolteachers that worked at the Picture Rocks High School. (Courtesy of Stewart Hill.)

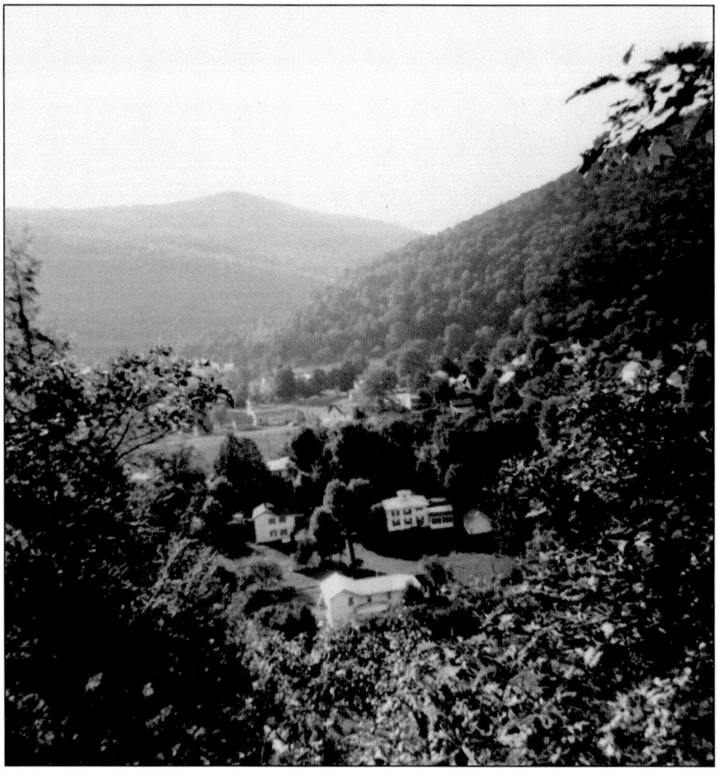

Picture Rocks is nestled at the base of a mountain. The entire town sits on only 58 acres of land. (Courtesy of Cris Gansell.)

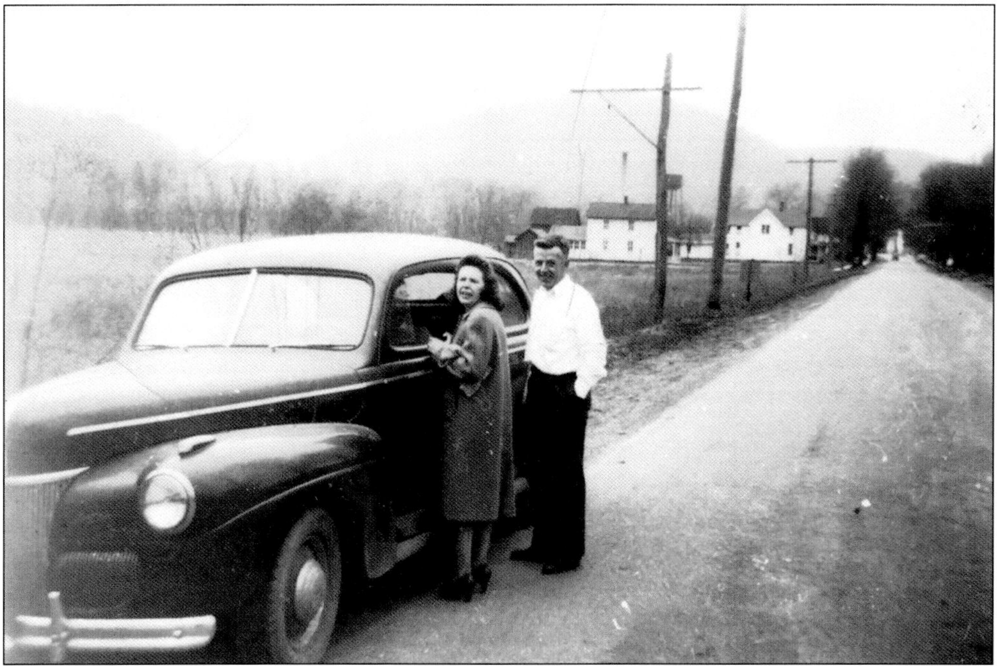

This photograph was taken along South Main Street looking into the main part of town. (Courtesy of Mike Bayley.)

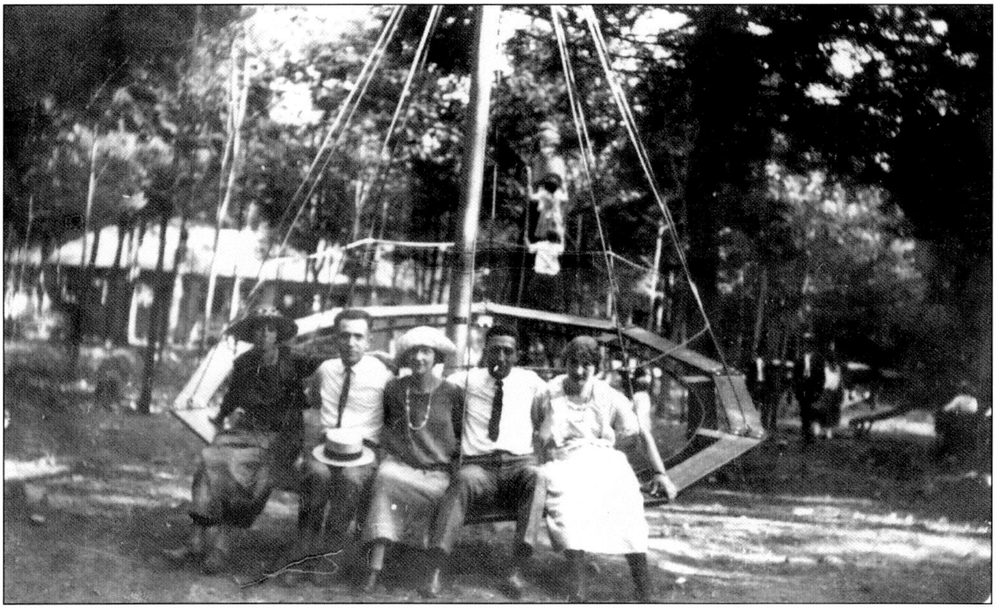

The park in town was named Van Rensselaer Park after Asa R. Sprout. One popular story of the park has to do with the ripcords. Youngsters used to cross the creek and head up the mountain, grab hold of the rip cord, and sail down the mountain over the creek and back into the park. (Courtesy of Janet Kohler.)

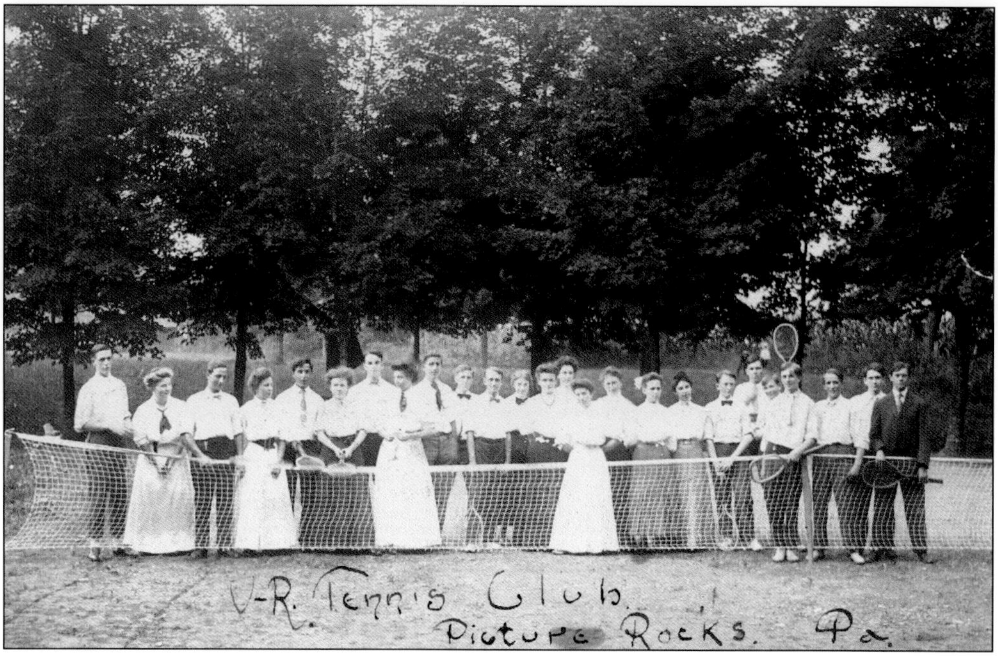

The Van Rensselaer Tennis Club existed before World War I. (Courtesy of Dot and Bill Sandmeyer.)

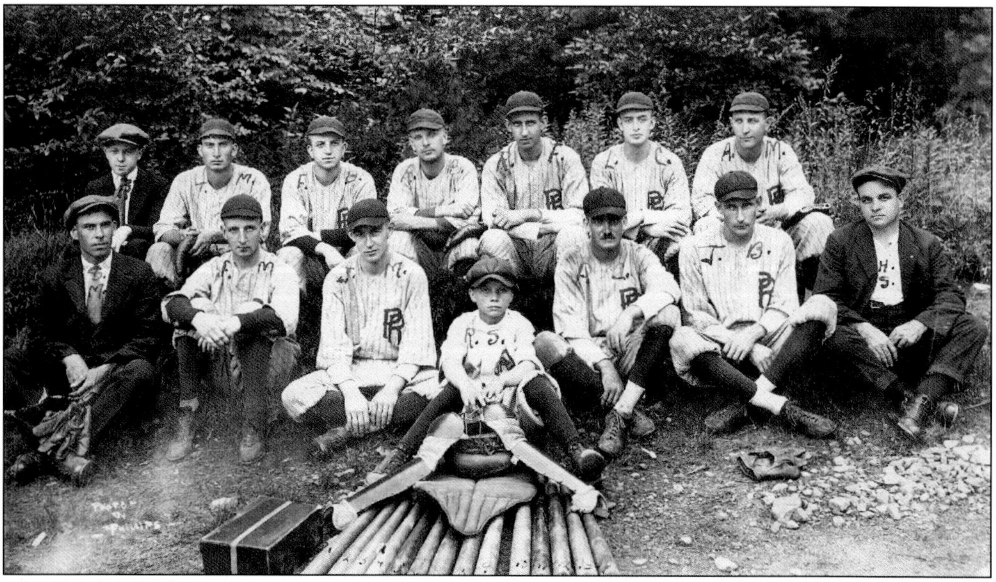
The first baseball teams in town were organized by the factories in town. The Burrows Brothers, H and E, and Lycoming Ladder all had their own teams. They played in a vacant lot behind the fire hall until the field and grandstand at Van Rensselaer Park was created. (Courtesy of Bob Roller.)

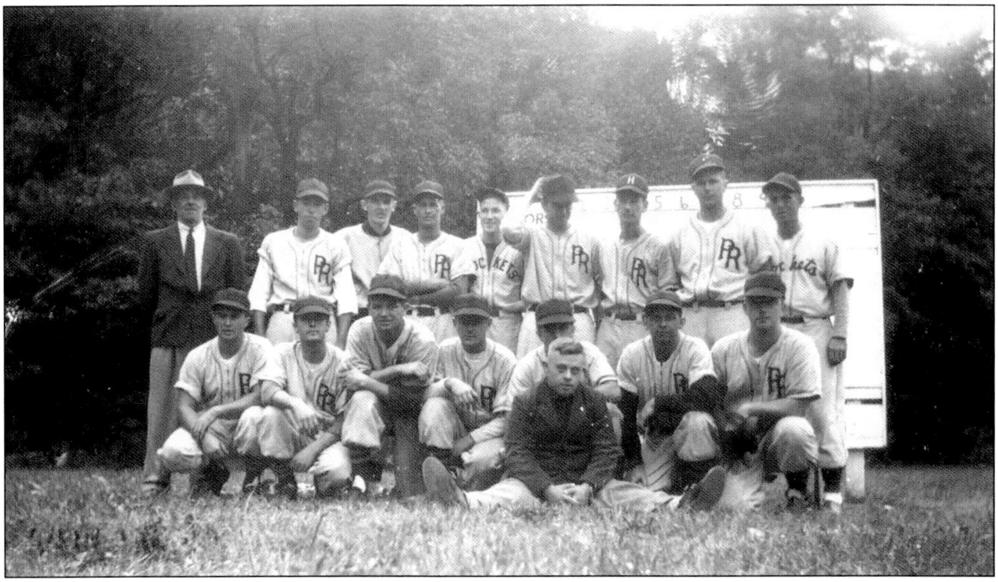

The Picture Rocks Rockets was the towns baseball team from the 1940s through the 1980s (on and off in the later years). (Courtesy of Bob Roller.)

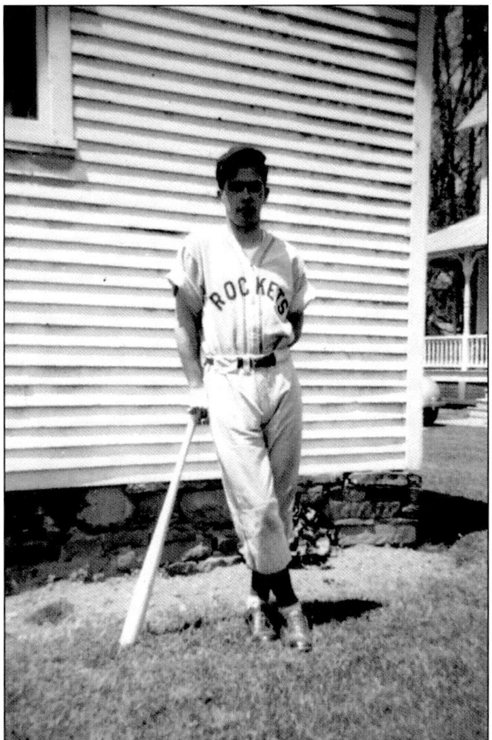

Charley Gansell was the catcher for the Picture Rocks Rockets. (Courtesy of Charley Gansell.)

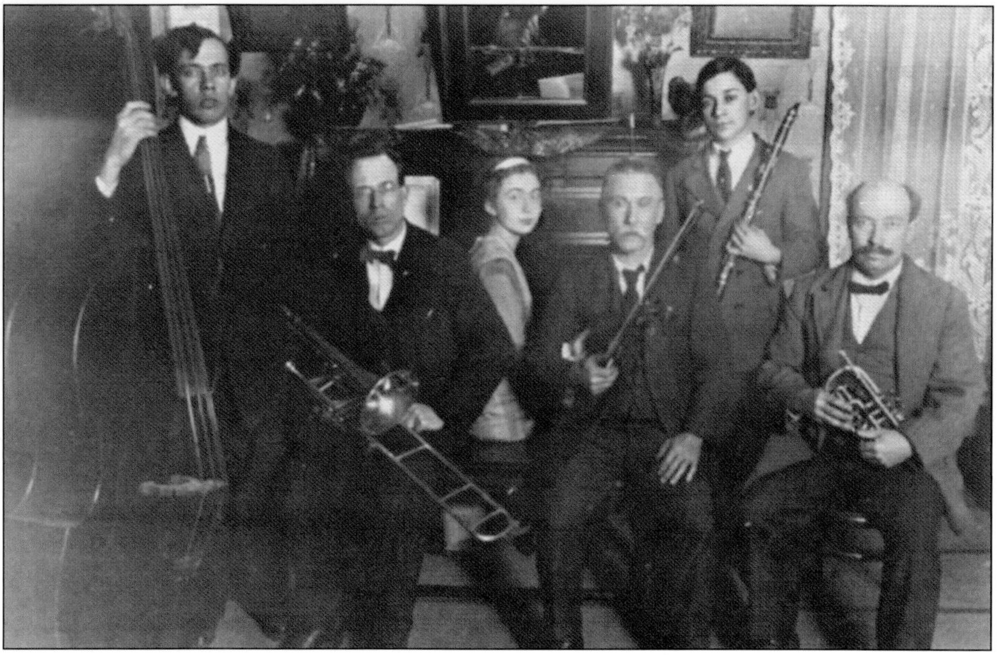

Not only was Picture Rocks a self-sustaining town, it was a self-entertaining one too. Pictured here is a small orchestra. From left to right, on string bass violin is Frank Rimert, on the trombone is Robert Archer, on piano is Edna Melhuish, on violin is J. R. Edler, on clarinet is Gray Rimert, and on cornet is Joseph Rimert. (Courtesy of *History and Pictures of Picture Rocks* by Ethel Cruse.)

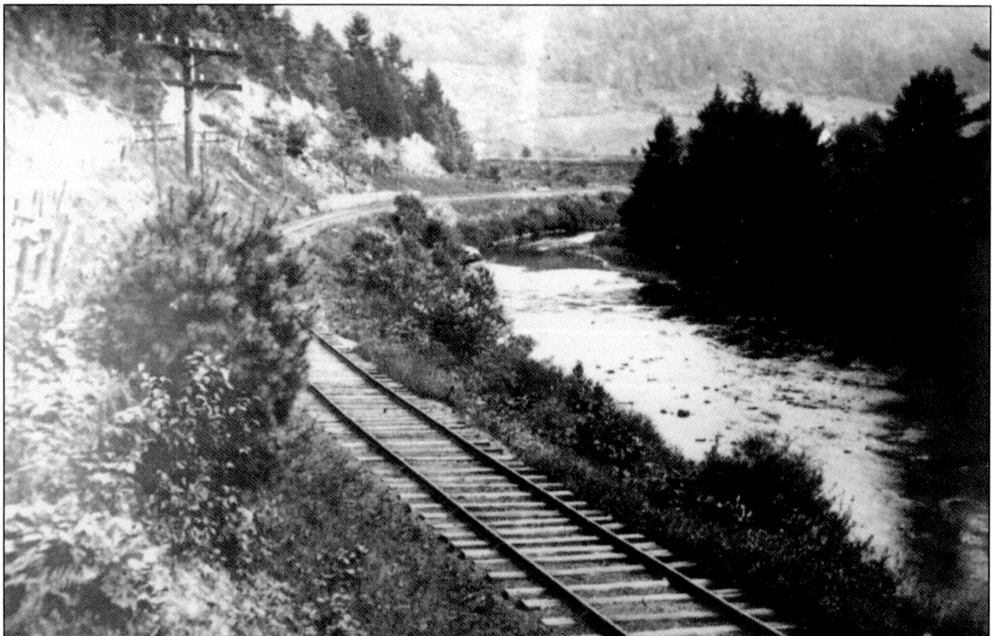

The railroad served two major businesses in town, the Burrows Brothers Furniture Company and the coal and lumber company owned by Edward Bayley. (Courtesy of Wes and Pat Sprout.)

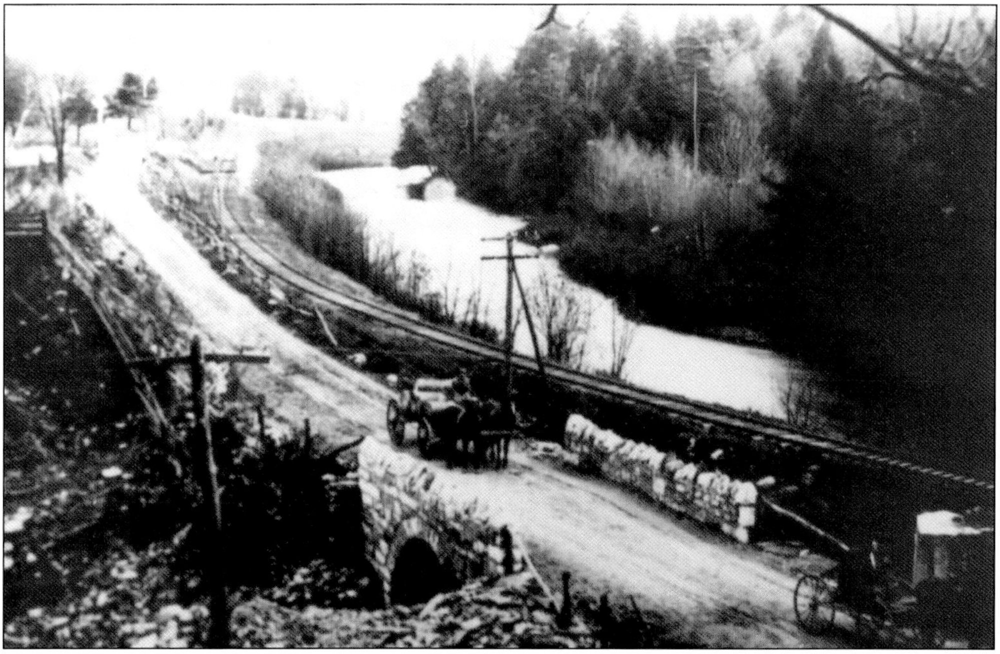

Beyond Picture Rocks was the Chamouni Station. From there, one could take a stagecoach to any of the hotels in Highland Lake where many of the hotels were owned by people from Picture Rocks. The Chamouni Station was later named Essick after one of the Highland hotel owners, who lived in Picture Rocks. (Courtesy of Wes and Pat Sprout.)

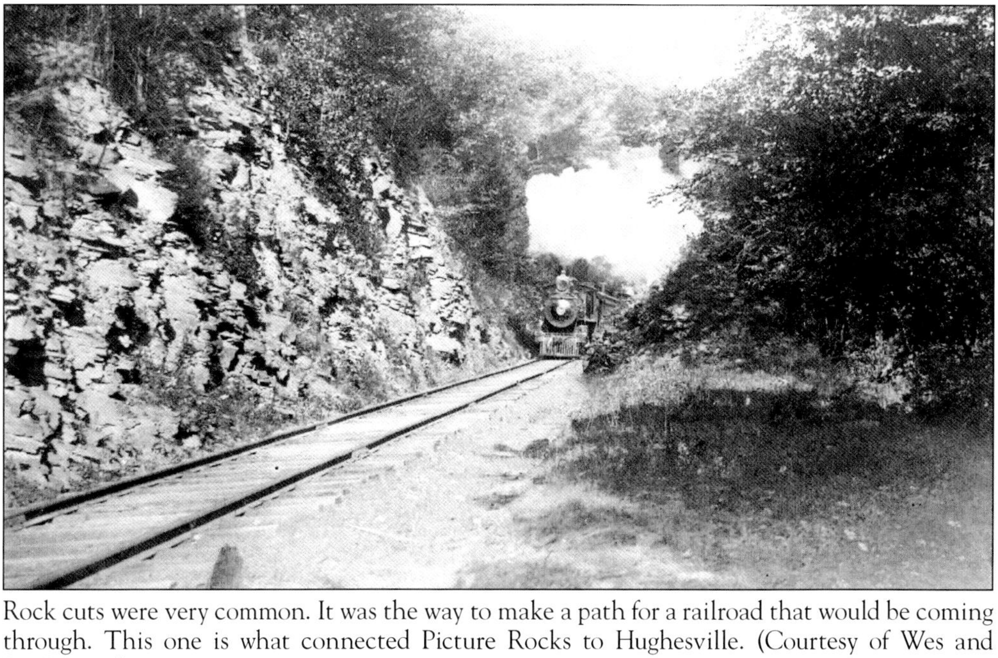

Rock cuts were very common. It was the way to make a path for a railroad that would be coming through. This one is what connected Picture Rocks to Hughesville. (Courtesy of Wes and Pat Sprout.)

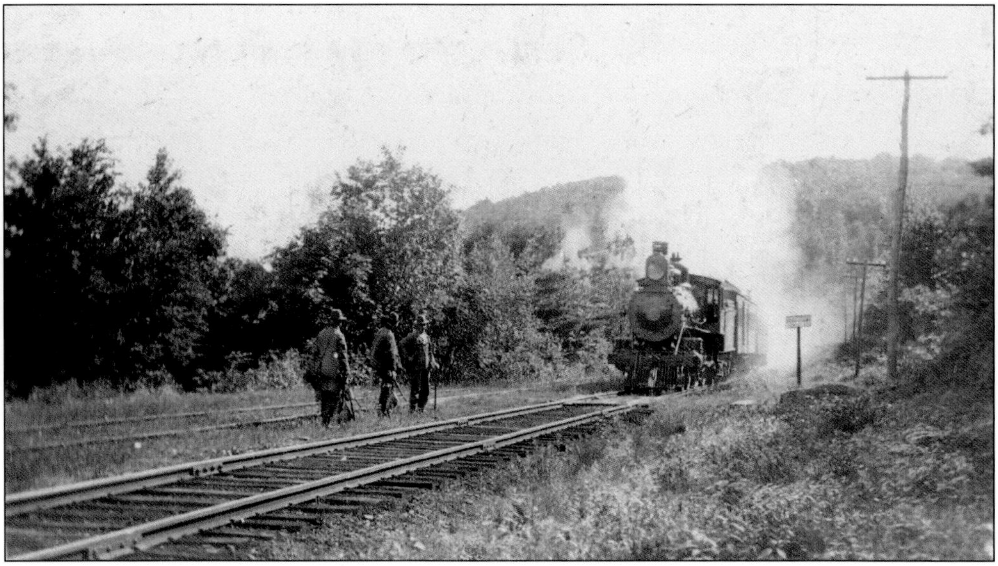

The Williamsport and North Branch Railroad came to Picture Rocks on March 14, 1884. To celebrate, the train made three excursion trips to Hughesville, allowing the townspeople to ride for free. (Courtesy of Wes and Pat Sprout.)

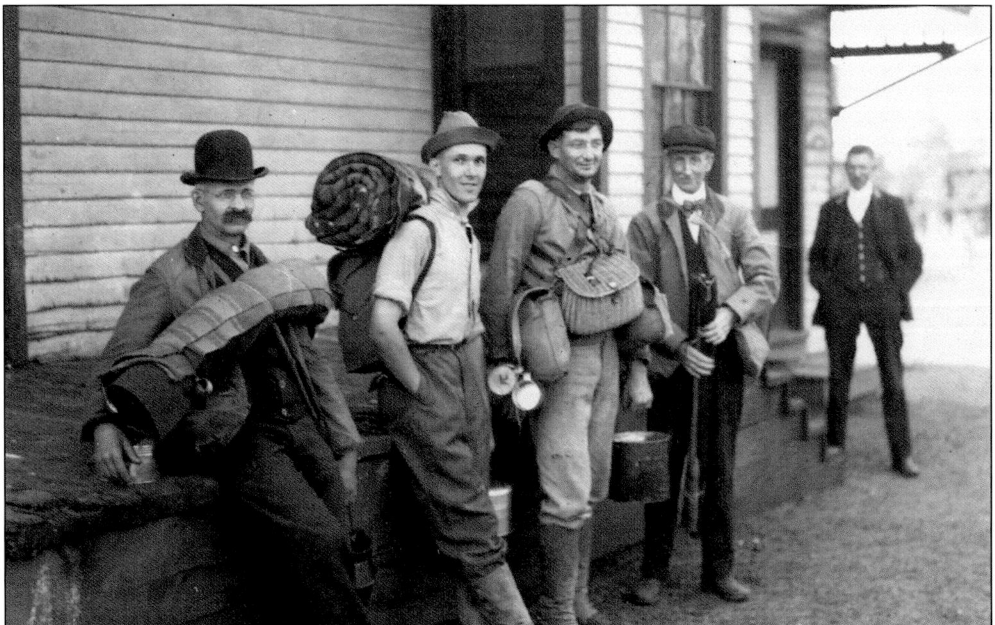

The train station that sat on Railroad Street is pictured here. The first station manager was John Dietrich Musgrave. The railroad was discontinued in 1937. By 1938, the tracks in town were torn up. (Courtesy of Wes and Pat Sprout.)

Seven

SURROUNDING AREAS

Friday December 23, 1870
Worked about 6 hours on the rails. Did chores. Two engineers employed by the Cattawissa R. R. CO. who are running the Muncy Creek route today stay with us tonight.

—Amos Sprout

If one had an able body during the building of the Williamsport and North Branch Railroad, chances are they worked on it. In 1864, work started on the railroad. For 74 years the railroad was in service. In 1938, the W&NBRR was traveled for the last time.

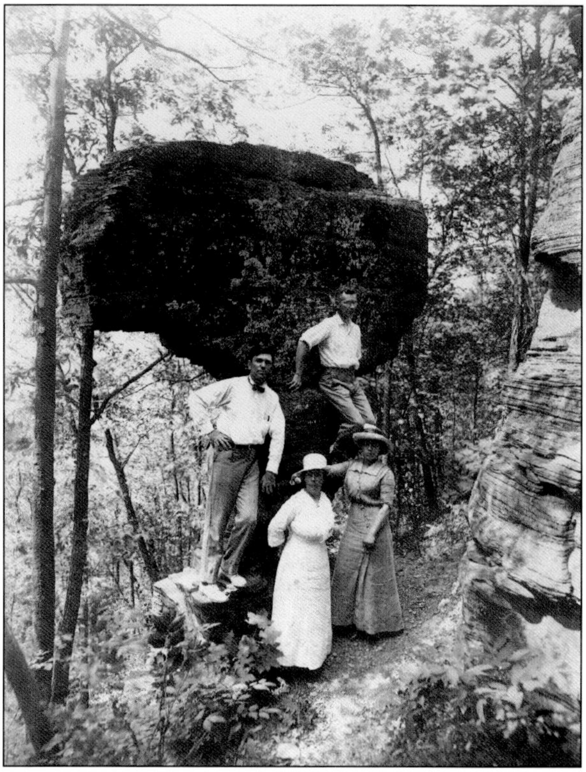

Fanny Painton of Picture Rocks poses with others at Ticklish Rock. (Courtesy of Bob Roller.)

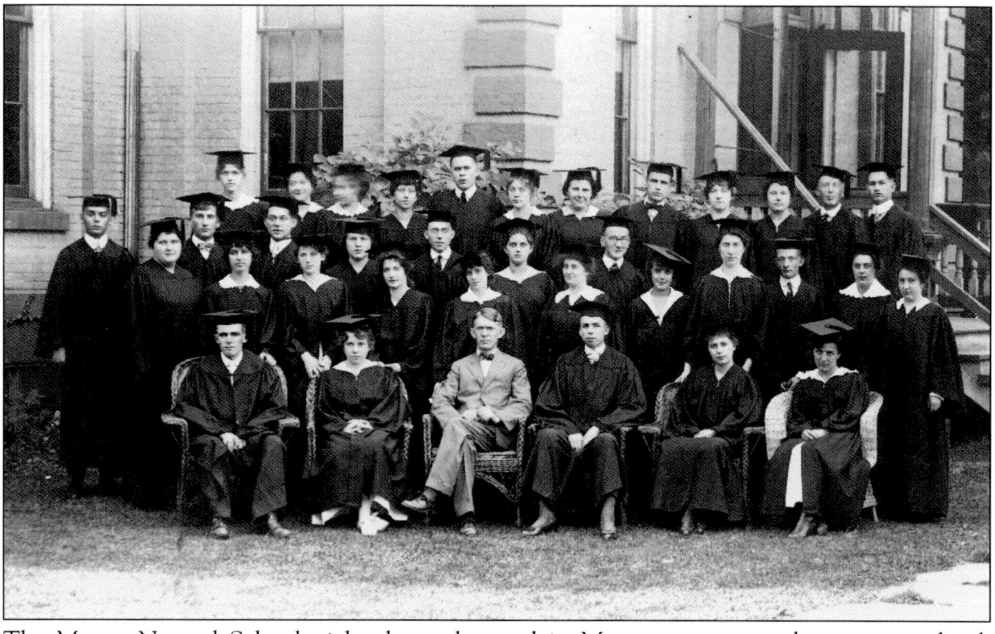

The Muncy Normal School, right down the road in Muncy, was a popular nursing school. (Courtesy of Cris Gansell.)

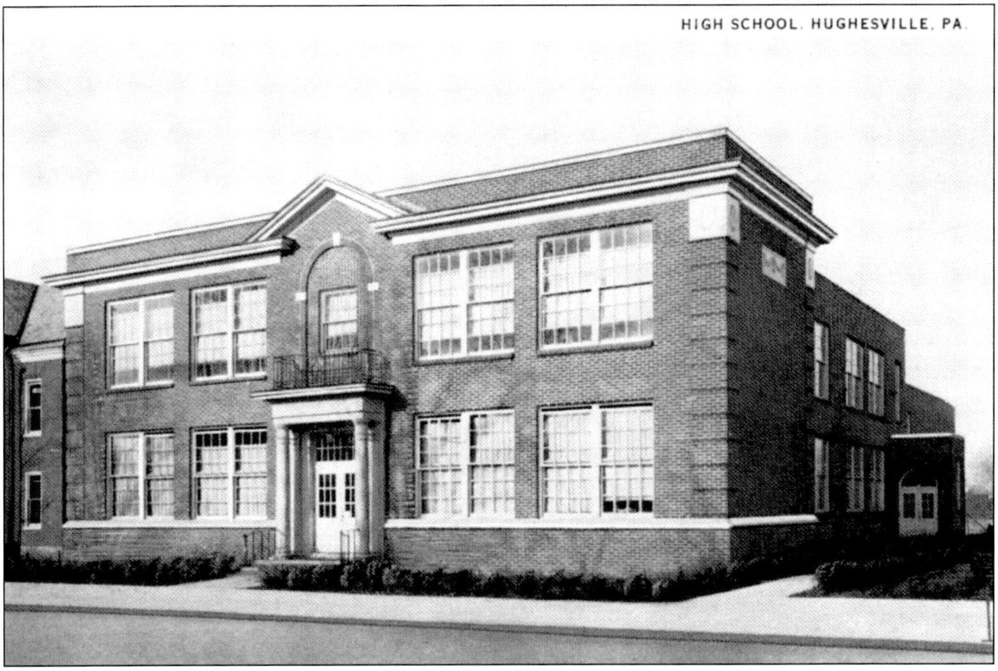

The Wolf School was the first high school in Hughesville. The Wolf School sat (the building is still present) along Main Street. (Courtesy of Cris Gansell.)

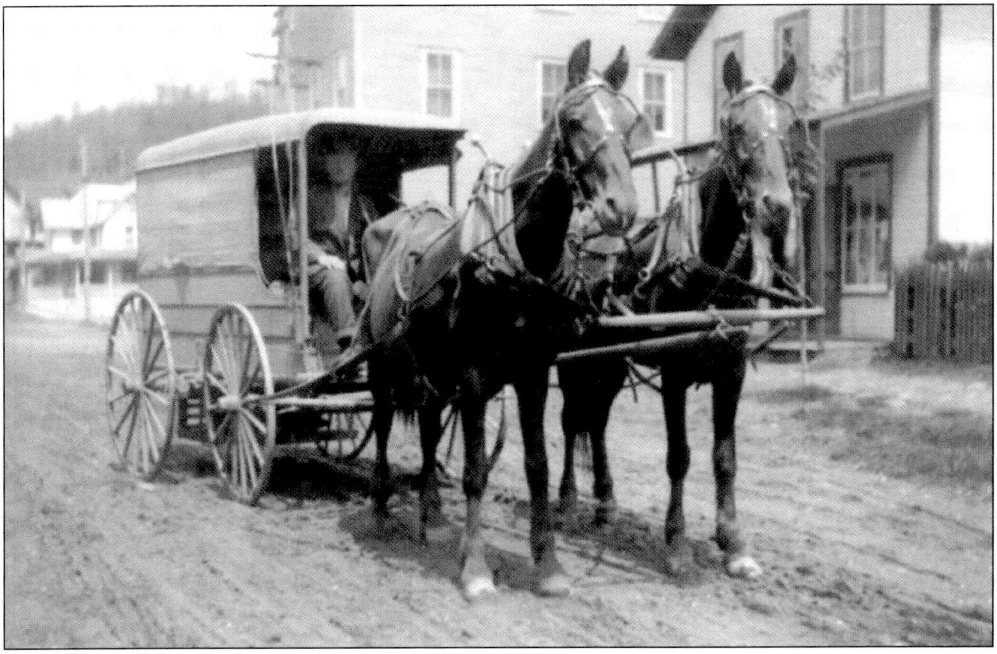

Arnold Price was Hughesville's butcher. Price used a horse-drawn wagon to deliver his product. He served the community for a number of years. (Courtesy of Stewart Hill.)

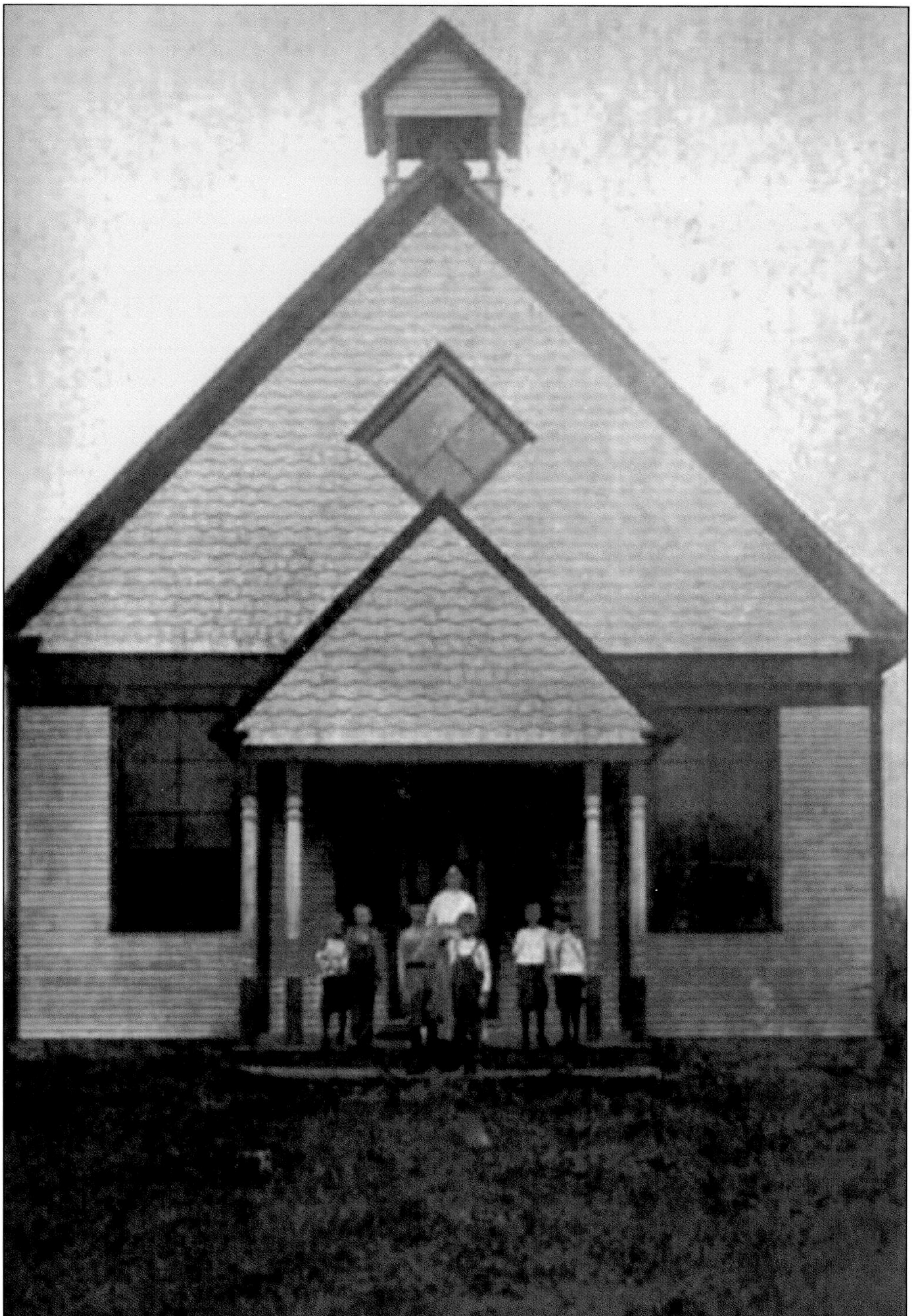

Hartley Hall in Halls Station was the epicenter of activity. The hall was used to conduct town meetings and social events. (Courtesy of Stewart Hill.)

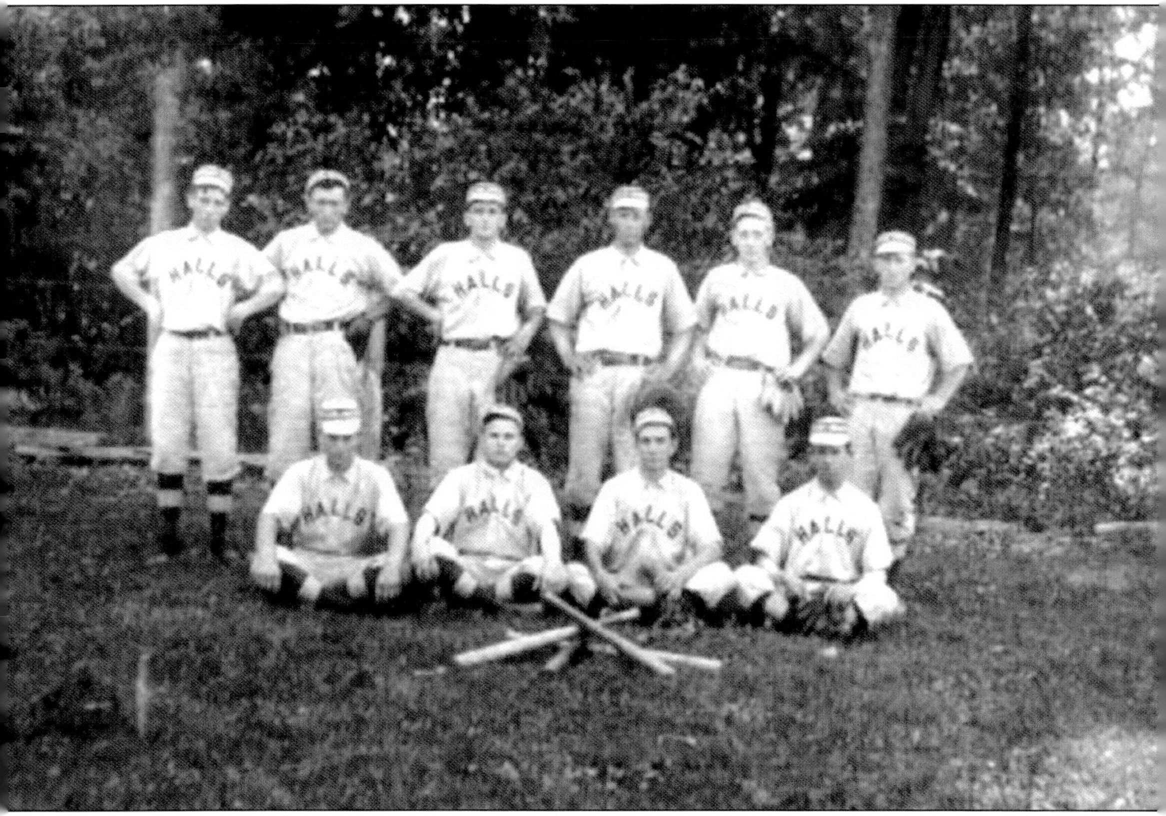

The Halls Station baseball team is pictured here. Like Picture Rocks and many other surrounding areas, Halls Station had a town team. The teams were generally made up of factory workers. (Courtesy of Stewart Hill.)

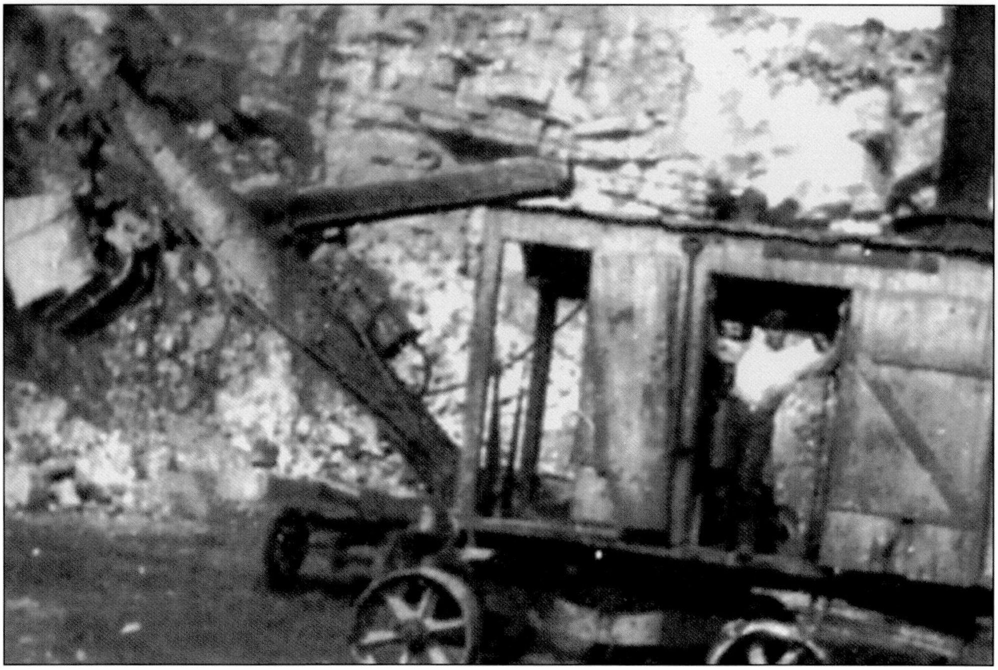

This steam shovel was used to make the rock cut in Bryantown. The cut would allow the train to go from Picture Rocks to Hughesville. (Courtesy of Stewart Hill.)

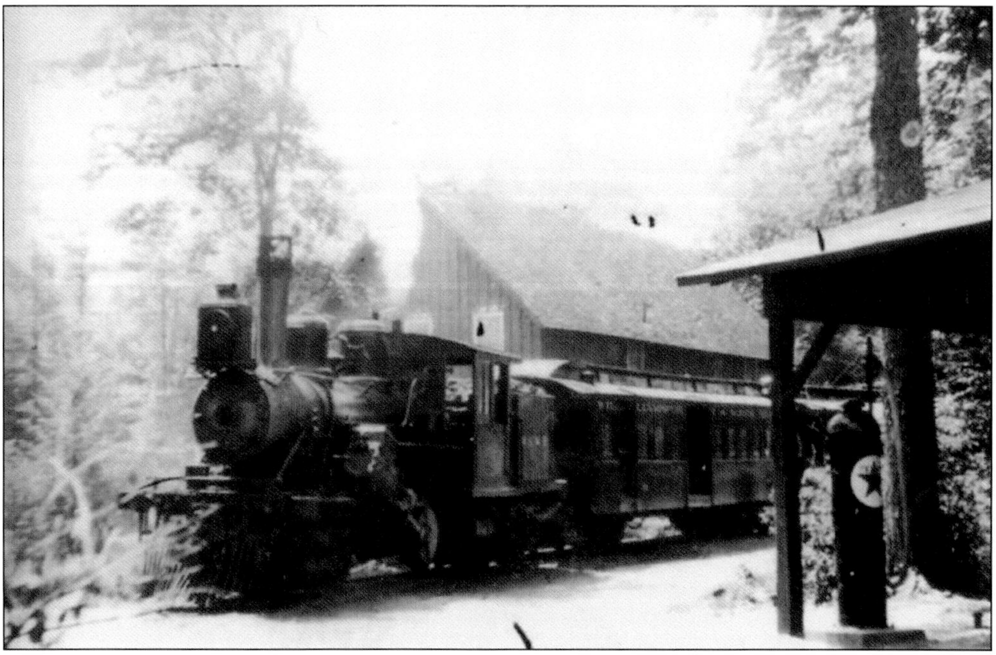

The Williamsport and North Branch Railroad (W&NBRR) opened in Picture Rocks March 14, 1884. It was a very popular way to travel to and from Hughesville. (Courtesy of Stewart Hill.)

The Williamsport and North Branch Railroad went under construction in 1864. However, before the W&NBRR ,there was the Muncy Creek Railroad and Coal company. The MCR&C was a forerunner to the W&NBRR. The W&NBRR picked up where the Muncy Creek Railroad left off. Eventually the W&NBRR went from Halls Station to Satterfield. (Courtesy of Stewart Hill.)

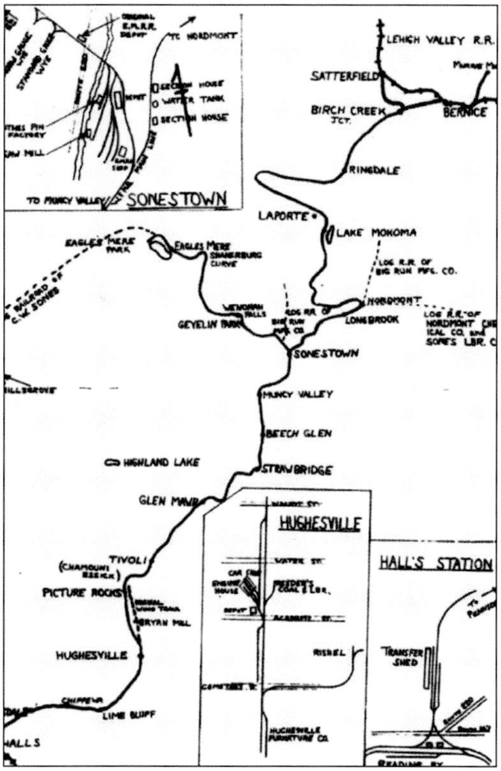

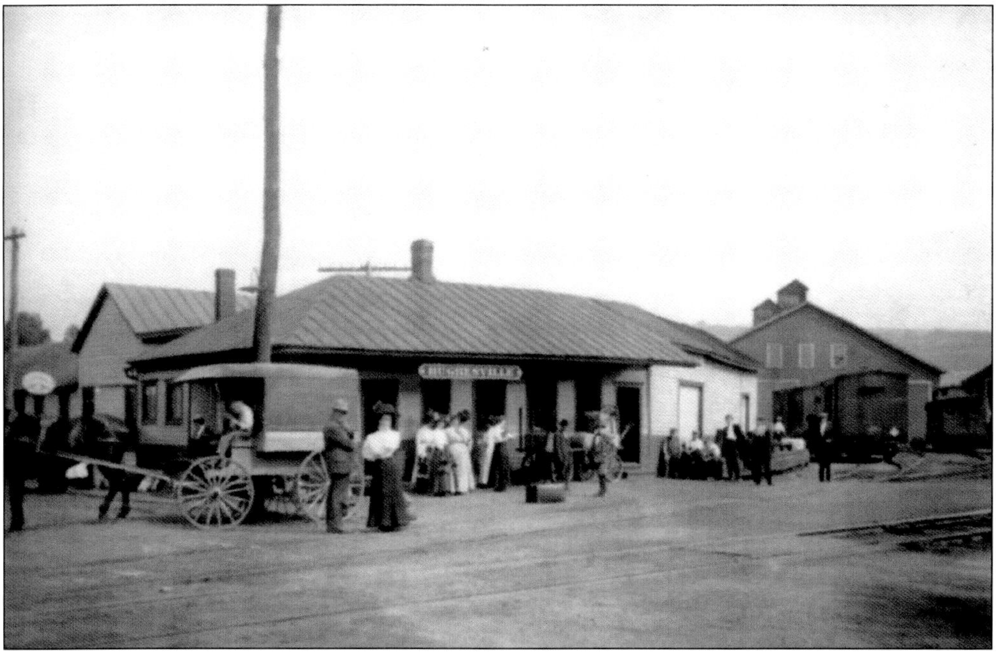

Hughesville was the biggest town along the railroad. It also served as a headquarters. Hughesville was also a popular stop because of its many shops in town. (Courtesy of Stewart Hill.)

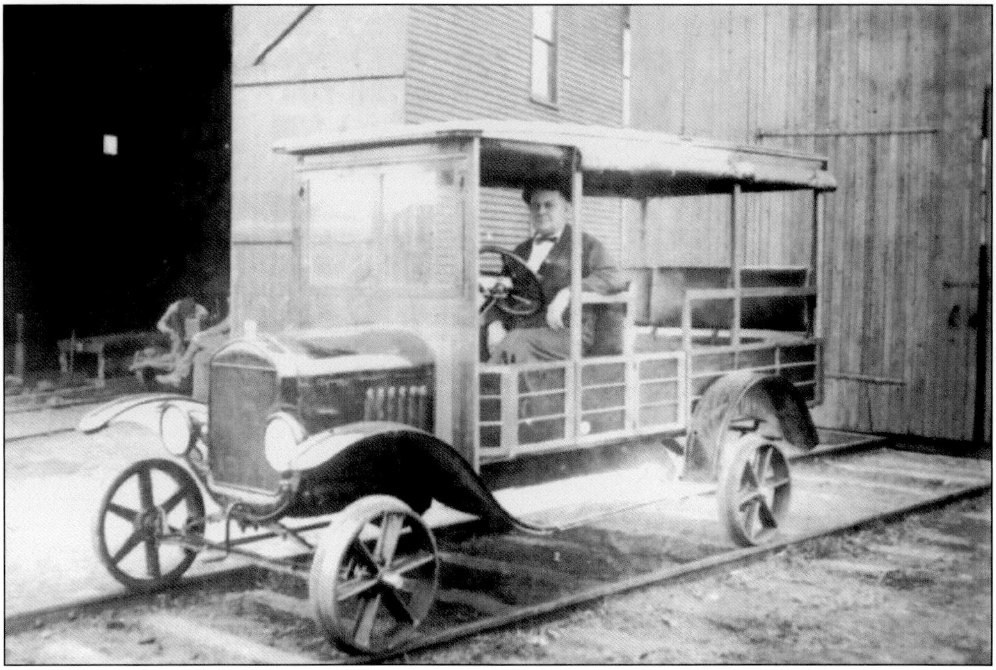

John Turner, a Hughesville Ford dealer, shows off this Ford Model T inspection car in 1924. This was a car that they actually drove on the tracks to do their inspections. (Courtesy of Stewart Hill.)

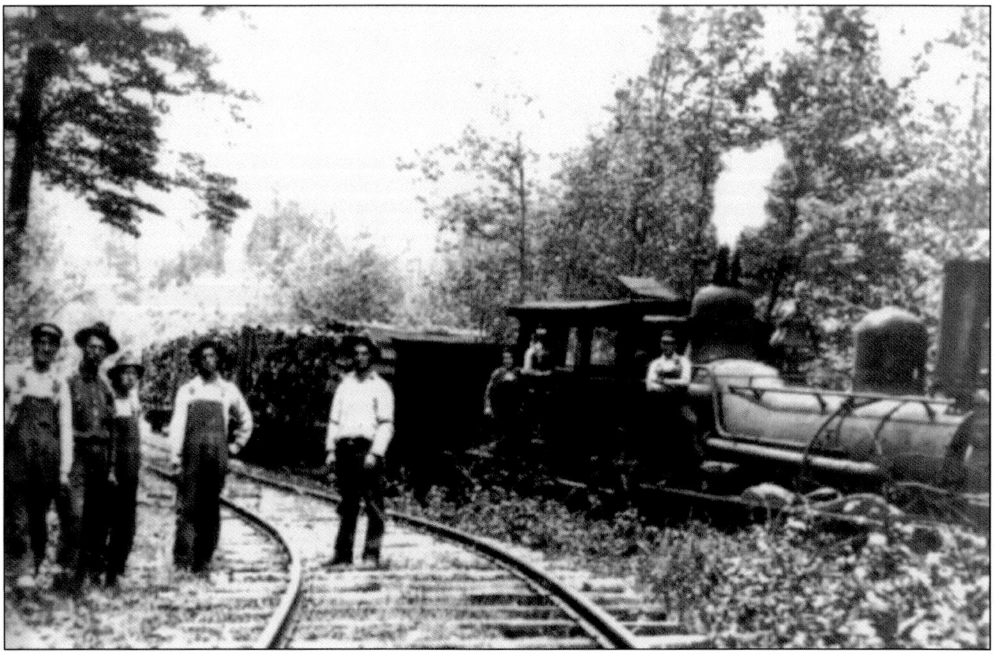

Work was steady on the railroad. The W&NBRR employed nearly 1,000 people. (Courtesy of Stewart Hill.)

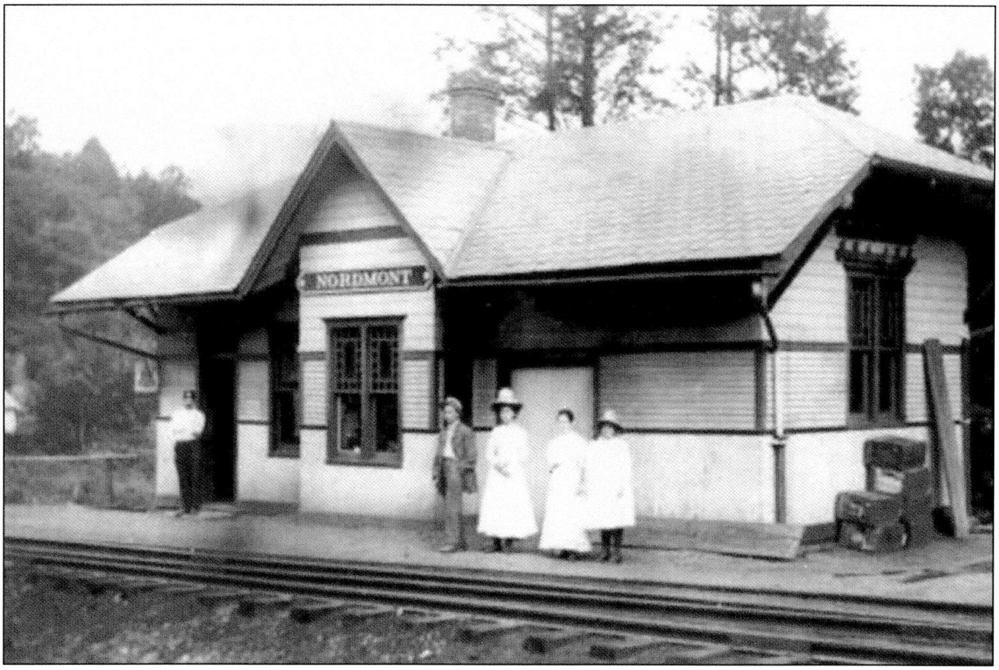

In 1884, construction was started towards Nordmont from Hughesville. The cost for construction was $30,000 a mile. It took three years for the W&NBRR to finally reach Nordmont. (Courtesy of Stewart Hill.)

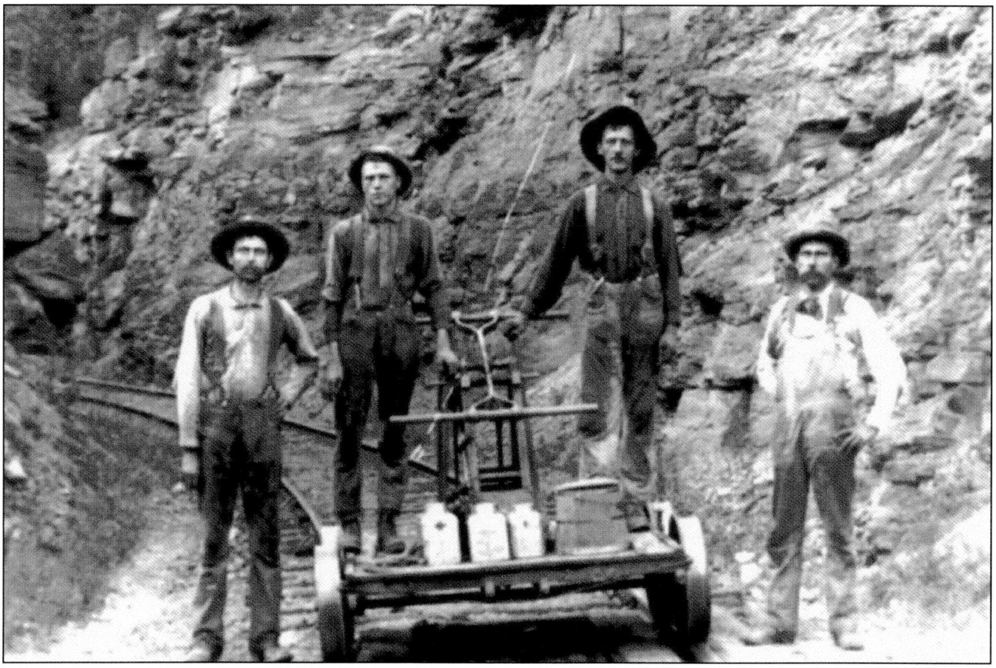
During the building of the tracks, many times workers would come from out of town for work. Those workers also stayed with other families while doing the work. Six miles was a long distance to travel. (Courtesy of Stewart Hill.)

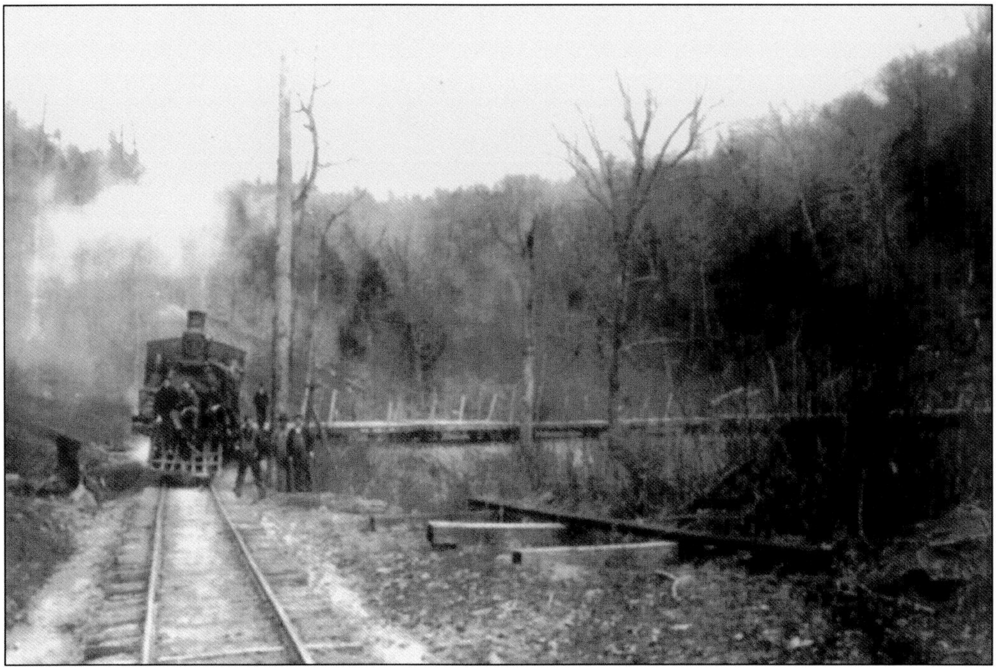

Another train and its crew are pictured along the Williamsport and North Branch Railroad. The railroad had approximately 25 locomotives between 1893 and 1938. (Courtesy of Stewart Hill.)

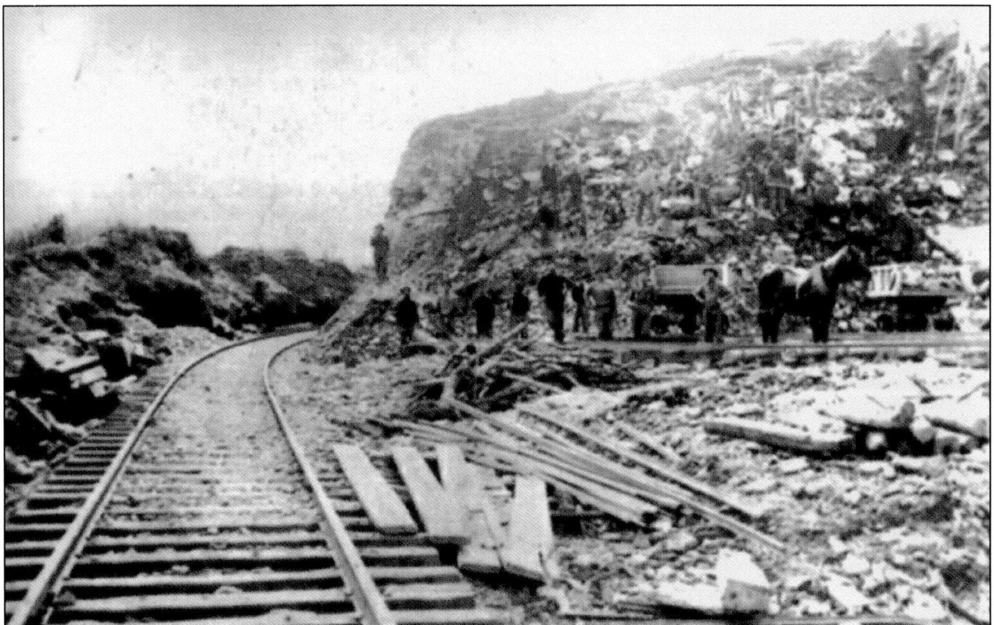

During the building of the railroad, workers could easily spend 11 hours a day working hard labor on the tracks. This was on top of caring for their homes and other obligations. (Courtesy of Stewart Hill.)

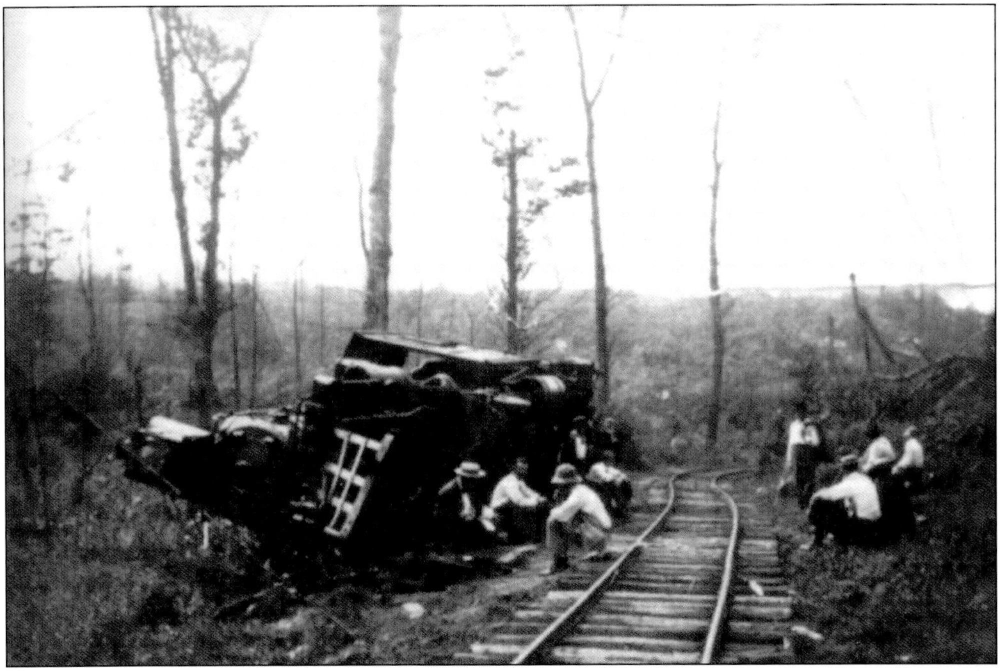

There were many train wrecks along the W&NBRR—some fatal, some on purpose. (Courtesy of Stewart Hill.)

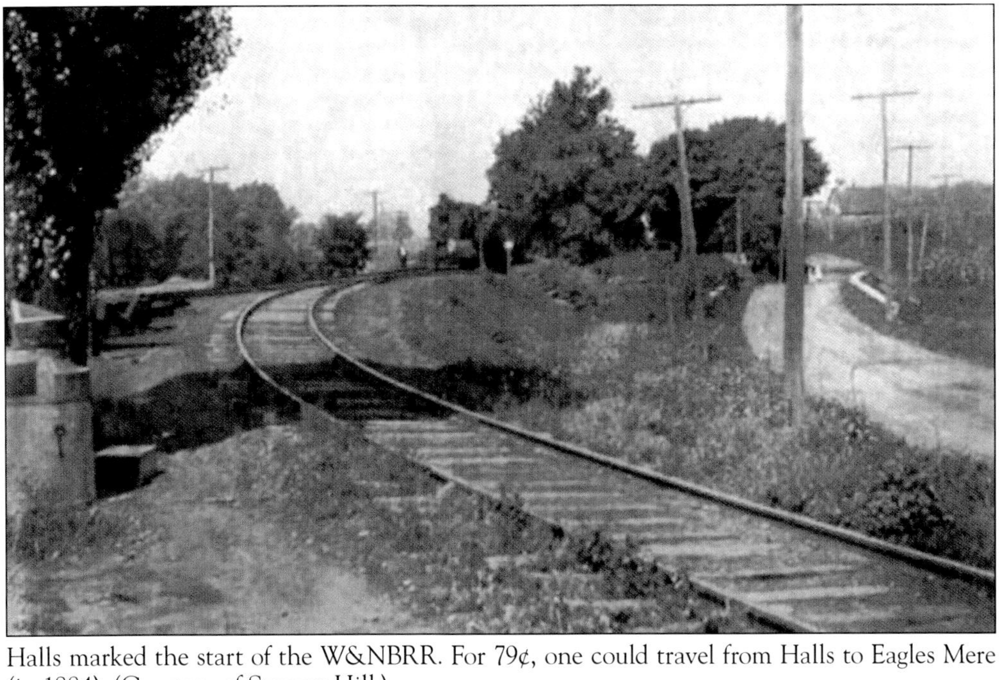

Halls marked the start of the W&NBRR. For 79¢, one could travel from Halls to Eagles Mere (in 1884). (Courtesy of Stewart Hill.)

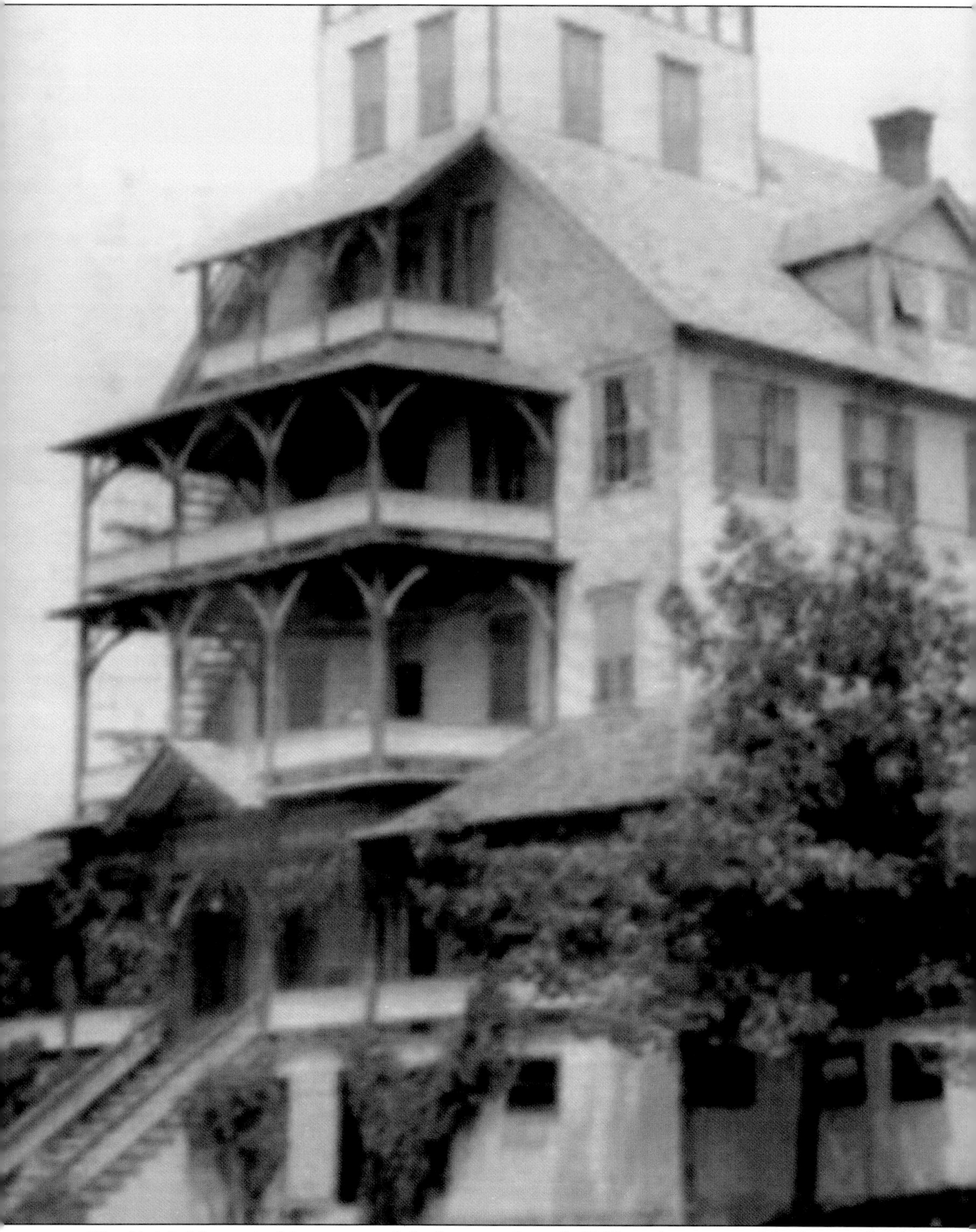

The Essick Mountain Home opened for business June 1, 1889, and was owned by Picture Rocks doctor H. M. Essick. The hotel had a nine-hole golf course and a two-story casino, which had two bowling alleys, a shuffle board, pool tables, a post office, and a place for dancing and gambling.

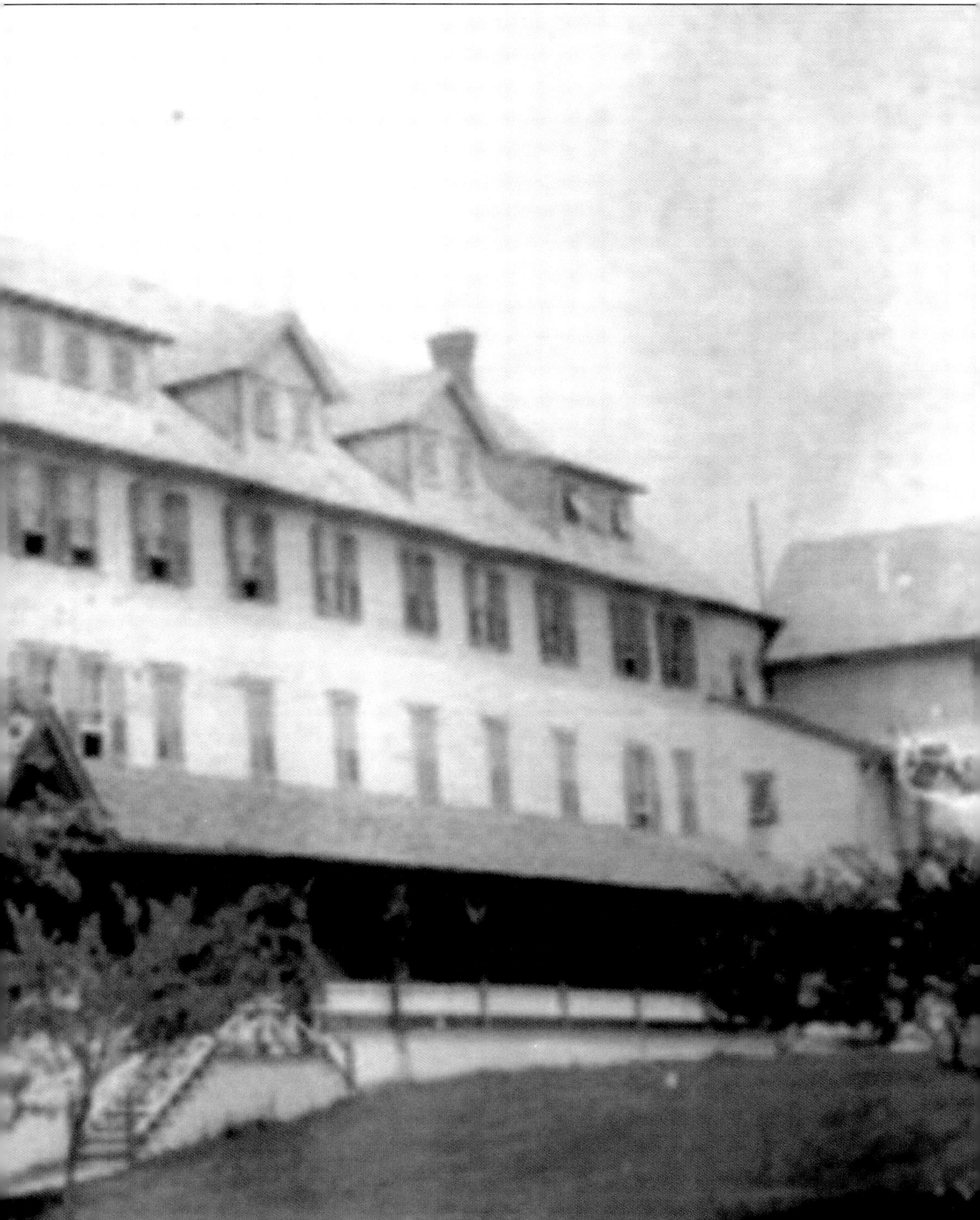

Dr. Essick also built Chamouni Drive, which connected his hotel to the railroad in present-day Tivoli. The hotel was destroyed by fire November 15, 1916, causing Dr. Essick to go into bankruptcy. (Courtesy of Stewart Hill.)

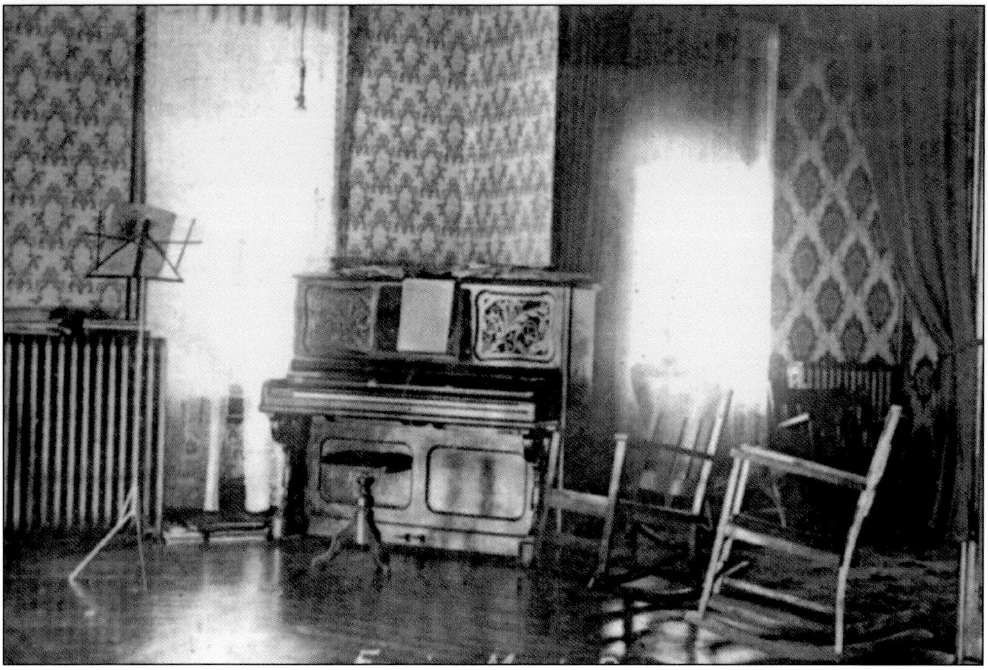

A select orchestra gave daily concerts and played music for dances at the Essick Hotel. Religious services where held on Sundays. (Courtesy of Stewart Hill.)

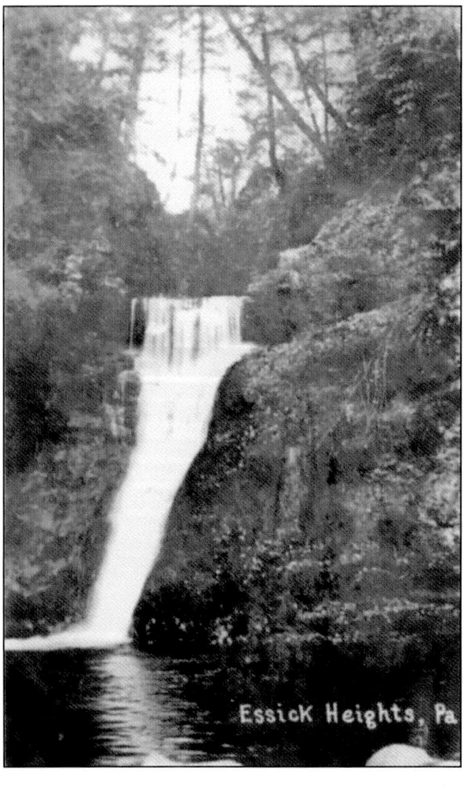

Essick Heights sat on 150 acres of land. This secluded waterfall also sat on the land. (Courtesy of Stewart Hill.)

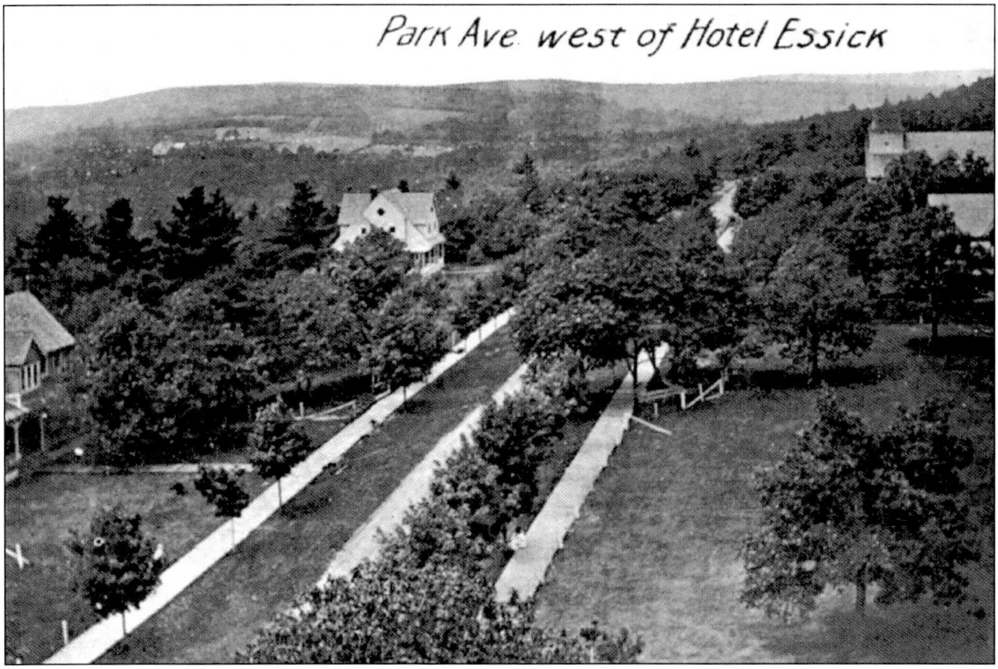

Park Avenue, west of Essick, is pictured here. (Courtesy of Stewart Hill.)

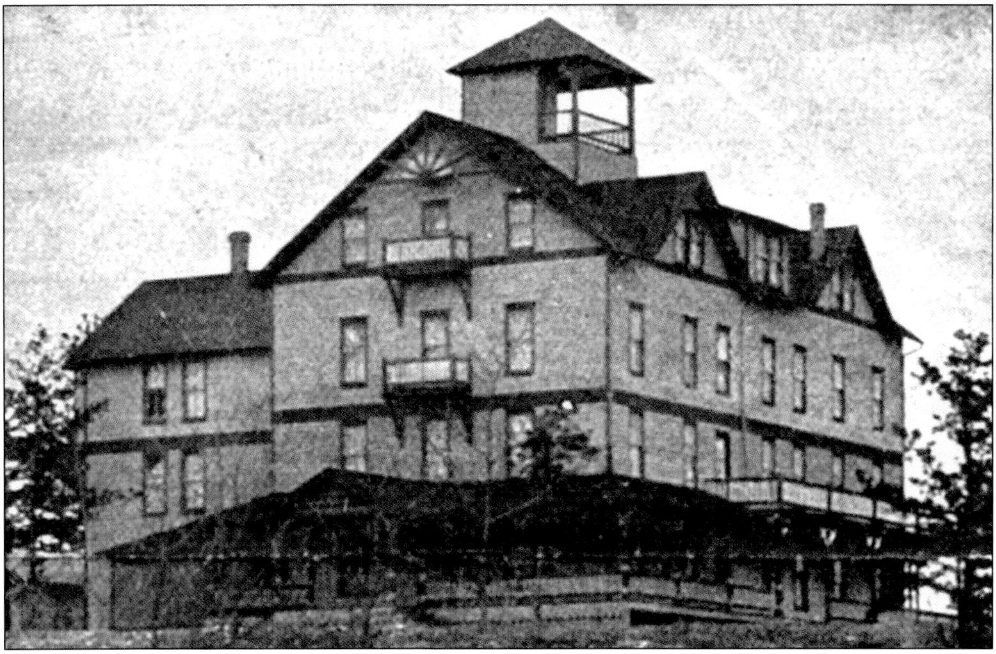
The Highland House was the first of two hotels at Highland Lake owned by Amos E. Burrows of Picture Rocks. It was also the first hotel built at Highland Lake. Sabin Burrows, son of Amos, built the hotel and it opened in 1878. Sabin and Charles Burrows were also proprietors of the Highland House. (Courtesy of Stewart Hill.)

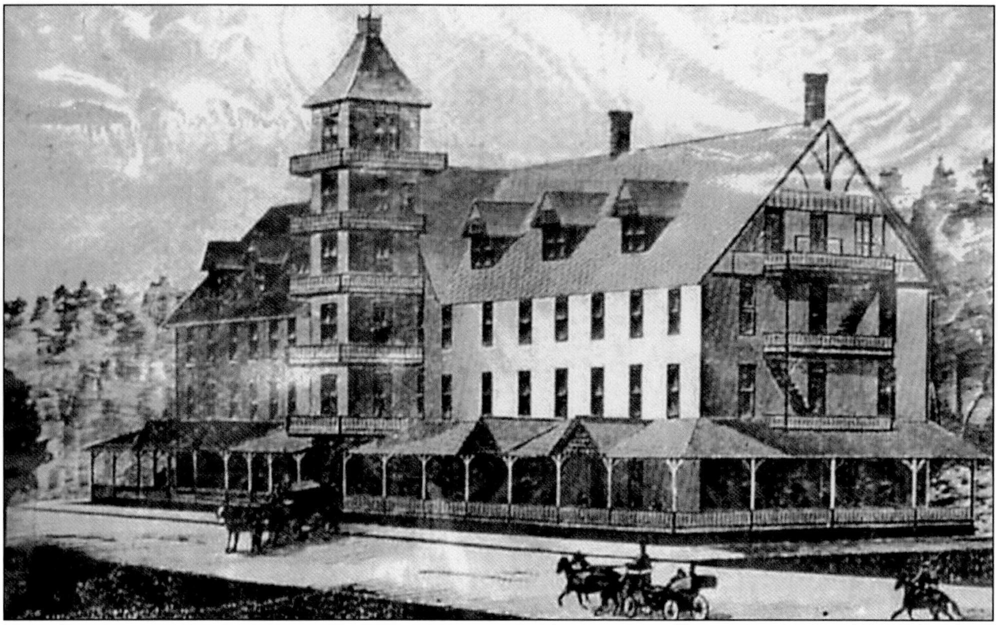

The Hotel Grandview, built in 1886, was set upon 180 acres in Highland Lake in Shrewsbury Township. The hotel was incredible in size. It was three stories high with water on every floor. The Hotel Grandview was furnished by the Burrows Brothers furniture factory in Picture Rocks, very fitting because the hotel was owned and built by Amos E. Burrows. (Courtesy of Stewart Hill.)

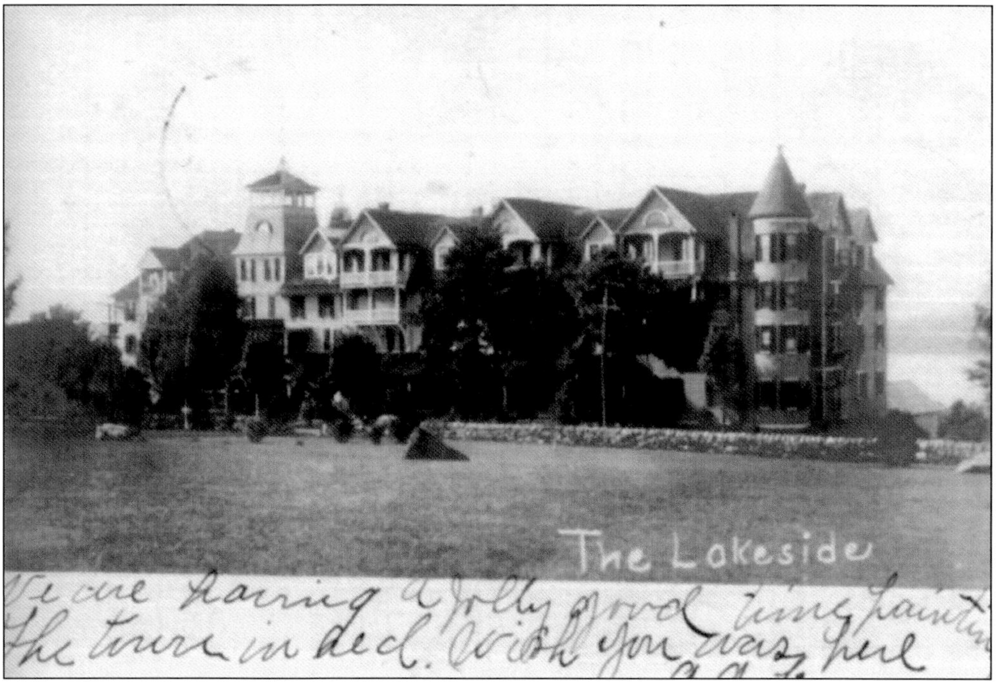

Located in Eagles Mere, this was the Lakeside Hotel. (Courtesy of Stewart Hill.)

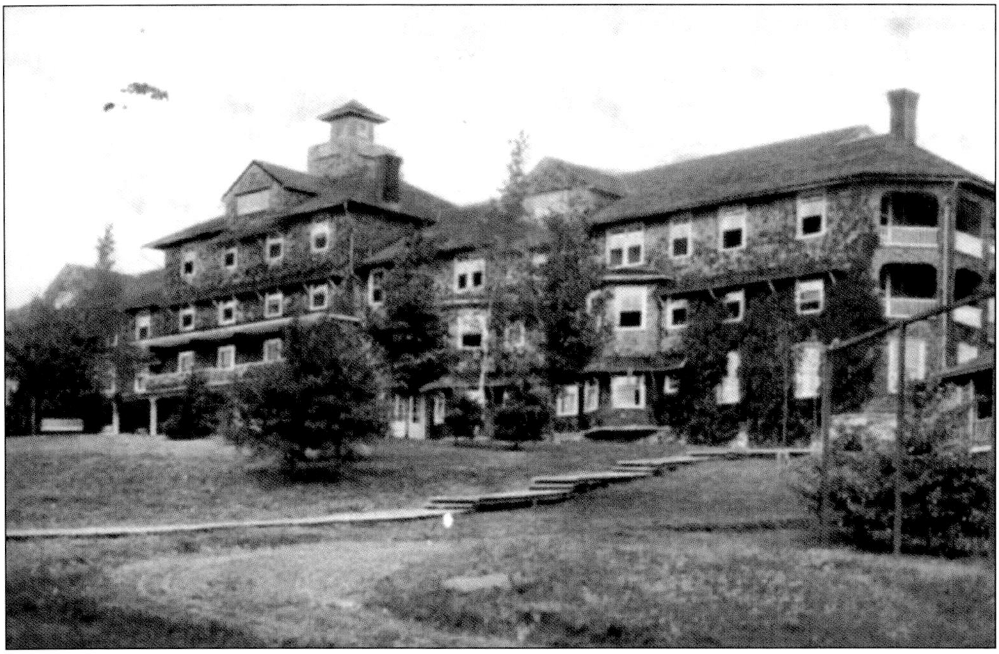

The Crestmont Inn is pictured here. (Courtesy of Stewart Hill.)

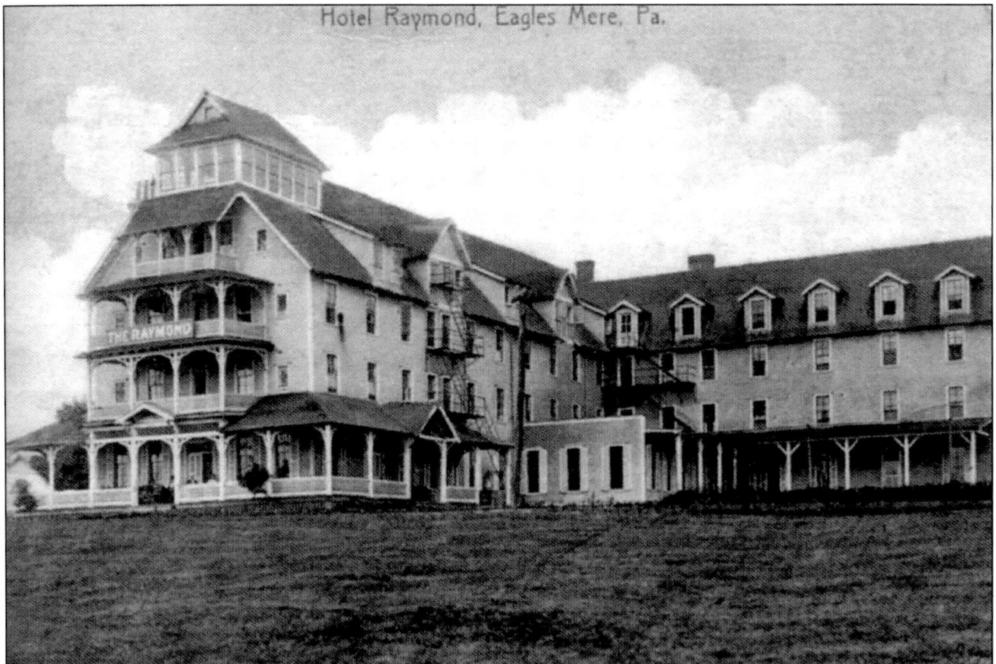

Another popular hotel was the Hotel Raymond located in Eagles Mere. (Courtesy of Stewart Hill.)

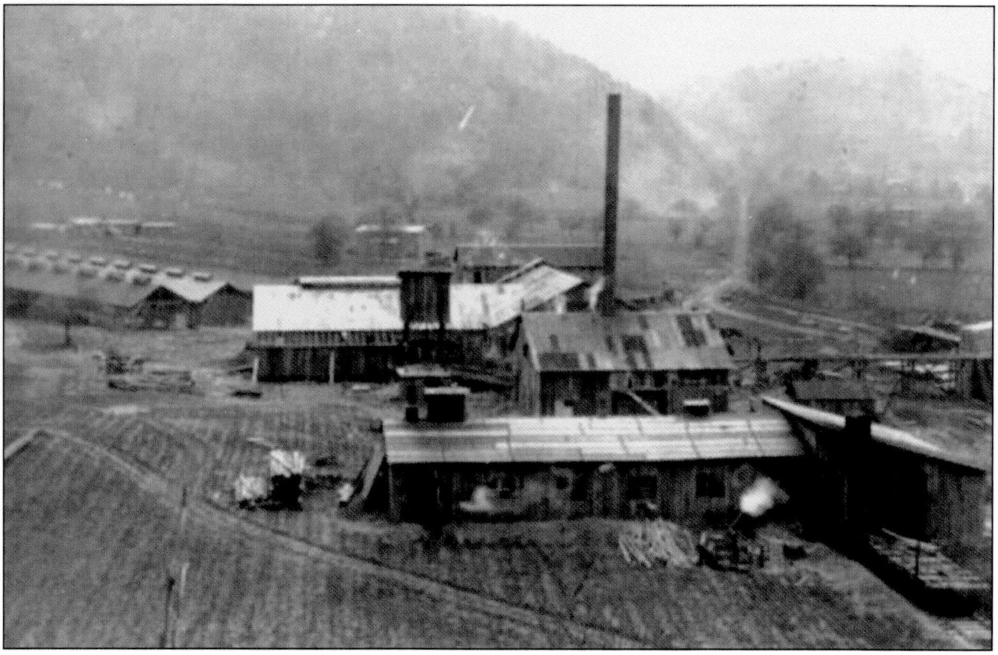

The Stove Factory in Sonestown, or also known as the Big Run Manufacturing Company, only operated for eight years. It was closed down in 1914 when the lumber they needed was no longer available. (Courtesy of Stewart Hill.)

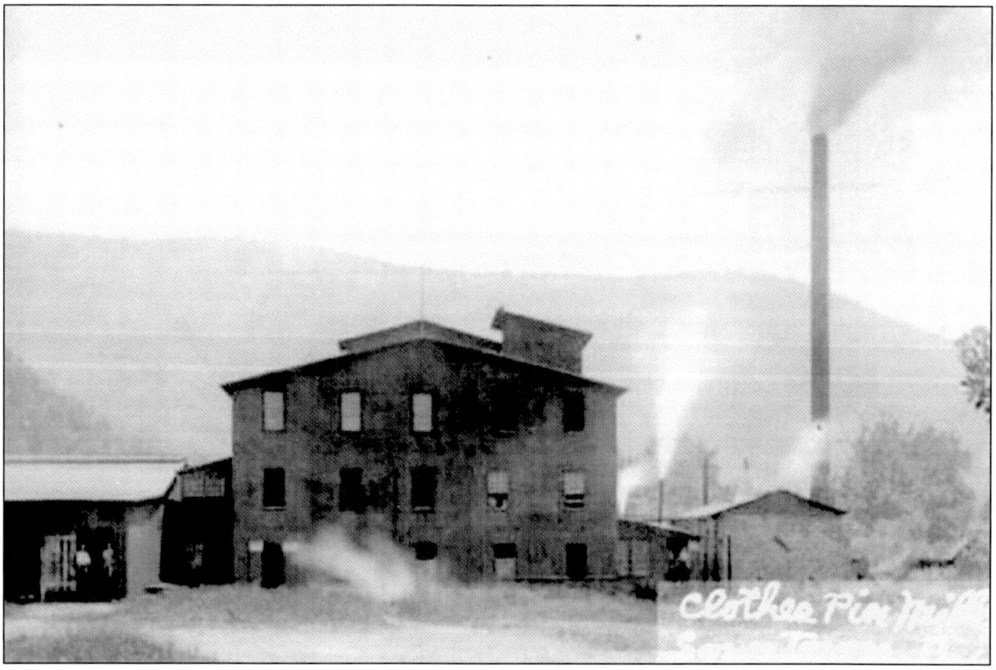

From 1903 to 1931, the Clothes Pin Factory in Sonestown was a staple in the community. It saw many different owners, even C. W. Sones who became a state senator. (Courtesy of Stewart Hill.)

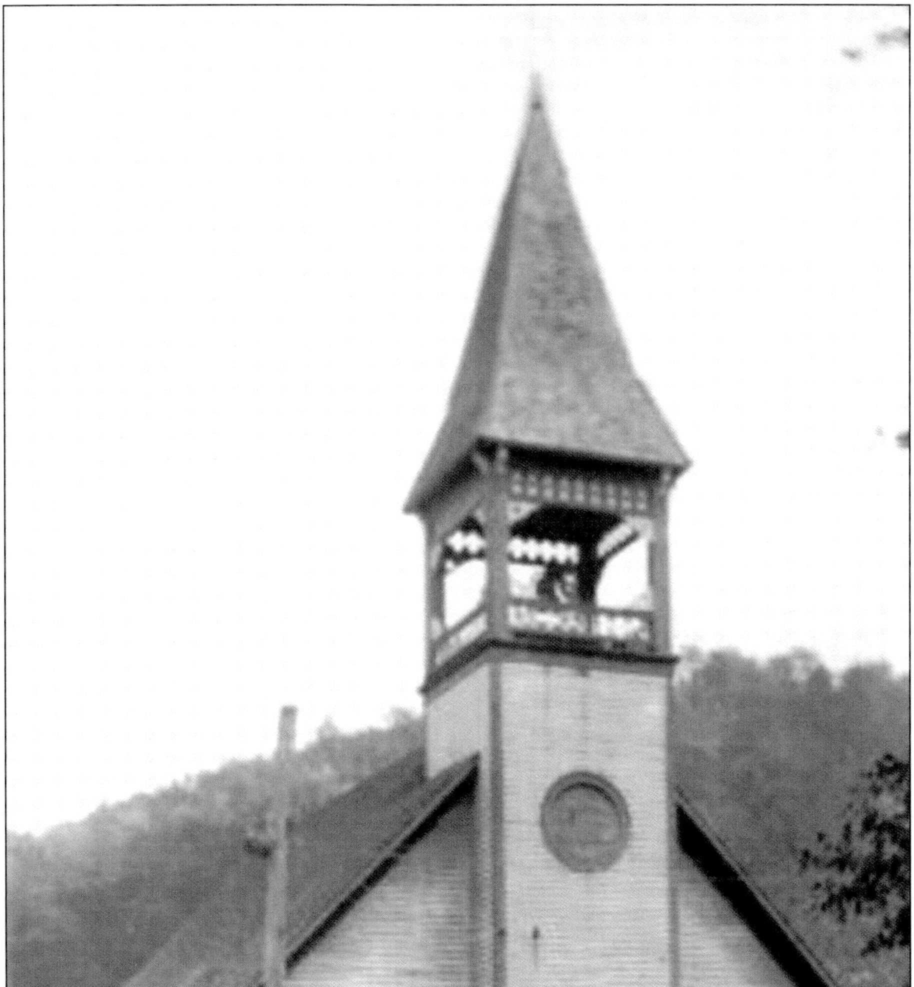

Pictured here is the Methodist Church in Sonestown. (Courtesy of Stewart Hill.)